BUSINESS/SCIENCE/TECHNOLOGY DIVISION
CHICAGO PUBLIC LIBRARY
SOUTH STATE STREET
CHICAGO, IL 60605

SE

D0225369

Chicago Public Library

REFERENCE

Form 178 rev. 11-00

DISCARD

Ordinary
Consumption

Studies in Consumption and Markets

Edited by

Colin Campbell, Department of Sociology, University of York, UK

and

Alladi Venkatesh, Graduate School of Management, University of California, Irvine, USA

Consumption has become a major focus of research and scholarship in the social sciences and humanities. Increasingly perceived as central to any successful understanding of the modern world, the meaning of the individual and collective consumption of goods is now a crucial issue at the heart of numerous contemporary debates on personal identity, the social and cultural structure of postmodern societies, and the historical development of modern industrial society.

This new interdisciplinary series will publish work on consumption-related topics in the fields of sociology; anthropology; material-culture studies; social, economic and cultural history; media and cultural studies; psychology; communication; human geography; marketing; economics; and art and design.

The series will publish the results of empirical research which employs an ethnographic, historical, or case-study approach. Theoretical and conceptual discussions will also be included, either those which represent original perspectives on the study of consumption or those which constitute critical commentaries on existing theories.

Volume 1   *The Dynamics of Advertising*
            Barry Richards, Iain MacRury and Jackie Botterill
Volume 2   *Ordinary Consumption*
            Edited by Jukka Gronow and Alan Warde
Forthcoming Volume
            Food and Cultural Studies
            Bob Ashley, Joanne Hollows, Steve Jones and Ben Taylor

Ordinary Consumption

Edited by
Jukka Gronow
University of Helsinki
Finland

and

Alan Warde
University of Manchester
UK

London and New York

/ HC 79 .C6 O73 2001

Ordinary consumption

First published 2001
by Routledge
11 New Fetter Lane, London EC4P 4EE

Simultaneously published in the USA and Canada
by Routledge
29 West 35th Street, New York, NY 10001

© 2001 Routledge

Routledge is an imprint of the Taylor & Francis Group

Typeset by Expo Holdings, Malaysia
Printed and bound in Great Britain by MPG Books Ltd, Bodmin

All rights reserved. No part of this book may be reprinted or reproduced or utilised in any
form or by any electronic, mechanical, or other means, now known or hereafter invented,
including photocopying and recording, or in any information storage or retrieval system,
without permission in writing from the publishers.

British Library Cataloguing in Publication Data
A catalogue record for this book is available from the British Library

ISBN: 0–415–27037–5

BUSINESS/SCIENCE/TECHNOLOGY DIVISION
CHICAGO PUBLIC LIBRARY
400 SOUTH STATE STREET
CHICAGO, IL 60605

R03035 06406

IN MEMORY OF DR. DAVINA CHAPLIN

Table of Contents

INTRODUCTION

Jukka Gronow and Alan Warde

The essays in this book originate from several conferences held under the auspices of the European and British Sociological Assocations between 1996 and 1998. Together they represent an attempt to broaden the understanding of contemporary consumption behaviour by exploring some central conceptual and empirical issues which, despite the explosion of interest in the field of consumption in the 1990s, have suffered comparative neglect.

THE DEVELOPMENT OF THE SOCIOLOGY OF CONSUMPTION

The study of consumption emerged as a sub-disciplinary specialism of sociology only in the mid-1980s. Though much of its intellectual inspiration came from France (from Bataille, Baudrillard, Bourdieu, Castells, de Certeau and Maffesoli), the sociology of consumption was developed most enthusiastically in the north west of Europe, in the Nordic countries and the United Kingdom. Its emergence coincided with the maturation of mass consumption in northern and western Europe and an impending threat of fiscal crisis of the welfare state. Unprecedented private affluence, represented by high average levels of personal consumption, fuelled increasing household expenditure on items like leisure, clothing, domestic technologies and automobiles. Simultaneously, the neo-liberal critique of the escalating cost and detrimental effects of collective state provision sought to rehabilitate faith in markets as the most appropriate mechanisms for the distribution of goods and services. One ideological effect was to affirm the legitimacy of the principle of consumer sovereignty—that people should be permitted, some would say obliged, to determine for themselves the means for the satisfaction of their wants without external guidance or regulation. Against this background, mass consumption was re-evaluated.

Prior to the 1980s, sociological reflection had concentrated almost exclusively on the negative aspects of private consumption. Prominent themes included the deprivations associated with poverty in market societies, the impact of the manipulative techniques involved in mass marketing, the perceived inferior quality of mass culture, and the malign effects of invidious social comparison. This last concern with the social effects of conspicuous consumption—the expression of social distinctions by groups and classes through their possessions and cultural competences—had constituted the major contribution of sociology during the 20th century.

The subsequent decade witnessed a significant transformation in the sociological understanding of consumption. Negative connotations were exorcised. The presentation of the consumer as a dupe of capitalist producers was supplanted by a model of an active, creative, self-reflexive agent. The aristocratic critique of popular culture as inferior was widely derided as misplaced and unsustainable, as well as offensively elitist. And the understanding of consumption as a means of displaying social status and class position was challenged from several angles.

The new, revised analyses which emerged had various intellectual sources which were often inter-disciplinary in scope (see Miller, 1995). Cultural studies, especially influential in the UK, provided a strong defence of the value of popular culture and a demonstration of the ways in which sub-cultures improvised with consumption items to express personal and collective resistance to hegemonic cultural understandings (e.g. Willis, 1990). New developments in social theory generated models of the self-reflexive actor who, having become aware of the plasticity of personal biography, was forced constantly to choose among alternative courses of action through which the self came to be constituted. It was argued that the creation of self-identity was substantially achieved through symbolic consumption decisions which formed an individual's lifestyle (eg Bauman, 1988; Giddens, 1991; Beck, 1992). The intellectual ferment of postmodernist thought added many additional, complicating elements.

When, in 1990, Featherstone surveyed studies of consumer culture, he identified three operative analytic perspectives. One put emphasis on the effects of the logic of capitalist production, as for example did the Frankfurt School. The second, best exemplified by Bourdieu, concentrated on 'the mode of consumption', the way in which different groups enaged in consumption practice. The third was very heterogeneous, being still in the process of formulation, but was essentially a portfolio of themes which subsequently came to be understood as the characteristics of postmodern consumption. Concerned with the 'dreams, images and pleasure' associated with consumer culture, the emergent concerns identified by Featherstone as deserving of further attention were: issues of excess and waste, after the fashion of Bataille; carnivalesque events; the 'dream worlds' of department stores and arcades; the creative potential of mass culture and the apparent collapse of the boundary between high and popular culture; the aestheticisation of everyday life; and the collapse of the boundary between the artistic avant-garde and the new *petite bourgeoisie* represented in the plural lifestyles of the new cultural intermediaries. Investigations of the 1990s did indeed pay considerable attention to these topics, resulting in an extensive literature.

OLD AND NEW AGENDAS

A review of the first generation of textbooks on the sociology of consumption which began to emerge in the mid-1990s reveals a field which remains fragmented and theoretically disputatious (Corrigan, 1998; Gabriel & Lang, 1995; Lury, 1996; Miles, 1998; Slater, 1997). Nevertheless, it is clear that much was learned from the revisionist endeavours of the previous ten years. The extent to which consumption might be transgressive, absorbing, remarkable, identity-forming and hedonistic was increasingly appreciated. Consumption was rescued from the ascetic presumptions of much previous critique. It was widely affirmed that consumption was better understood for its symbolic and communicative significance than for its capacity to meet practical needs. The role of the emotions, of desire and of concerns with pleasure were recognised. In addition, analysis was increasingly distanced from the unrealistic assumptions of orthodox economics. But while the sociology of consumption was substantially altered thereby, it was, we contend, at the expense of ignoring some equally central phenomena. It is to the outstanding gaps that a new agenda for research should be directed.

The analysis of glamorous and spectacular activities is not objectionable, but undue concentration may be misleading if other, equally important, practices, which are less flamboyant or visible, operate in accordance with a different logic. The theories of consumption inherited from the last decade of scholarly inquiry have particular emphases, on choice and freedom, taste and lifestyle, identity and differentiation, image and appearance, transgression and carnival. However, these considerations left out a good deal of the substantive field of consumption. Those actions which required little reflection, which communicate few social messages, which play no role in distinction, and which do not excite much passion or emotion, were typically ignored. The overall thesis of the book is that the sociology of consumption has concentrated unduly on the more spectacular and visual aspects of contemporary consumer behaviour, thereby constructing an unbalanced and partial account. Social scientific investigations have, arguably, concentrated excessively on musical taste, clothing fashions, private purchase of houses and vehicles, and the attendance at 'high' cultural performances like theatre and museums, to the exclusion of everyday food consumption, use of water and electricity, organisation of domestic interiors and listening to the radio. At the very least, these activities appear to require a different approach and a different set of concepts to understand their social uses. However, a stronger case might be made, that these are the prototypical activities of consumption, which define the character of consumption, but which have become so mundane, so taken-for-granted, so normal, that most people, including scholars, fail to appreciate their significance.

We are of the view that, previously, too much emphasis has been placed upon

- extraordinary rather than ordinary items
- conspicuous rather than inconspicuous consumption
- individual choice rather than contextual and collective constraint
- conscious, rational decision-making rather than routine, conventional and repetitive conduct
- decisions to purchase rather than practical contexts of appropriation and use
- commodified rather than other types of exchange
- considerations of personal identity rather than collective identification.

Each essay in the book addresses one or more of these points, mostly using new empirical material from several different national contexts as illustration. In order to describe generically those aspects of routine, practical usage, etc., we have recourse to the not entirely satisfactory term 'ordinary' consumption. We offer no formal definition at this stage. However, the idea of ordinary consumption refers to those items and practices which are neither highly visible nor in any way special and which often stand in a subsidiary relation to some other primary or more conscious activity. Ordinary items might include the petrol for the car, the electricity for the light and the water for use in the new bathroom suite. Petrol, electricity and water are products which are essential but, if brought to mind at all, tend to be considered subordinate, instrumental to a more meaningful activity. Such items, mostly taken entirely for granted and without symbolic communicative potential, are typical examples of ordinary consumption. However, the term does not necessarily imply that such consumption is common to the majority of people. Nor does it necessarily relate to activities which are undertaken very frequently—though some of the most obvious examples are—for instance, routine shopping for groceries, turning on an electric light, drinking a glass of tap water, or listening to the radio while driving home from work.

We thus propose consolidation of the sociology of consumption in the awareness that there has been excessive concentration on some topics to the exclusion of others. Our contention is that these ordinary practices comprise a significant proportion of the total range of activity that might be called consumption, and that they are not ones readily explained by the dominant theoretical approaches of the recent past. It therefore requires theoretical renewal and development, and the deployment of some different conceptual tools, as well as empirical study of relevant behaviours, to be able properly to appreciate the importance of ordinary consumption.

THE CONTENTS OF *ORDINARY CONSUMPTION*

The chapters of the book address conceptual and empirical issues. In chapter 1, Kaj Ilmonen, contesting the applicability of the model of voluntaristic and reflexive individual agency, analyses the concepts of habit and routine. He explores instances of ways in which consumption becomes routinised and identifies implications for consumer behaviour and the sociological research agenda. Bente Halkier, in chapter 2, engages in more extensive empirical analysis of the relationship between reflexive decision-making and routine conduct, reporting on a study of environmental considerations involved in food purchasing by young Danes. She uses her data to demonstrate that it is impossible to maintain a sharp distinction between reflexive and routine consumption practices, and indicates how features of each mix together in everyday activity. Elizabeth Shove and Heather Chappells, in chapter 3, take up the theme of ordinary consumption by examining the relationships between providers and consumers of two largely inconspicuous and unglamorous items, water and electricity. They identify some of the distinctive properties of these utilities, for instance that they are typically used indirectly, without reflection and in amounts determined by the routinisation of other daily activities.

They are then able to isolate some remarkable features of demand for these utilities which result in complicated and unexpected systems of co-provisioning. The complex overlapping of production and consumption is the central theme of the fourth chapter by Davina Chaplin. Based on a study of the experiences of Britons owning second houses in France, she reflects on the work involved in restoring and using rural properties as holiday homes. Routines and rituals of everyday consumption intertwine with extensive productive activity to constitute highly active and purposive, yet unspectacular, forms of leisure. Drawing on the theory of Bourdieu, Shou-Cheng Lai, in chapter 5, sketches a framework for explicating the role of social capital in establishing social relations around consumption. In the context of contemporary Taiwan, he demonstrates the role that processes of circulation of information and mutual cooperation within social networks play in determining what should be purchased, and by whom. His study highlights the importance of collective over individual decision-making procedures, showing that social capital is mobilised differently with respect to the acquisition of ordinary and extraordinary items. Chapter 6 also addresses critically the role of individual choice in the process of consumption. Examining the origins and implications of the notion of choice in a historical perspective, Roberta Sassatelli shows its complex association with the modern sense of individuality. The modern individual is one who has an obligation to pursue his or her personal desires, but only in a disciplined and purposive fashion. The legitimised conception of a 'tamed hedonism' has profound implications for consumption of everything from body maintenance services to recreational drugs.

The next four chapters comprise studies of the acquisition and use of common consumer goods. In chapter 7, Pasi Mäenpää examines the use of a new consumer item, the mobile telephone, which has been very rapidly diffused in Finland. He shows how a distinctive and profoundly mundane culture of use has bedded down, in a form probably not anticipated by its designers, with potentially profound impacts upon urban life and public space. Listening to the radio is an even more widespread, but now unremarkable, activity. In chapter 8, Brian Longhurst, Gaynor Bagnall and Mike Savage report on interviews with the middle classes of Manchester regarding their patterns of radio use. Respondents explained their preferences in terms of conjunction with other activities and in the context of everyday practical routines. These are expressed in narratives about their tastes and cultural preoccupations which centre less on the pursuit of distinction than an aspiration to ordinariness. Tim Dant and Pete Martin, in chapter 9, reflect on the phenomenological aspects of mundane car usage, enumerating the many everyday satisfactions delivered to the driver of an automobile, none of which relate to its potential function as a symbol of social status or identity. The place of motoring in modern life is much more complex and integral. Dale Southerton, in chapter 10, also examines consumption practices which are very much taken-for-granted. On the basis of interviews with house-holders, he describes how people of different social classes conceive of the content and design of their kitchens. Systematic variation of aesthetic principle and customary practice is related to social differentiation by class position, geographical mobility and degree of integration into social networks.

The influence of state provision on patterns of private consumption is not a topic that has received much attention, a feature associated with more general neglect of non-commercial channels of consumption. In chapter 11 Terhi-Anna Wilska engages in a comparative analysis of the consumption patterns of young adults in Britain and Finland in the early 1990s. The effects of the character and level of state welfare provision are explored in the context of the polarisation of consumption opportunities for rich and poor and its implications for citizenship rights. In the final substantive chapter of the book, Katja Oksanen-Särelä and Mika Pantzar explore the ways in which scenarios of the future construct or imagine the consumer with respect to potential technological innovation. Interrogating a sample of futurological texts for their portrayal of the putative application of novel domestic technologies, they isolate authors' assumptions in order to expose and challenge the appropriateness of models of instrumental agency which abound in such accounts.

The empirical topics analysed are diverse, including shopping in Taiwan, second home ownership in France, food choice in Denmark, body maintenance services in Italy, new mobile telephones in Finland and kitchen design in England. The chapters undertake clarification of key concepts like tradition, routine and habit, as well as making some new conceptual distinctions. The overall effect is of sustained critical engagement with versions of postmodernist interpretations of consumption. Chapters mostly explore fields of practice in everyday life where postmodernist accounts have very little purchase. By beginning to demarcate the limits of such an approach, we hope to advance a critique of recent work and sow the seeds of a distinctive alternative approach to the analysis of the central practices of consumer society.

Chapter 1

SOCIOLOGY, CONSUMPTION AND ROUTINE

Kaj Ilmonen

'Paradoxically, we are trapped into the web of habit when we try to develop means of protection against routinized practices...' Barbara A. Misztal (1996, 111).

There have been at least three phases in the sociology of consumption. The last of them began at the end of the 1970s, when Pierre Bourdieu published his seminal work, *Distinction*. Since then the sociology of consumption has not, however, mainly followed the path opened by Bourdieu. Rather it has become anchored in the Anglo-Saxon tradition where the most powerful conception has been the idea of agency, an idea well formulated in Anthony Giddens' major work *The Constitution of Society* (1986 [1984]).

In this pathbreaking and influential book, Giddens writes about a reflexive agent who is doomed to making choices and who is also 'able to do otherwise' at any time. With this idea in mind, it is easy to understand why such a large part of the new sociology of consumption deals with questions of taste, style, and the construction of identity. These are, naturally, legitimate subjects. However, most types of consumption do not fit the idea of agency very well. When we are dealing with commodities, in the long run there will emerge consumption habits in the same way as all our other fields of activity are habitualized (Weber, 1964, 372). Through habits 'we also in-habit the world. It becomes [with the help of them, KI] a home, and the home is a part of our every experience' (Dewey, 1958, 104). It is not so easy to change this 'home' as agency theory claims. Therefore, it is appropriate to devote some attention to the forms of consumption that do not fit in with that theory. I call these forms 'consumption routines'.

I begin by making a distinction between action and behaviour, because it is of great importance for our understanding of routines. Then I will discuss what routines are and how they have been interpreted in social theory. Thereafter, I will show how routine behaviour is connected with consumption. Finally, I will make some comments on the sociology of consumption from the viewpoint of consumption as a matter of routine.

ACTION AND BEHAVIOUR

As noted above, the new paradigm of the sociology of consumption deals mainly with agency. This is understandable especially if we keep in mind that this paradigm has been a counter-reaction to the view, taken by earlier critical theory, of consumers as victims of production and mass-marketing. However, while the new paradigm stresses the importance of agency in consumption, it too often takes the actor's power (to do otherwise) for granted. This is surprising, because the nature of the accomplishment of an action is in itself problematic. As Campbell puts it, 'individuals do not always succeed in their attempts to implement their decisions'. Failures naturally happen due to opposition from other people and structural hindrances, but also because individuals simply do not manage to or want to 'implement their will and therefore "to act"' (Campbell, 1996a, 157).

Campbell thus clearly separates action from non-action. The former has to do with willing or will power and its practical implementation. This emphasis shows that action should be seen as voluntary and meaningful conduct (Campbell, 1996a, 25). Non-action, by contrast, is connected with involuntary reactions and conduct. It is governed by more or less unmotivated practices. They are repetitive and unreflected, following principles that are known neither to the individual nor to a larger public (see Bauman, 1990, 223). This latter type of conduct is called behaviour.

This distinction between action and behaviour was already made by Max Weber when he regarded the routinization of action as 'one of the principal continually operating forces in everyday life' (Weber, 1964, 372). However, he talked of the trichotomy of behaviour, action and social action. The difference between the second and third was that action did not orient itself according to the conduct of others, while social action did (88). This difference has important implications from the point of view of his action theory, but perhaps not so important as the distinction between action and behaviour later applied by Alfred Schutz, William Thomas and Florian Znaniecki, among others.

Like all dichotomies, the distinction between action and behaviour is not absolute. Weber, too, pointed out that these modes of conduct are ideal types that include each other in reality. In practice, according to him, behaviour seems to 'shade over' into action (Weber, 1964, 116; see also Campbell, 1996b, 95). By this expression Weber wanted to stress that human conduct is always a mixture of behaviour and action. If this is accepted, one must conclude that in a strict sense categories such as 'action' do not exist at all. However, one does not have to take such a standpoint even when using Weberian action theory, because in the end behaviour consists of 'merely "decayed" versions of earlier "true" actions', as Campbell, echoing Durkheim's formulations, puts it (Campbell, 1996a, 57; Durkheim, 1983, 38, 79, 83) and because only some behaviour is of this kind (e.g. ceremonies). In any case, it remains wise to distinguish, at least analytically, between these two categories of human conduct.

CIRCUMSTANCES AND FORMS OF BEHAVIOUR

If behavioural conduct starts as action and later becomes behaviour, it is necessary to ask two questions. First, it is useful to know what circumstances are most likely to promote this transformation of conduct. Second, it is necessary to know what form behavioural conduct takes as a consequence of this transformation.

In order to answer the first question, it is useful to contrast two situations. The first is where an ideal type of agency, (i.e. a decision maker who applies his/her will power and promotes his/her interests), prevails. The second concerns the circumstances in which a prototypical form of behaviour (i.e. a repetitive, ritualistic and unmotivated performance) governs people's conduct. The former comes close to utilitarian and strategic reflective conduct (Camic, 1986, 1047). Micro-economic theory, and economics in general, rests mainly on the presumption of this ideal form of action, of rational decision making.[1] The second form involves conduct that is unmotivated, repetitive and largely ritualistic (Giddens, 1979, 218). Anthropology has dealt extensively with ritualistic behaviour (see e.g. Bell, 1993). It is useful to see what these two approaches offer with respect to understanding routine conduct.

According to economics, rational decision making is strictly bound by the epistemological aspects of probability, or in Giddens's terms, to knowledgeability. John Maynard Keynes, for instance, held this view. According to him, in situations where the probability of a certain outcome is relatively high—in other words, where all relevant aspects of a decision are well known—it is possible to implement the model of the rational, willing decision maker and the individual has a good chance of being a real agent of his or her own future. However, when uncertainty increases and the probability is unknown, the situation changes in ways that are well reflected in capital investment decisions.

How do investors make investment decisions under great uncertainty? In his *General Theory,* Keynes emphasizes the importance of 'devices' in making investment decisions in uncertain situations. According to him, such 'devices' include conventions, mimesis, fashion and habits. They allow behaviour that 'saves our faces as rational, economic men' (1964, 114–117, 152).

Anthropological theory draws our attention to ritualistic behaviour. It deals with ritualism in two different contexts. In the Durkheimian tradition ritualism is seen as proper conduct for strengthening group solidarity (Durkheim, 1912, 214; Douglas, 1982, 14), thereby creating social order out of disorder. When rituals succeed in this task, they decrease uncertainty and increase the predictability of the group's action. This interpretation of the function of rituals brings us close to the second context in which rituals are used. According to Bronislaw Malinowski, rituals are common in magical thinking, which flourishes when an outcome is important but individuals have no control over that outcome (1948, 79–81). In other words, Malinowski assigns rituals (and other superstitions) the same role as Keynes assigns to 'devices'. That is probably no accident, because Malinowski was strongly influenced by neo-classical economics. In other words, rituals are a way of coping with things in highly contingent circumstances. They are 'devices' that reduce the anxiety caused by decisions that have to be made in uncertain situations. This interpretation has also been made by anthropologists after Malinowski.

Rituals, of course, are not the only form of such devices. As already noted, Keynes also talks about fashion, habit, convention and mimesis. In making this list he was, however, not very analytical. Fashion and mimesis do not belong to the category of 'device', insofar as we understand them as forms of behaviour. In a sense, they are located between agency and behavioural forms. Old experiences can be recalled and utilized selectively in new situations (one can 'do otherwise'). According to theories that stress the mass or imitative nature of fashions (Tarde, 1903; Simmel, 1957), fashion is followed blindly, but this is not always so. To follow fashion may also imply self-reflection on an individual level. This places the individual in the position of an agent. He or she must decide whether to put old experiences into practice and whether or not to follow fashion.

Habits and conventions, by contrast, have a different status in our conduct. They are followed without conscious reflection. We have to think about them only when we happen to get into extraordinary circumstances where we might face difficulties in applying our 'devices'. When circumstances are again normalized we will return to our habits and conventions. They form, so to say, the nucleus of our behaviour (Durkheim, 1983, 83).

Rituals, habits and conventions are all social mechanisms designed to reduce uncertainty in complex decision situations, but they also differ from each other. Since Durkheim, rituals have been connected with the sacred part of our lives. They are a way of approaching sacred objects and ideas that are considered to belong to the 'pure' side of our reality (Durkheim, 1912, 209; Douglas, 1984, 8–9). They are also usually formal by nature, which makes them easy to control. Habits and conventions, by contrast, belong to the profane sphere of our behaviour. They both belong to the behavioural categories of routines that are part of the mundane mess of daily life. They are usually neither formalised nor closely reflected upon. They cannot be identified in terms of what is done, 'but only in terms of how it is done' as Campbell stresses (1996c, 161). The most striking point of difference between routines and rituals, however, is their relationship to rules.

In his highly innovative study *How Societies Remember* (1989, 30–34), Paul Connerton differentiates between rule-oriented and habitualized conduct. Rituals belong to the former category. They are forms of collective memory that follow relatively strict rules. A breach of these rules is interpreted by society as an offence against the sacred, and usually sanctions are imposed. The threat of sanctions reminds us that breaking the rules always involves risks, which helps maintain consciousness of the rules.

When we are carrying out our daily routines, our relationship to rules differs completely from that found in ritual behaviour. In order to understand this we must separate rules from their applications. This separation is fundamental to our understanding of learning processes. It is clear that knowledge of the grammar of a language is not a sufficient condition of its mastery. Only after exhaustive rule-following conduct, such as the use of a given language, has become habitualized can we cease to think about grammar, and our language use becomes automatic. This has its advantages. When we have 'learned by doing', we have no need to turn to grammar books any more. When this phase is reached, the pattern whereby a rule is followed by its application is turned upside down. The application starts to maintain the rule

(Connerton, 1989, 34). At that stage we are conscious of the rule only in exceptional circumstances, for instance, when we get into trouble with language use.

Nor are we so aware of our routines. They are, in a sense, 'our second nature', too close to us. One reason for this closeness is that rule-supporting behaviour is incorporated in our daily gestures, ways of walking, the routes we choose, etc. In other words, habits are enduring features of our being—'remembrances of the body'—which express our individuality. They are, however, not only individual, but also social features. They also reflect social categories (gender, age, etc.) and affective attitudes (aversion, liking, etc.), the individual totality of which Pierre Bourdieu named—borrowing a word from Latin (and Weber)—'habitus'.

It would, however, be wrong to see our incorporated routines or habituses only as a cultural code of class, gender, etc., or as a form of individual staging. They also manifest the accumulated knowledge and mimesis in our bodies, appearing as the 'armorization' of our muscles and stiffness in our gestures. In this sense, routines are not only means of coping with contingent circumstances and easing our everyday lives. Transformed into habituses, they are means of giving ourselves a feeling of normality. This feeling is 'the most common way in which we relate to the world surrounding us, and at the same time the most obvious frame of reference for attitudes of general trust'. Even in the most extreme circumstances, as in concentration camps, people try to maintain a state of 'practical normality' by repeating daily routines 'as though nothing had happened' (Misztal, 1996, 198). However, the feeling of normality is not achieved without cost. Routines are also impeding structures that narrow down our alternatives for action.

ROUTINES AND FORMS OF CONSCIOUSNESS

Routines have not attracted very much attention in the social sciences, although they play such a fundamental part in our everyday lives. In a way this is, however, not very surprising, considering the sociological tradition. True, the forefathers of sociology, like Durkheim, regarded habitual practices as 'real forms that govern us' (1956, 152), or as a matter of 'automatic reaction' (Weber, 1964, 116). They were, however, 'intentionally expunged from the vocabulary of sociology', not only because modern people were said to be less tradition-bound, but also because this step was considered necessary in order to gain distance from behaviourism and to establish sociology as a scientific discipline (Camic, 1986, 1061, 1077). Perhaps another reason for avoiding the concept of routine in sociology has been that it has been seen as a hybrid concept uniting controversial elements. Like habit, it is 'at once mentalistic and observational', individual and social (or historical). Moreover, it is at the same time causal and persistent (Turner, 1994, 16, 50).

In the last few years routines have, however, attracted some attention. Of the contemporary sociological masters Anthony Giddens and, to a lesser extent, Pierre Bourdieu have tried to get to grips with routines. In *The Constitution of Society* Giddens gives routines a notable status in his theorising.[2] He refuses to give priority to either agency or structure, referring instead to the 'duality of structure'. By this, Giddens means that social structures are both creations of human activity and the means of shaping and directing this activity (Giddens, 1976, 121; 1979, 24). According to this view, every act by an agent not only influences the world but also reproduces it. This is true even when an action breaks existing social norms or conventions. Action is even then maintained by the structural features of society and by the existing social order and conventions. Giddens calls this relationship between the production and reproduction of the world the 'recursive nature' of social life (1986, 2).

The recursiveness of social life means several things in Giddens's structuration theory. I can refer to only one of them here. Recursiveness is strictly connected to the 'knowledgeability' of agents. According to Giddens, agents are (by their very nature) 'knowledgeable subjects'. Giddens has taken this idea from ethnomethodology, and says that although action is not, in the strong sense of the word, conscious conduct, an agent still monitors the consequences of others' and his or her own activity and tries to give an account of ('rationalize') it. This accountability of action means, in turn, that an agent has 'theoretical knowledge' that connects action to the prevailing conditions and helps to make it relevant from the viewpoint of external circumstances (Giddens, 1986, 4–5).

The term 'theoretical knowledge' has intentionally been put into quotation marks, because the reflective monitoring of one's own activity is not so conscious an action that it could be presented in a discursive form, i.e. be explicated. This observation (or contention) forces Giddens to develop his own theory of consciousness. He criticizes Freud, and explains that to be 'conscious' means a variety of different things. According to him, it must be possible to separate these meanings: consciousness, as sensual awareness; memory, as the temporal constitution of consciousness; and 'recall, as the means of recapitulating past experiences in such a way as to focus them on continuity of action' (Giddens, 1986, 49).

Giddens ends up considering recall and its different modalities as the best means of differentiating the forms of consciousness. Two of them refer to the psychological mechanisms of recalling and one is outside the reach of direct recall (1986, 49). Giddens names the former two 'discursive' and 'practical consciousness'. Like Freud, he calls the latter 'unconscious'. Discursive consciousness refers to those modes of recall that can be expressed verbally. Practical consciousness is closely related to Husserl's and Schutz's concept of natural attitude, which refers to the frame of reference that is used in observing and interpreting the surrounding world. It is fundamental to note that, according to Schutz, an agent is not conscious of this framework of his or her observation and interpretation processes (Schutz, 1962, 299). Giddens echoes this conception by saying that practical consciousness refers to the recall that takes place in an agent such that he or she is unaware of it and unable to express it verbally (1986, 49).

Practical consciousness is perhaps the most central element in structuration theory, as Giddens himself acknowledges (1986, xxiii), because the reflexive monitoring of actions takes place at this level of consciousness. At the same time it is, according to Giddens, the most dominant mode of consciousness because it corresponds to the dominant mode of everyday action, namely routinized action, which is another cornerstone of the theory (op.cit., xxiii).

The expression 'correspond to' is actually somewhat imprecise. As a matter of fact, routines materialize practical consciousness. To have routines is, in effect, 'to have a particular kind of mental cause operating' (Turner, 1994, 16). They incorporate the contents of practical consciousness. It might be that Giddens does not accept this, but in my opinion Pierre Bourdieu's views of sport fits in well with the analysis of the relationship between practical consciousness and routines. According to Bourdieu, training in sport is about the cultivation of the body. As a result of physical exercise, a sportsman/woman learns to 'understand' his or her body. Training is, in other words, nothing other than learning with the whole body, and an athletic performance is nothing more than the repetition of everything that has been learned (see Bourdieu, 1990, 166).[3]

The verb 'understand' has been put in quotation marks in order to emphasize that this understanding is not a conscious act, but a form of memory that is incorporated not only in our thoughts but also as steady features in our body language. As has already been said, this kind of understanding has great advantages. Routines are not only a means of reducing uncertainty (or, in Giddens's words, of maintaining 'ontological security'), they also save energy and make everyday life easier. They 'put it in order'; make it, in Dewey's words, 'habitable'. When we follow our routines, we do not have to start everything from the beginning and ponder the options that are available to us. We can just go on as before. In terms of economic theory, routines help to reduce 'transaction costs' and make social life predictable. From this latter point of view they construct a frame of reference for considering a person as trustworthy from a point of view of people close to him or her (Misztal, 1996, 68).

Routines thus seem to fulfill several functions at the same time. They are a) a means to reduce the complexity of decision-making and save one's energy. In addition, from the point of the view of ourselves they are b) a means to create a safe, habitable world and a feeling of normality. Moreover, seen from the outside they c) make our behaviour predictable and, in that sense, trustworthy. These functions of routine make our everyday lives run smoothly. This helps us to understand why it is so difficult to get rid of routines even though they restrict the range of options open to us, and confine us to a limited number of set behaviour patterns.

When we have been habituated to these forms, and routines become a fundamental part of ourselves or our 'character' (Camic, 1986, 1052), it is very difficult to change routines, or to create new ones without great effort. We are in a sense imprisoned by learned routines. Therefore, it is not easy to proceed from practical consciousness and the related internalized routines to an agent who is, by Giddens's definition, free to 'do otherwise'. Because Giddens, in his structuration theory, emphasizes this sort of agent, he sets aside routines, stresses the discursive side of the agent's consciousness and thus ends up closer to the idea of the voluntaristic, reflective agent which features in economic theory.

ROUTINES AND CONSUMPTION

Now, one can ask, how do routines relate to contemporary everyday life and especially to consumption? There are many obvious answers. I want here to point to only one.

There has recently been a great deal of talk among sociologists about the contingent nature of modern societies and their growing complexity.

Many of the arguments put forward are still under discussion, but at least one thing is certain. In consumption there is a growing insecurity regarding consumption choice (see Ilmonen, 1987). There are many reasons why this is so, but here I will content myself with naming only some. First, the average layman's knowledge of the origin, component materials, and functionality of commodities has decreased, while the technical complexity of production processes has increased and markets have been globalized. Second, the more unstable the (global) markets are in terms of prices, the more special offers there are, and the more the markets are characterized by superficial variation among goods, the more difficult is it for consumers to know, let alone compare, the prices of goods. Third, the growing emphasis on design (not only in the ordinary sense of the word, but also including, for example, the manipulation of smell), the promotion of brand images and new methods of packaging make rational calculation difficult when making choices. Fourth, because other consumers participate more and more in the final production of commodities, they may also influence transaction costs in unforeseeable ways. For instance, the success of a package tour depends not only on the services and helpfulness of their guides but also on other participants on a tour, on their experienced pleasantness, activity or passivity in relationship to other participants, their curiosity about travelling, etc.

Such trends put us, as consumers, in a very unpleasant situation. The growing variety of commodities not only increases the choices available to us (providing that we have sufficient economic resources), but it also makes it more difficult for us to know whether we are making the right choices. Still, we are condemned to choose. It would be a real miracle if a consumer were to be capable of rational decision-making in such circumstances. To avoid making irrational purchases, one would expect him or her to seek to minimize uncertainty and ease decision-making through routines, among other things. This supposition can be tested by drawing attention to five different phases in consumption, namely a) the decision of what to buy, b) the decision of where to buy, c) our behaviour/action at the place of purchase, d) the actual use of consumer goods and e) our ways of handling waste. Space does not permit me to deal with all of these phases in detail. I will touch on them only briefly and restrict my attention to the first four phases—although the fifth phase of consumption is also of great interest because we do not only throw away used commodities, but we also, for one reason or another, store them in the way Claude Levi-Strauss' *bricoleur* is supposed to do.

In purchase choices, routines are expressed in the repetition of the same solutions and in brand loyalty. This behaviour is, however, not necessarily reflected upon. As Deborah Lupton asserts, 'food preferences may be acted upon in a totally unthinking way, as the product of acculturation and part of the habits of everyday life' (1996, 155). The routinization of the choice of foods can be seen in Finland and Sweden, for example, in the fact that dishes traditionally linked with agrarian society are still as popular as ever. Despite the fact that the Scandinavian diet has become more international and the consumption of pre-processed food has been increasing since the 1960s, the list of the ten most popular dishes has remained virtually unchanged (Ilmonen, 1991, 170–171). For example, the traditional soup dishes—pea, meat and fish soup—have maintained their popularity. Nevertheless, they have not remained totally unchanged. Their salt and fat content has been diminishing, spices and herbs have been added to them, but there have not been any essential changes in the dishes.

Brand loyalty is apparent in the repeated favouring of one brand name over another. Even if new, tempting and cheaper alternatives become available, the individual does not give up the familiar brand. As market researchers have been able to show, brand loyalty remains even if a competing brand is sold at a reduced price (Tucker, 1968, 119; Hoyer and Brown 1990, 141–148). However, it must be added, there are exceptions to that rule. Producers know fairly well that brand loyalty varies considerably according to the type of commodity purchased. The decisive factors seem to be the extent to which a given product can generate emotional commitment in the consumer, and how sizeable an investment the purchase of the product is in relation to the consumer's income. When a product is one of the cheap staples, the degree of emotional commitment and brand loyalty is likely to be low. In Finland this is true of clothes pegs, detergents, toilet paper, and so on. When, on the other hand, the commodity is one of the rarely purchased, expensive capital goods, or is one of the frequently purchased staples with a strong emotional charge, the buying habits that support brand loyalty are quite evident. (In a sense, one could say that especially in the case of the latter type of products, consumption routines seem to explain continuing consumption routines). Cars and perfumes are a good example of the former type of goods, whereas examples of the latter type include (in Finland) motor oils, breads, beers, and the previously mentioned popular foods (Seies 1986, 87).

The choice of the place of purchase also depends on whether the intention is to buy staples or capital goods. In the former case, routinized practices are prevalent, whereas the latter are purchased so seldom that no routines can develop. Because of this, when buying capital goods consumers have to rely on conscious deliberation more than usual. The rules regarding the purchase of staples seem to be that most of the commodities purchased on weekdays are bought from a local shop, often regardless of the price. In the Nordic countries, as recently as the 1950s and 1960s, the choice of the shop—if there were more than one local shop—was dictated by factors other than economic ones. Most often the choice was based on the consumer's ideological commitment to either cooperative or private enterprise (see Böök and Ilmonen, 1989). These days, the choice of the shopping place is based on the consumer's impression of price versus quality in a given shop, or merely on practical considerations (i.e. transaction costs). During weekends, when larger quantities of goods are usually bought at one time, people go to the supermarkets. In developing a preference for a particular supermarket, the individual becomes its regular customer, although special offers may occasionally break this routine behaviour.

As already noted above, there has been a long-term trend toward shifting more and more of the labour costs of production, and especially the cost of services onto consumers. This has its risks. If consumers act without restrictions, the result may be chaos. The availability of services must be guaranteed, and the stress on other consumers and service workers must be minimized. That is why attempts have been made to standardize and routinize the actions of consumers. The strength of this effort is revealed by several recent books on ways of making customers more profitable (Fuller and Smith, 1991, 1–16). In practice this effort can be seen in the way consumers have to follow certain routes in stores, as well as in the placement of commodities so that they are easy to pick up in a shopping cart. Within the restaurant business this standardization can be seen most clearly at McDonald's, where the flow of customers in and out is regulated through a number of cues, and where they are almost unknowingly forced to follow a script written for the employees. This creates the feeling of safety among customers and they, therefore, are prone to choose McDonalds restaurants even abroad (Leidner, 1993, 68–74). (On the other hand, this kind of policy implies also great risks. If restaurants are too stylized, they might be experienced as too boring and customers will avoid them in order to find new ones where they have more use of their 'creativity').

Although there are no thoroughgoing studies of the routine use of commodities as such, the sociology of food offers something of an exception. It shows that in many countries people prefer home cooked food, since it is 'food they are used to' (Lupton 1996, 49). Further, food patterns seem to be relatively stable. A breakfast is understood to be different from a lunch, which, in turn, is defined differently from a supper (Douglas and Gross, 1981, 6–8; Murcott, 1982; Prättälä et al., 1993). Much the same food items are eaten on ordinary weekdays when the nutritive aspect of food seems to have a great importance. (It is no wonder that every day food is called 'staples' in English). For instance, most Norwegians used to eat meatballs, pasta and sausages for dinner during the working week (Wandel et al., 1995, 165). Habits and 'household traditions' still play a great role in Finnish every day eating (Palojoki, 1997, 124–125). Weekends and visitors seems to break through this repetitive eating behaviour when another sort of mechanism enters to govern the choice of food: as Päivi Palojoki says 'then taste is the most important factor regardless of the type of food or homemakers' values' (126).

Similar patterns have been observed for some other kinds of consumption, especially commercial TV and the Internet. It is, for instance, well known that people follow for years the very same TV-serials (like Dallas, Ally McBeal, Twin Peaks etc.) that are usually on during prime time. Also large numbers of general public 'are making Internet news reading a routine part of their daily life'. One of the latest surveys in the USA shows that 22% of those who use the Internet as a news source use it every day of the week (Levins, 1998). Moreover, time budget studies show that other sorts of media are followed steadfastly every day and almost the same amount of time is spent on them. Time budget studies also suggest that people devote the same amount of time day after day to all kinds of productive consumption. They clean their homes, prepare food, wash dishes, etc. every evening and conduct these activities in the same order (e.g. Niemi and Pääkkönen, 1989; Liikkanen and Pääkkönen, 1993).

Most of the empirical material on consumption routines is focused on consumption objects and activities that have been in use for a long time. There is less research on the routinization of consumption of novelties. But from our own experience we know that a similar logic is at work in the habitualization of any novelty—despite the variation introduced by different types of commodities—a process which Bourdieu describes so nicely in his analysis of sports training. We learn, little by little, to know these novel commodities through our bodies, their properties and the activities that they imply. This learning process might take a shorter or longer time, but when we no longer need concentrate on these commodities and their related activities, their use becomes routine and that does not demand our attention. Spectacles might serve as an example. Having purchased their first or a new pair of glasses, people tend to be very conscious of them because they feel strange for a while. But once the eyes and nose have become used to the glasses, people will no longer even notice them. Cycling is routinized in essentially the same way. At the learning stage riding requires the individual's undivided attention and conscious maintenance of balance, but once riding starts to come naturally, the body begins to react automatically and the rider's attention shifts from the bicycle to the environment. Once the environment, too, has become familiar, the cyclist may ride for long stretches without even 'perceiving' the surroundings. Only when something exceptional happens in traffic do we once again pay attention to our riding.

ROUTINES AND THE SOCIOLOGY OF CONSUMPTION

I have been able to offer only a few examples of the routinization of consumption. This is partly because of the scantiness of existing research on this topic. However, it would be very difficult to conduct such research. Routinization is a long process, which progresses very smoothly and in an almost unobserved way. The same goes for consumption routines and for the research of the routinization of work and work routines. Robin Leidner, who has conducted an interesting inquiry into the work routines at McDonald's, writes: 'I asked about variations from the routine...and about workers' responses to customers. However, the interactions between workers and customers at McDonald's are over almost as soon as they begin, and others are immediately under way... it was very difficult for the workers I interviewed to call such minute incidents to mind' (1993, 239).

That consumption is routinized unobserved is one obstacle to its study. Yet the most difficult obstacle to overcome in studying consumption routines is probably the fact that they are intertwined with action. Because routines also 'shade over' into action in consumption, one needs to be able to separate 'true' action from consumption routines. This would require a researcher to have an intimate knowledge of her or his informants and to follow them in all the above mentioned consumption situations.

Although not easy to study, consumption routines exist; and they play a large part in the consumption process. Consequently, it is not enough to focus on consumption mechanisms such as fashion, style, etc. in order to grasp the role that consumption plays in modern life. These mechanisms imply agency, and are related to the meanings of consumer goods and acts of consuming. Naturally, routinized consumption may also express certain social and cultural meanings, as Bourdieu has shown, though this is not always the case (see Campbell, 1996a, 97; Camic, 1986, 1052). When consumption carries some meaning, the meaning is often neither intentionally and willfully produced (in the strong senses of these terms) nor reflexively monitored. Therefore the scope of the sociology of consumption should be expanded in the direction of consumer behaviour.

To focus on consumption routines would lead us to a completely different kind of world from the one revealed by fashion etc. If we pay attention to consumption routines on a micro level, this would obviously take us to more or less unseen consumption practices that occur in everyday life, ones indeed that have been demonstrated in much feminist research. Secondly, it will also draw our attention to the hidden abilities that are so important in carrying out our daily lives and which have also been shown to be so essential a part of women's work. Thirdly, it would probably give a good picture of what is considered 'normal' in particular societies.

Notes

1 It must, however, not be confused with the theory of rational choice. It considers the most effective means to attain to aimed preferences, but the preferences themselves are taken for granted. Because of this the theory of rational choice approaches a habitual, routinized behaviour (Pantzar, 1996, 5).

2 To him routine is a historical concept. In a class-divided (feudal) society routine is concealed by tradition. Only in a modern, class society (in capitalism) does routine become a specific practice, because the role of tradition changes (Giddens 1979, 221). This view, however, is not easy to defend. All routines in class-divided societies are neither bound to traditions, nor is all traditional conduct routine. They have been reflected and include variation.

3 Jeffrey Alexander criticizes Bourdieu by arguing that he does not have any place for the self in his theory of practices and that the theory is, therefore, 'too practical'. He may be partially right. Alexander's criticism, however, is unfair. He claims that Bourdieu 'employs his special kind of sociologized biologism', as for him 'a practical belief is not a state of mind...but rather a state of body' (1996, 144). This is overinterpreting Bourdieu. What he aims at is simply that states of mind, intended performances, are transformable by practices into states of the body. Cultivation of the body, in other words, incorporates a state of mind, an idea of how an athletic effort should be made.

Chapter 2

ROUTINISATION OR REFLEXIVITY?
CONSUMERS AND NORMATIVE CLAIMS FOR
ENVIRONMENTAL CONSIDERATION

Bente Halkier

Ascribing normative and political responsibilities to consumers and thence problematising consumption practices is not an entirely new phenomenon. Historically, several phases can be identified. Early in the century, the consumer movement was dominated by the co-operatives that began fifty years earlier, e.g. in the pioneering co-operatives in Rochdale, England. The next wave, from the 1930s to the 1960s, was dominated by the 'value-for-money' organisations that set up test boards for goods and published their tests in consumer magazines. From the 1960s, the consumer movement began to integrate broader issues into new and more radical consumer organisations or campaigns concerned with social justice and critical awareness towards producers. The number and visibility of consumer boycott campaigns and support organisations grew. In the same period, the institutions and procedures of formal consumer policies were consolidated and, from the 1980s, consumer policies as well as the consumer movement became significantly international (Gabriel and Lang, 1995, 152–72; Ilmonen and Stø, 1997; Lupton, 1996, 68–93; Vogel, 1995, 150–95).

Consequently, a variety of ways of politicising consumption now exist: green consumption, ethical consumption and a number of single issues. Internationally, the well-known single cases in recent years include: the boycott of Shell in relation to their dumping plans for the oil platform, Brent Spar, the boycott of British beef due to concern about 'mad cow disease', the boycott of French goods as protest against French renewal of nuclear tests in the Pacific, boycotts of goods produced using 'child labour', and boycotts of different foodstuffs due to risk-perceptions such as irradiated and genetically modified items and items produced with growth hormones. Examples of internationally prominent long-term consumption issues are the environment, animal welfare, and fair-trade. At the same time, a variety of campaigns by the state, attempting to prompt people to change their consumption patterns—quit smoking, adopt a less fattening diet, support national products during periods of economic crises etc.—are common in many countries.

Compared to earlier waves of consumer activism and consumer policies, the new feature of the problematisation of consumption in the 1990s is the focus on the choices and responsibilities of the individual consumer to her or himself. As Ulrich Beck (1992, 137) has argued, due to increased individualisation and the increased instability of social frameworks of orientation in late modern societies, choice has become an unavoidable element of daily life for the individual. Or, as Giddens (1994, 75) put it, 'In post-traditional contexts, we have no choice but to choose how to be and how to act.' The individual belongs to a plurality of different important relationships, and has access to a large variety of social and cultural knowledge, which provide them with more scope, but also more uncertainty and more work in integrating their lifeworlds (Beck, 1992, 128–136; Gullestad, 1989, 103). The plurality and uncertainties in the lifeworlds of individuals open up social space for reflections and negotiations about understandings, choices and routine practices. People negotiate how to act and how to choose the right thing. Hence, there is also potential social space for problematising, discussing and negotiating consumption choices and everyday routines connected to consumption on political or moral grounds. This type of social space has become accepted broadly throughout society, at least in Western societies (Bauman, 1995; Gundelach and Riis, 1992).

This chapter is concerned with what happens in everyday life when consumption is problematised via normative claims. I take the example of food consumption practices being problematised via claims for environmental consideration. Those claims come from government campaigns, consumer organisations and other consumers, and consumers 'meet' the claims in indirect mediated and institutionalised relations as well as in direct personal relations. But the concrete questioning and choosing takes place in consumers' direct interaction in everyday life. Everyday consumption practices are as often, if not more frequently, characterised by habits and routines as by intentional reflection and choice. And the first consumption practices to become politicised via the environmental debate in Denmark and other European countries have been the more mundane areas of consumption such as food, energy, garbage and cleaning. These are characterised by embodied routines and tacit knowledge rather than symbolically more 'noisy' types of consumption such as clothes and music.

The purpose of the chapter is to show that a sharp distinction between reflexive and routinised consumption practices is impossible to sustain in empirical analysis. This holds even when studying cases of problematised consumption which might be expected to exhibit clear-cut reflected practices. Hence, some of the assumptions in contemporary fashionable diagnoses of modernity, regarding the role and scope of reflexivity in social life, are criticized. Tentatively, the chapter suggests some conceptual development whereby the sharp distinction between the routinised and reflexive aspects of consumption practices could begin to be overcome.

Firstly, the chapter presents a theoretical understanding of consumption, integrated in everyday life analytical concepts. Secondly, a number of examples of how routinised and reflected aspects of consumption are intertwined are presented, using a Danish study of young consumers' handling of normative environmental claims in food consumption. Finally, the conceptual implications of these examples are discussed.

EVERYDAY LIFE AND CONSUMPTION

Private consumption at household level forms an important part of everyday life. First and foremost, everyday life is connected with the social space where people take part in creating and reproducing meaning by attempting to knit together the different roles and experiences of life (Gullestad, 1989; Luckman, 1989). Thus, everyday life analysis sheds light upon this sociality (Maffesoli, 1989, 11)—how lived socio-cultural practices take place. Using the term sociality should thus be seen as an underlining of the processual modality of social life (Bauman, 1992, 190), a notion originally inspired by Georg Simmel's understanding of social life as interaction or, as he termed it, sociation (*Vergesellschaftung*) (Simmel, 1998, 25).

This does *not* imply that everyday life analysis deals with a cosy micro sanctuary for social relations, characterised by closeness, familiarising and mutuality, resting in its own common sense taken for grantedness. On the contrary, late modern everyday lives are embedded in larger, ambivalent societal dynamics, such as enhanced individualisation and enhanced institutionalisation. Among other things, these dynamics prompt more indefinite social processes, more compelling choice for the individual, and more dependency on mediated institutional dynamics (Bauman, 1992; Beck, 1992; Giddens, 1990). Individual citizens participate in a plurality of shifting social belongings with unclear rules for interpretation and action in different relations and situations. At the same time, far reaching institutional dynamics such as the welfare state, the world market, mass media and expert knowledge are directly present in citizens' most intimate activities. The institutional dynamics constitute conditions in daily life, but everyday activities would also be impossible without being able to draw on the institutions. Hence, everyday life is ambivalent as it contains meaningful solidarity and meaningless fragmentation as well as problematic choices and liberating systems.

The normative demands on consumers to integrate environmental consideration into their daily lives are examples of this entanglement between individualisation and institutionalisation in everyday sociality. Environmental problems of society, closely related to institutional structures of production, reproduction, consumption, infrastructure and resource management, are being placed on the kitchen table agenda of each individual household. Trivial practices of individuals and families can be questioned, and consumers forced to 'take a stand' and perhaps make new choices in complex daily situations.

Understanding everyday life as sociality implies working with anti-essentialist analytical concepts,[1] where it is not assumed that social phenomena such as consumption practices contain a true essence which the researcher can eventually find. Sociality implies a dynamic and open view of the interplay between subjects and their conditions as well as between subjects themselves. Thus everyday life can be seen as being characterised by contingency. That is to say, social life is neither entirely coincidental nor entirely determined (Mortensen, 1991, 54).

The key concept of my everyday life analytical framework is experiences, and three subconcepts relate to it, practices, interpretations and interactions. *Experiences* are the basis of and the result of practices and interpretations in interaction with others in concrete contexts (Lave, 1988, 178–79). Experiences are concrete 'meetings' with phenomena in everyday life. Such experiences can have a sensate as well as a cognitive character (Hastrup, 1992, 27–39; Hastrup, 1995, 182–84). What do people do, where, when, with whom, how do they experience it, and how are these experiences used to produce meaning in other contexts? This is how the build up of socio-cultural knowledge and expectations takes place over time (Berger and Luckmann, 1987, 33–48; Schütz, 1975, 23–41). The possibilities and limitations of resources, living conditions and social networks obviously also influence which experiences the individual makes.

Practices are the activities of the individual in sociality. Most everyday life analysts work with a continuum of activity types that can be simplified into two types of practices, routines and actions. Routines consist of the continuous stream of activity that is taken for granted and they work on the basis of tacit knowledge in the practical consciousness. Actions consist in intentionally chosen activities that the individual is explicitly capable of accounting for and work on basis of reflected knowledge in discursive consciousness (Giddens, 1984, 5–14; Gullestad, 1989, 34–37). Hence, by reflexivity I mean social reflection that is intentional but not necessarily rational in the strict sense. Contrary to two other important understandings of reflexivity, of ethnomethodology and Habermasian critical theory, I understand it as social reflection which is motivated by problematised practices.

Actions do not solely take place as single incidents that the individual voluntarily chooses to let happen. As actions are part of sociocultural patterns too, actions are often immersed in social rules, irrespective of whether they are based on rules, chosen contrary to rules or attempting to reflect upon, negotiate and revise the rules. On the contrary, routinised practices are not in need of rules, since practice is embedded in what is done. In the same sense, routines constitute practices that the body stores and remembers, in which case it is very difficult to reflect actively on these practices. In this way, routinised practices are part of how people sustain an experience of normality, which the more reflected actions can break or actively legitimate (Ilmonen, 1997, 4–5).

In spite of all the differences, the two types of practices overlap, and routines make as much a difference in the world as intentional actions, partly because of the unintended consequences that both types of practices produce (Giddens, 1984, 27). Such overlaps between routines and actions are related to one of the main problems in this agency-oriented definition of practice: the problem of autonomy of practices versus the conditions of practices. I suggest that the degree of autonomy and conditionality of practices is dependent on the specific characteristics of the actors and the degree of structuring of the context which relates directly to the contingency of the social relations of everyday life sociality.

The remaining two subconcepts also fit into the contingent sociality understanding. *Interpretations* are open ascriptions of meaning to phenomena where in time, they can become typifications—'one of a particular kind' (Luckmann, 1989, 23–25). Interpretations are formed in a process where individuals bring their socio-cultural pre-understandings into play in order to understand a phenomenon (Gadamer, 1993, 265–277). Thus, interpretations never express totally closed structures of meaning but more often, changeable compositions, drawing on several different available practices and discursive repertoires (Antaki, 1994, 119). *Interactions* are the carrying out of practices and interpretations as part of social relations. Such relations are formed with known others in social networks as well as distant others in imagined communities (Anderson, 1983). Interaction produces and reproduces social relations. The participants form the results of the interaction as well as the interaction forming the participants (Goffman, 1959, 245). Interactions are a prerequisite for subjective experiences to turn into socio-cultural knowledge.

The concept of consumption can be integrated into the framework of everyday life analysis. This conceptual integration serves the purpose of avoiding the well-known polarisation in sociology of consumption: between seeing consumption as an appendage to production or letting consumption float into free individual choice and aesthetics (Featherstone, 1990). Consumption is a particular field of practice in everyday sociality, which combines the satisfying of needs with expressions of identity. Consumption covers not only activities of buying but also social relations connected to provision, use and disposition of goods and services. I draw upon three sources to establish the concept of consumption. The first is Alan Warde's understanding of consumption as 'who obtains what goods or services, under what conditions are they delivered and to what use are they put' (Warde, 1997, 19). The obtaining, provision and use take place within a framework of exchange value, use value and identity values (*ibid.*, 197–98). Second is Pasi Falk's understanding of consumption as a primary space for personal and social identification. Consumption is here related to the processes whereby goods are taken in as well as kept out, materially and symbolically (Falk, 1994, 134–37, 144). Third is Jukka Gronow's understanding of identification as *bricolage* of different elements of consumption into styles (Gronow, 1997, 91–92, 170–71).

Consumption experiences regard bodily practices whereby goods and services are obtained, used and disposed of. Such practices are characterised by routinised as well as reflected activities whereby goods and services are taken in and kept out. Interpretations of consumption are particularly related to individual and social belonging and distancing. Such practices and interpretations take place in interaction with relevant others and across different 'zones' in contingent everyday life sociality.

The next section gives a number of empirically based examples of consumer experiences with (environmentally) problematised consumption practices which show how it is impossible to operate with a sharp distinction between the routinised and reflexive aspects of ordinary consumption.

ROUTINISATION AND REFLEXIVITY IN PROBLEMATISED CONSUMPTION

In Denmark, following shifts in the public discourse on environmental problems and solutions, the individual consumer or household is ascribed direct co-responsibility for solving environmental problems by redirecting their consumption choices and everyday habits into less polluting and resource consuming practices (Læssøe, 1990). These claims for environmentally friendly consumption practices (EFCP)[2] are present in a number of societal activities: in public and private campaigns addressing consumers such as handbooks on behaving in an environmentally friendly manner (Danmarks Naturfredningsforening, 1989); in policy initiatives such as the Danish product-oriented environmental policy (Miljøstyrelsen, 1996); in citizen initiatives such as the organisation of 'Green Families' (Læssøe et al., 1995); and in the retail sector where a growing variety of types of environmentally friendly products are available, due to successful alliances between specific supermarket chains, alternative producers and state controlled eco-labelling schemes for foodstuffs (Klint, 1996). The latest representative surveys of the Danish population estimate that 37% of Danes report that they always, or often, buy organic foodstuffs (Gallup, 1999), and the total market share for organic products is between 4 and 5% (Vestergaard, 1999).

Thus, in various ways, environmental claims become part of people's shared everyday life experiences in Denmark. Different consumers manage the presence of the normative claims for environmental consideration in consumption[3] very differently, and not just in Denmark (e.g. Eden, 1993; Finger, 1994; Joy and Auchinacie, 1994; Lavik and Enger, 1995; Læssøe et al., 1995).

My own research on young Danish consumers contains parallel findings of vast socio-cultural differences in their experiences of environmental consideration in consumption, and their ambivalences in their practical handling of such problematised consumption (Halkier, 1999). These data form the background for establishing the ideal types around which the following discussion of routinised and reflexive consumption evolves. An in-depth qualitative empirical study, the data consist of two qualitative interviews (Kvale, 1996; McCracken, 1988; Spardley, 1979) with nine young consumers who have just started their own household. They were interviewed about their life story, everyday food consumption and experiences with the environmental problematique. Data were also obtained in five focus groups (Morgan, 1997) with the key informants and participants from their social network about norms on environmental consideration and consumption.

Routinisation and reflexivity mixed

A common assumption of research on consumers' environmental behaviour is that either their practices are greened as a result of reflection or they are not greened as a result of the routine character of consumers practices (e.g. Stanley and Lasonde, 1996; Thøgersen, 1994). A slightly different argument assumes that consumers begin to incorporate environmental consideration into their practices via reflected choices but that these choices over time become silent and non-reversible habits. This kind of assumption seems to lie implicit in some of the research that divides consumers into a continuum of segments from light-green to dark-green (e.g. Enger, 1995). The mutual problem of the two sets of assumptions is their insistence of maintaining a separation of intentional action and silent routines in real life socialities. Even in such a narrow corner of consumption practices as those related to environmental consideration, the two types of practices are much more intertwined.

Helga[4] is an unemployed woman of 21 who primarily understands normative claims for environmental consideration as creating everyday dilemmas, often without solutions, as this has been her most recurrent experience. For example, she and her flatmate are sorry to throw out a huge pile of packaging after returning from the supermarket, but take it for granted they don't have other shopping possibilities to avoid over-packaging. Once they go into a supermarket, packaging follows: 'But it's also easy in a way to disclaim responsibility and say, but I can't help that they pack all their goods in those things, then, you can say, that's a way to evade. That...but it's also difficult to put a finger on because...there are so many...things that are just natural, that you don't think about...whereas perhaps you ought to have moral scruples, ugh, but there are suddenly some things that have become so integrated into our daily life, that...it would be unnatural otherwise.' During the interview process, she begins to reflect upon the relationship between what she hears herself saying about her shopping routines and what she hears herself and her social network saying about their wishes to improve environmental degradation. As a consequence, she changes practices to buying organic milk and eggs. Hence, she makes a couple of reflected consumption choices, but they are continuously part of the overall routinised pattern of her shopping.

Nis is an unskilled worker of 21. He is not reminded about environmental problems in his everyday life. His friends served organic milk to him once, without talking about it, and this sensate experience of tasting such milk reminded him of milk from his childhood. The experience was so positive that he now buys and uses several types of organic foodstuff: '...as far as I can and can afford it, I buy organic, it's a way to begin to think about not getting all those artificial shitty stuff that they put in the food and sort of trying to get things raw from the nature.' He still doesn't talk to his friends or colleagues about environmental considerations, so explicit discursive interaction about EFCP is not a part of his experience. But he makes sense of the silent bodily incorporation of EFCP by making them a part of his everyday speculations on the relations between man and nature. Thus, he sees organic foodstuff as more natural and pure and less dangerous to himself than ordinary industrialised food. Hence, consumption practices located in his practical consciousness are linked to and supported by reflexivity.

Morten, a 20 year old shop assistant and vegetarian, includes a large number of different EFCP in his consumption. To him, buying organic foodstuff, non-harmful washing powders and saving water have become natural habits that he doesn't reflect upon any more. He simply does not reach out for cauliflower from Italy outside the Danish season, when he is out shopping: 'I just think...then, it's just become such a natural part of my day...think about it, really it's just...ok, you think about it, but it's just become natural, it doesn't occur to me to buy the other goods...' At the same time, he often introduces normative discussions in all parts of his social network about environmental considerations in consumption and what the individual consumer ought to do: 'Ok, at least they always get a kick, if they have bought milk that's not organic, such things that are so easy to get hold of. In that way, we talk about it...'. Thus, Morten's EFCP apparently are characterised by a mixture of solitary tacit knowledge and social active reflexivity.

The potential conceptual implications from this mixture of routinisation and reflexivity point towards problematising or making more subtle parts of the sociological diagnoses of late modernity, embraced by a large number of consumption analysts, including myself. Ulrich Beck (1992, 137) and Anthony Giddens (1994, 75) both argue that the individual and social subjectivity of late modernity concerns the individual being forced by individualisation to reflect and choose intentionally to a larger extent, and in many more areas of life, than previously. Although they recognise the existence of a large area of people's everyday practices being routinised, a clear separation between routines and reflected actions is being maintained, and consumers including EFCP are categorised as reflected practitioners of life politics or subpolitics (Giddens, 1991, 215; Beck, 1992, 184–87). Instead, I suggest using a parallel to the notion of contingency in everyday life sociality. Contingency means that social relations are neither determined nor coincidental, and indeed they might be both at the same time. Consumption practices are neither entirely reflected nor routinised, and may be both at the same time. But in order not to lose the analytical capacity for distinction in this understanding, contingency should be framed as a contingency scope of practices. A contingency scope allows for different distinctive 'creolised', or mixed, positions between routinised and reflexive aspects of consumption practices.

Routinisation negotiated via reflexivity
The young Danish consumers studied do not exhibit consistent environmental consumption behaviour which is put into practice in all areas of daily life, not even those for whom environmental consideration plays an important part of their identification. This generality of practices is often assumed in the segmentation studies on consumers and environment, mentioned above.

The normative handling of the claims for environmental consideration in consumption common to all the young consumers consists of something else. The concept 'immediacy of responsibility' denotes a particular way of negotiating normative claims in everyday life, in this case environmental claims (Eden, 1993, 1748). The daily lives of people are full of different problems and responsibilities, which make it necessary for the individual to prioritise between responsibilities. Often, the responsibilities that get priority on consumers' kitchen table agenda are those that consumers experience as close to them. Secondly, prioritised responsibilities are often those that give consumers space of action and where actions are perceived as making a difference to problems. Thus it often seems more important and consequential for consumers to take care of the immediate needs of partner, children or job rather than the problems of global climate changes or pesticide use in agriculture. The young consumers negotiate their concrete environmental responsibility with themselves and their network along one or several of these dimensions of the immediacy of responsibility.

Such processes highlight the role of the institutional conditions of practices and changes of practices. When consumers change into less environmentally damaging consumption practices, one should distinguish between the practices that can be carried out within the existing institutional conditions and those that demand going beyond these conditions. For example the mother of Helga, the unemployed young woman, buys organic meat directly from the farmers in the area where they live instead of going to the supermarket that is the more normal institutional frame for food shopping. But such a change in practices would be quite unlikely among the young consumers living in the city, due to the lack of practical and economic possibilities to engage in them. Therefore such consumption choices would often not even be a part of the negotiations related to the immediacy of responsibility.

Anne is a clerk apprentice of 19 who associates the environmental problematique with boring school subjects and who interprets organic goods as being an exaggerated fashion phenomenon. She is not reminded about the environment in her daily life, so it is not a part of her practical experiences or her social reflections. If she were to include environmental consideration in consumption, it would only be if the government established the infrastructure and support to make EFCP as easy for her as her current routines—such as waste sorting systems: 'The more in favour of it, the faster it goes or the better it becomes. But there will also always be some people that won't do it. I think, if it comes out what you say about every family is to have more responsibility for what they consume, I will do it too. I do think a little about it, I don't walk around and pollute on purpose.' Hence, Anne negotiates whether, and when, to change her food routines on the grounds that she doesn't have the necessary space for action.

Signe is a high school pupil of 19. She doesn't think it is her responsibility to solve environmental problems if other consumers don't. She doesn't believe in an imagined community of green consumers, numerous enough to produce an aggregate effect large enough, because members of her own social network are worried but mainly passive. Her social interaction thus is not characterised by negotiations of what to do about the environment. Like Anne, she ends her negotiations with herself by placing responsibility with public authorities and experts. She typifies such actors as more likely candidates to make a difference to environmental problems than herself: '...and when I take a glass of water from the tap, I don't think about how dead polluted our ground water has gradually become, because I think, if it was that polluted, they would do something about it. Then they would say, don't drink from the tap...'. Signe doesn't have her food routines such as drinking water disturbed by environmental consideration in daily life, but accounts for this non-disturbance via her reflections upon her own status as societal actor when social surroundings demand an explanation.

20 year old Anders studies biology and comes from a family where organic foodstuffs were consumed routinely. He buys and uses organic goods regularly, if quality, price difference and effect on environmental problems are in a reasonable relation to each other. This he believes to be the case for oat flakes, milk and eggs, but not for meat (because of the price) and not for foreign citrus fruits (because of the environmental effect of transport). Thus, he negotiates situationally his familiar habit of using organic goods: 'With daily goods, you ought to do something, if you can afford it.'

Routinisation negotiated via reflexivity, expressed here in terms of the immediacy of responsibility, can be seen as a particular incidence of mixed consumption practices, a particular position in the contingency scope that has to do with ambivalence. The examples suggest that consumers are quite capable of handling ambivalences without necessarily being burdened by anxious crises of identity based on the insecurity of social choice in a world of fragmented knowledge, as Bauman argues (Bauman, 1992, 187–95; Warde, 1994, 65). Rather, the negotiated combination of some predictability via routinisation and some degree of choice via active reflection suggests that consumption practices operate in a way consistent with Jukka Gronow's interpretation of Simmel's notion of fashion (Gronow, 1993, 90; Simmel, 1991, 69). The ways in which consumers form their own styles offer them the possibility of expressing subjectivity. But at the same time, fashion gives them a certain security for choosing in a socially correct manner. Hence, consumers are capable of handling ambiguities of practices in normalised ways in everyday life.

Reflexivity drowning in routinisation—or in stylisation?
As underlined above, even those young consumers to whom environmental consideration is important to their personal and social

identification negotiate their green reflections in relation to other and more habitualised practices. These negotiations entail a certain degree of intentional reflection over the taken-for-grantedness of their routines. In some cases, routinisation of consumption practices 'drown' reflections, so in particular 'zones' of life the young consumer is not reminded at all about the environmental aspect in the getting along of daily life. To put it another way: environmental consideration can be part of the person's discursive consciousness in general, but is perhaps only part of her or his practical consciousness in particular everyday areas. Hence, consumption practices are characterised by compartmentalisation in relation to environmental consideration (Iversen, 1996, 48–49).

Sonja is 20 years old and works as a postwoman. She gets reminded about environmental problems when shopping for food, cooking and eating. She buys organic food, goods with less environmentally damaging packaging and locally produced foodstuffs. She expresses lack of trust in the edibility of industrialised food. She feels she can handle the risks towards her body by using foodstuffs which she interprets as being of better quality such as organic goods: 'Everything must be rinsed very thoroughly before I eat it,' cause I don't know what they have sprayed it with. From oranges to carrots to apples, everything must be rinsed, because you can't count on anything. You don't know what's genetically manipulated and what's not. I take care to rinse what I buy and try as far as possible to buy organic, so I can count on the animals to have had a good time or the vegetables to have grown in earth that's not too pervaded.' The consumption practices of her partner and friends—with whom she shares most meals—are similar, and they differentiate themselves from other Danes whom they perceive as over-consuming materialists. Hence, Sonja identifies with the consumption-based lifestyle of her network group. But Sonja is only reminded about environmental problems when it has to do with food getting into her body. Even the packaging around foodstuffs is judged on criteria for whether parts of its plastic or metal can sift into the food and she might incorporate it. She is not reminded about the environment when taking a shower or buying clothes, and she finds it tiresome to locate a bottle bank. Hence, her main experiences of environmental consideration in consumption are related to handling of risks against her body, and this is perhaps the key point of compartmentalisation for her.

The unskilled worker Nis who buys some organic goods is a similar example of compartmentalised consumption practices. He reflects upon and includes environmental consideration in his food consumption, since he had a positive sensate experience with organic milk. His own expression for environmental consideration is 'to take care of what you go around and do'—not to hurt animals and plants. But his hottest consumption desire is to get a car as soon as he can afford it, and he doesn't associate environmental damage with that. He takes it for granted that you have got to have a car to get around.

Conceptually, both examples point towards the usefulness of Trine Iversen's concept related to compartmentalisation—tactility of practices (Iversen, 1996, 80–82). This means the importance of the tangibility or physical sensitivity of practices for whether and how consumers carry them out. Her point is that consumers maintain or shift to an environmentally friendly practice, if the environmentally friendly element can be physically felt—visible, touchable, tasted etc.—towards which routinised practices are often oriented. In Sonja's and Nis' cases, the sensation of taste is important. Hence, in other consumption zones of their lives, their reflections upon normative environmental claims cannot be linked to something tangible and drown in the tangibility of these other routinised practices. Some forms of compartmentalisation however take other forms than routinised tangibility and have more to do with social relations.

Lena, who is 20, works as a home help. She grew up in a family where her mother insisted on the family participating in their household becoming a more sustainable one by changing many routines. Today, Lena is not reminded about environmental problems in any tactile sense in her daily life, and she doesn't carry out any EFCP. Her life is currently much more centred on going out with her friends who are not interested in environmental considerations: '...but certainly, I think it's something you ought to think about, but it demands that you change your habits totally, and that demands some time. And I don't have time now, and I don't think very many young people have that.' But she accounts discursively for her understanding of consumers as having normative responsibility towards environmental problems, and she feels guilty about not acting upon this herself. Sociality drowns her environmental reflections—not her consumption routines as such and this is related to her moving away from family to live with friends.

The shop assistant, Morten, who routinely, as well as reflectively, undertakes a large number of EFCPs, identifies himself with being anti-materialist and is identified as such by his social network. But in a number of consumption zones, he doesn't include environmental consideration because he enjoys the pleasures of the material consumption itself, and the specific practices are used in his styling of his personal and social identification. He buys and dresses in a lot of trendy clothes, likes to buy the latest pop music cds and occasionally eats at McDonald's. In his case, social styling drowns environmental reflexivity.[5] He makes a point of explicitly accounting for what he sees as materialist consumption practices to the interviewer as well as in his network group. Apparently, this is to signal social normality. Environmental consideration is the dominating uniting element in his *bricolage* of consumption based identification. Socially, he is a lifepolitical activist in his social network, questioning the routines of his friends and colleagues. Hence, he styles himself as more 'average' and compartmentalised in order to belong to his network more easily: 'That's what makes it so cool to eat at McDonald's once in a while. It's just so extremely politically incorrect.'

Thus, compartmentalisation is a useful concept with which to examine mixed consumption practices. It can be used to analyse how reflected and chosen consumption practices can become 'crowded out' by tangible routinisation. But perhaps the two concepts should be more clearly distinguished in a contingency scope. Compartmentalisation can contain more dimensions than tactility, namely the socialising and styling elements involved in keeping green reflections out of certain practices. Thus, compartmentalisation seems to be the more creolised concept of the two, whereas tactility seems closer to the routinised aspect of consumption practices.

Routinisation as relief from reflexivity

Several sociologists argue that the individual has increasingly become an autonomous moral agent as a consequence of fragmentation or weakening of the systems of traditional codes for social behaviour (Bauman, 1993; Wolfe, 1989). The ascription of environmental responsibility to each household and consumer seems to be one clear example. None of the informants or focus groups entirely rejected the normative legitimacy of the consumer's environmental responsibility. But such arguments tend to overestimate the burden of normative reflexivity by underestimating the role of routinised normative practices.

Zygmunt Bauman (1995) works with two types of ethical practices. In the ethics of conformity, the individual is responsible *towards* a social code or institution, and she or he can routinise practices. In the ethics of responsibility, the individual is responsible *for* something or somebody, and he or she has to reflect and decide upon—and possibly also negotiate with others—which practices to choose. Hence, his argument about moral conduct is that the ethics of responsibility gradually replace the ethics of conformity.

Among the young consumers, the ethics of responsibility is certainly at work, since it is never entirely rejected, and some of the young people carry out practices related to ethics of responsibility, such as the life-political shop assistant, Morten. But as mentioned earlier, the normative dynamic of the immediacy of responsibility is present in all of the young consumers' daily lives, regardless of their other differences. They all negotiate their concrete environmental responsibility in relation to other responsibilities and conditions, as well as in relation to the possibilities of actions and the effects of actions. Some of their negotiations and expressions related to the immediacy of responsibility suggest that the ethics of conformity still seems to be necessary for society, because the ethics of responsibility in consumption is experienced as a burden and an inefficient space for action.

The clerk apprentice, Anne, and the high school pupil, Signe, are the clearest examples. They both emphasize that industry and agriculture damage the environment as much as consumers. They feel that on their own initiative it is difficult to contribute effectively to solve environmental problems connected to consumption practices, because of lack of serious space of action and lack of committed fellow consumers. Thus, both want to be relieved from having to reflect and choose among their consumption practices by public authorities—the system world if you like. In their view, public authorities should provide more institutional and economic support and infrastructures to act in an environmentally friendly manner as well as obliging all societal actors to participate. Then it could become easy and routinised to 'do the right thing', and the sheer amount of EFCP could become large enough to redress environmental damage.

The ethics of conformity can be seen as a kind of routinisation of normative claims on consumption practices, a way of willing away personal moral responsibility for large societal problems. Such routinisation works as a relief from being forced to reflect and relate oneself actively in every situation (Ilmonen, 1997, 4–5), which can be quite stressful, especially in a context of uncertain knowledge and ambivalent possibilities for action. Even the lifepolitical activist of the young consumers, Morten, has routinised particular parts of his consumption practices. Thus he reduces the burden of doubting, checking and reflecting as a critical consumer. Some practices are safe and predictable, and he doesn't have to question them. These examples can be seen as a specific normative variety in the contingency scope of consumption practices being creolised between routinisation and reflexivity.

Routinisation legitimised by reflexivity

The empirical examples of the mixing of routine and reflected aspects of consumption practices illustrate a point made many times by anthropologists, symbolic interactionists and conversation analysts: tacit knowledge and routinised practices become rationalised socially when accounts of them are being requested (Antaki, 1994, 107; Coffey and Atkinson, 1996, 100–05; Potter, 1996, 43–46). As shown in some of the earlier examples, the young consumers do not treat the normative claim for environmental consideration in consumption as a binding moral rule. Rather, different versions of environmental claims are used as drafts for social norms that can be negotiated in relation to different consumption practices and consumption situations. This is in line with contemporary research on social norms. Here it is argued that the traditional concept of norms as being rules people ought to follow must be supplemented with at least two other ways of acting normatively. One is reflexive norms, where people reflect, discuss and negotiate what would be the right thing to do. Another is facticist norms, where people refer to fact-like conditions as reasons for what they do in situations of normative choice (Mortensen, 1992, 197–201). This last type of norm is what the examples from the young consumers' reasonings and negotiations are about. They constitute examples of the young people legitimising their routinised exclusion of environmental consideration in consumption practices through the discursive accounts for their own practices which their common negotiation on norms force them to give.

There are negotiations about three different ways of facticist legitimisation in both Helga's and Sonja's network groups: personal, societal and sensate facticism. The common characteristic of the three types is that arguments are based on some sort of reification of practices that is not questioned but taken for granted. This is the way things just are.

Personal facticist arguments are of the form: this is the way things just are for me. To consume organic goods is just too expensive.

Declarations on goods are too technical to find out which is the least environmentally damaging choice. Systems for sorting waste are not sufficiently detailed. Shopping for organic goods takes too long a time. We cannot afford to go to special shops. Food is something to get over and done with. When you live on your own, you spend less money on foodstuffs.

Societal facticist arguments take the form: this is the way things are in general for people in this society. This is a normalising device. The supply of environmentally less damaging consumption possibilities is just not available yet. No young people have a salary sufficient to buy organic goods. Everybody has a right to prioritise their consumption practices. We cannot live in this society without having a lot of material things.

Sensate objections against organic goods and environmentally friendly packaging obtain their facticist character from not being questioned. In other words, the young consumers accept each others' bodily and aesthetic experiences as legitimate in themselves. Organic carrots are full of earth. Organic vegetables are sloppy and look uninteresting. Frozen, chopped, organic meat looks disgusting. It's not possible to feel any difference between environmentally friendly washing powder and conventional powder. Fat lumps in organic milk are unpleasant. Environmental packaging looks boring. Organic cotton clothes are extremely boring.

Even Morten, the lifepolitical activist, uses a sensate facticist legitimisation when accounting for his consumption of clothes: 'But I won't call myself an over-ecological consumer. Surely, I don't care to walk around in those puke-white coloured clothes...' Hence, these examples show that routinisation can be used as a part of reflexivity.

CONCLUSION

I have argued that it is impossible empirically to maintain a sharp distinction between reflexive and routinised consumption practices. This is so even when ordinary consumption such as food practices become potentially extra-ordinary through normative environmental problematising at which point more clear-cut reflected 'green' practices could be expected. The background for this apparently 'messy' empirical condition can be understood by taking a closer look at the analytical context of private household consumption. Consumption is a particular field of practices in the sociality of everyday life. Understanding everyday life as sociality implies a dynamic and open view on the interplay between subjects and between subjects and their conditions. Hence, everyday life is characterised by contingency: social life is neither entirely coincidental nor entirely determined.

At the most basic level, routinised and reflexive consumption practices in relation to environmental consideration are mixed. This is not taken account of in segmentation and lifestyle studies, typical of the research field of consumers' environmental behaviour. This creolisation of reflexivity and routinisation is also neglected in some of the fashionable sociological diagnoses of social life in late modernity which maintain a clear separation of routines and reflected actions. As a tentative alternative—which needs more conceptual development—I suggest the use of the notion, the contingency scope of practices. A contingency scope allows for different distinctive positions of mixes between routinised and reflexive aspects of consumption practices.

The remaining four types of mix between reflexive and routinised consumption practices in relation to environmental consideration in consumption constitute different specific positions in the contingency scope. Firstly, routinisation can be negotiated via reflexivity. Hence, consumers are capable of handling ambivalences in practices in normalised ways. This forms a parallel to Jukka Gronow's argument about the ways in which fashion works to offer consumers the opportunity to express individuality, while at the same time enjoying the security of doing that within normalised frames. This position in the contingency scope also contains a critique of Zygmunt Bauman's arguments about consumers being burdened by crises of identity due to compelling constant choosing. Secondly, reflexivity can 'drown' in context, because consumption practices are compartmentalised. The point here is that this context can be tactile routines, but it can also be social stylisation. Thirdly, routinisation can work as a relief from reflexivity. This position in the contingency scope challenges Zygmunt Bauman's argument about moral conduct in late modernity, that the more individualised and reflected ethics of responsibility has replaced the more socially institutionalised ethics of conformity. Finally, routinisation can be legitimised by reflexivity, which illustrates a well-known point in anthropology and conversation analysis, that tacit knowledge and routinised practices can be rationalised when accounts for them are being requested. Looking at routine and reflexivity in ordinary consumption practices does not necessarily imply an unpleasant choice between reductionist categories or boundless contexts. Rather, it implies a challenge for development of context sensitive but analytically precise concepts.

Notes

1   This requires us to rely less on traditional and new taxonomic concepts within everyday life analysis such as social class (Olin Wright, 1979), habitus (Bourdieu, 1984) and lifestyle (Weber, 1978), that have difficulties in catching the contingency of everyday sociality.

2   For example sort the waste, buy organic goods, buy locally produced goods, use detergents and hygiene goods without damaging chemical substances, recycle, save resources, use collective transportation or bike, lower the level of material consumption etc.

3   I define environmental consideration in consumption as 'behaviour which is intended to produce environmentally favourable outcomes, regardless of whether they do in fact do so.' (Eden, 1993, 1744).

4   All names are pseudonyms.

5   Related to the bodily dimension of consumption is another explanation for his compartmentalisation, and the historically contested space of the body between pleasures on the one hand, and rationality, self-discipline and social control on the other is very much related to the ways in which the young consumers related to environmental claims in their consumption practices (Halkier, 1997).

Chapter 3

ORDINARY CONSUMPTION AND EXTRAORDINARY
RELATIONSHIPS: UTILITIES AND THEIR USERS

Elizabeth Shove and Heather Chappells

INTRODUCTION

Water and electricity supplies permit such routine and ordinarily invisible practices that it is difficult to imagine how research in these areas might advance consumption theory or an understanding of the dynamics of demand. Though useful and perhaps necessary, the 'utilities'—a term which is about as unglamorous as the sectors it describes—have failed to attract much analytic attention within consumption studies (Shove and Warde, 1998). This is not the realm of identity politics nor is it an arena in which there is extensive scope for the expression of taste and difference. Until recently utility companies have had a correspondingly low profile, either as monopoly providers or as rather anonymous regional water or electricity suppliers. Though valuing an image of consistency and invisible reliability these organisations have no history of competitive differentiation. What they sell is uniformly unremarkable and for the most part uniformly uninteresting.

Nonetheless, expenditure on fuel and power accounts for up to 10% of average UK weekly household expenditure (King, 1997). More than that, the proliferation of all sorts of domestic devices, ranging from the electric carving knife to the power shower, requires such resources and promotes their consumption. Taking a still broader view, power cuts and prolonged droughts remind us of the extent to which 'normality' now depends on the steady and secure supply of electricity and water. A recent report on power blackouts in New Zealand suggests that 'It's this kind of reality that rams home to ordinary people what otherwise exists only as a theory. Electricity is not a commodity like a designer dress where an interruption of supply poses no wider consequences; it is a precondition for successful modern life' (Hutton, 1998, 24). If our focus is on *ordinary* consumption we should at least take note of the issues involved in acquiring, using, and providing the essential ingredients of normal life.

A second justification for thinking about utility provision, and one which motivates this discussion, is the prospect of learning more about relationships between consumers and providers not just at key moments of exchange but in terms of the social and technical organisation of what amounts to an intricate system of co-production. Electricity and water supplies may be a precondition for many ordinary actions and habits yet the provision and management of these key resources depends on a series of quite extraordinary relationships between consumer and provider. As we explain in the second part of the chapter it sometimes makes sense to view consumers as consumers, but it is also important to recognise their roles as non-consumers, and as co-managers of both demand and supply. Though extraordinary, these arrangements are not unique to the utilities hence prompting further thought about the conceptualisation of consumers within other systems of provision as well.

More immediately, this is as good a time as any to reflect on the buying and selling of water and electricity. Deregulation and privatisation of once state controlled monopolies is such that utility services in the UK are provided by companies whose interests span once distinct sectors and markets. Water boards dabble in electrons. Mergers between energy and water companies have, for instance, resulted in new multi-utilities, such as United Utilities which now has a 'regional stronghold' in the North West of England (Hawkins, 1998). Trans-national take-overs abound. The merger between Scottish Power and PacificCorp of the United States is one such example, also relevant since this once Scottish company now supplies electricity south of the border in England and Wales (Gow, 1998). Global trading and the separation of generation, transmission and retail functions has transformed the commercial landscape and led to the puzzling situation in which gas and water companies are to be found selling electricity along with offers of bonus air miles or new home repair services (Stuart, 1998; Waddams, 1998). From the consumers' perspective it is hard to figure out how different brands of electricity can flow from the same socket outlets, or how English water might be provided by a French company. Commercial re-configuration of the utilities seems to have the further effect of modifying consumers' perceptions of what water and electricity really are and allowing differentiation within what used to be mono-dimensional commodities.

For these reasons alone the utilities represents a promising sector in which to research and explore the characteristics of ordinary consumption. Rather than pursuing all the themes outlined above, this chapter focuses on the conceptualisation of consumer demand. Our review shows how theories of demand have evolved from an early preoccupation with planning and supply, through to more integrated notions of efficient service provision (Guy and Marvin, 1996; Wieman, 1996). Drawing upon the results of an EU funded project (DOMUS) [1], we argue that consumers are much more involved in managing electricity and water resources than even these models imply.

The concept of *co-provision* captures some of the interdependencies at play and helps make sense of such strange practices as the commodification of non-consumption. Given the need to match resource capacity and demand, utilities sometimes have a real commercial interest in restricting as well as increasing electricity and water consumption (Davis, 1998). Hence we find seemingly bizarre situations in which consumers become the providers of what Lovins terms 'negawatts'—that is the non-use of electricity (Lovins, 1996). Though the potential for such extreme role reversal, from consumer to provider and provider to consumer, is not unique to the utilities this case helps set out the issues at stake and so broadens the agenda of ordinary consumer research. Before taking these ideas further we begin by reflecting on what is involved in consuming and providing electricity and water.

CONSUMING ELECTRICITY AND WATER

From Victorian times onwards, maintaining the water supply has been seen as a public service or at least as a service in which there is strong public interest. The provision of power and water has been so closely associated with health and economic prosperity that the utilities have been, and still are, subject to all kinds of government control and regulation (Guy and Marvin, 1995). Though important in terms of investment and utility management, these relationships and controls are largely invisible at the level of the individual household. Many consumers are still unsure who their local supplier is and as Garrett (1997) observes when consumers do identify with their utilities the image is generally one of a bureaucratic but essentially faceless institution. Utility companies are struggling to overcome this history of anonymity in an effort to distinguish themselves from their competitors (Stone, 1997) but the reality is that consumers rarely know where these taken for granted resources come from or how they are provided.

Although households can now shop around and switch between suppliers, they are typically ignorant of the characteristics of their own consumption (Palast, 1998). Few people know how much water and electricity they use over the course of a year, or have a clear sense of when and how consumption takes place (Stuart, 1998). This is partly because electricity is itself invisible (Shove, 1997) and partly because consumption and payment are separated in time. Quarterly bills record the consequences of past actions and summarise the resource implications of a multiplicity of practices and habits (Stern and Aronson 1984; Wilhite, 1994). In addition, the many different moments of using resources, as when washing, ironing or television viewing, are lumped together and translated into the uniform languages of kilowatt hours or cubic litres per day.

As noted above, energy and water consumption can take many forms. What is important is that most of these forms are mediated by some intervening device. Water is used when washing clothes, flushing toilets, and doing the dishes. Similarly, electricity is consumed when making ice cubes, hoovering the floor, and illuminating the living room (Shove and Wilhite, 1999). While it is possible to simply drink a glass of water, electricity consumption inevitably depends on the development and diffusion of things like storage heaters, light bulbs and vacuum cleaners. Whatever the mediating technology involved, the general point is the same: energy and water are important not for themselves but for what they make possible, that is, cleaning, cooking, lighting, heating, and so on.

Since it is the services provided which count, not the resources themselves, more efficient technologies make it possible to do more for a given amount of water or electricity. Equally, new technologies, and new ways of using electricity and water generally increase demand. In short, consumption is mediated by a raft of everyday gadgets which play a tremendously important part both in determining the resource intensity of everyday life and in ratcheting up what become normal standards and practices of comfort and cleanliness.

The points above suggest that energy and water consumption share the following characteristics. First, electricity and water are implicated in the provision of a range of highly routinised services. The scale and character of consumption depends on a mixture of mediating domestic technologies alongside conventions of comfort, convenience and what constitutes a normal life. There is no easy way of revealing the resource implications of routines, habits and practices: although consumed continually, the raw materials of everyday life are only paid for once in a while. Finally, the systems and organisations of provision are typically obscure. Householders know relatively little about the networks and interests involved or the infrastructures which lie behind their taps and socket outlets.

The purpose of this brief review is not to argue that water and electricity are unique in all these respects (other services—for example, telecommunications—have many similar features) but to highlight aspects which have a bearing on conceptualisations of consumer demand and relationships between consumer and provider.

CONCEPTUALISING DEMAND

Given that water and electricity have so many end uses, one might expect observers and analysts to have struggled hard to conceptualise demand. In practice, this has not been the case. Instead of thinking about energy or water in use, discussions of demand have been dominated by the discourse of providers. Since the utilities have conventionally generated what they see as one commodity—that is electricity or water—these debates have circled around the need for somewhat mono-dimensional resources pumped into homes in standard form and destined to meet a variety of only vaguely articulated 'needs'.

Policy makers and utilities' representations of consumer demand have nonetheless changed over time. We identify three approaches. The first, especially relevant in the case of electricity, relates to the deliberate manufacturing of demand and the construction of consumer 'needs'. The second, associated with periods of major infrastructural development and investment, takes demand pretty much for granted. Consumers are positioned as the passive beneficiaries of supply side strategies designed to meet seemingly self evident 'needs'. The third approach, inspired by environmental, political or economic pressure to minimise resource consumption, draws consumers back into the frame and takes note of the potential for restricting demand without compromising the services provided. Though immensely influential in terms of policy and planning, all three perspectives obscure what we take to be important aspects of the ordinary use and management of electricity and water. Critically, they depend on a clear cut distinction between the role of consumer and provider. Even a brief review of the history of demand suggests that this is a misleading distinction and that the utility sector is marked by rather more complex relationships of co-provision and interdependence.

Manufacturing demand

The early history of electricity is a history of inventing uses (Hughes, 1983; Nye, 1992). Lighting was one of the first candidates and as long as it was used for this purpose alone electricity was only needed when it was dark. This did not make sense in terms of the investment and infrastructure required to produce and distribute electric power, hence the invention of other uses designed to spread demand more evenly through the day. During the early 1900s, an enormous variety of domestic appliances were produced including electric kettles, toasters and vacuum cleaners. These gadgets had the double effect of structuring and stimulating demand for electricity whilst also engendering and then establishing new concepts of cleanliness and convenience (Forty, 1986).

Meeting demand

The infrastructures which now surround us represent the physical embodiment of earlier efforts to construct, manage and anticipate peak demand. Those involved in energy and water supply, especially during the 1960s, made use of models and projections which relied on somewhat restricted theories of demand. The question was 'how many power stations do we need and how big should reservoirs be to meet present and future demand'? Consumers' resource needs were taken for granted and then taken into account in macro level estimates. In these scenarios, ever increasing demand figured as both a consequence of and a precondition for economic growth. Such an approach represents demand as a uniform requirement which has to be met and which is not in itself negotiable or malleable. This in turn justifies the construction of large reservoirs, major inter-regional water transfer schemes, and an extensive network of power stations sufficient to cope with seasonal and daily peaks in demand as well as with 'average' requirements (Guy and Marvin, 1995; Winpenny, 1994). The so called 'predict and provide' culture dominated utility planning until the late 1980s. Though demand was a central concept, utility planners dealt in aggregate data and at this stage had little interest in understanding how electricity or water was used in the home or what happened to it beyond the meter.

Managing demand

Energy and water systems are generally designed to meet peak loads and are consequently 'oversized' at other times of the day. Yet there comes a point when the ceiling is reached and the system cannot cope at moments of peak demand. One option is to then increase capacity. In the world of infrastructures of power and water systems, this generally involves significant additional investment (for example, building a whole new power station or reservoir), and often results in environmental anxiety about global warming or landscape degradation. Another option is to reduce or shift the peak and so defer the moment when new capacity is required (Osborn et al., 1998). A third route involves a more radical re-definition of what provision is really for. If energy and water consumption are relevant not in their own right but for the services they provide there may be less resource intensive means of delivering those same services. Viewed from this perspective, measures to increase efficiency and reduce wastage increase the effective capacity of a power station or reservoir, again deferring the need to extend the macro infrastructure itself (Siohansi and Davis, 1989). This is an important conceptual development for it means thinking about the multiple uses of what were previously seen as mono-dimensional resources, and it means understanding much more about the services which households have come to expect (Lovins, 1996). Understanding the dynamics of daily demand then becomes a real priority.

Such ideas have led to development of techniques like 'demand side management' and 'integrated resource planning', the aim of which is to identify the most efficient means of providing services, rather than to simply calculate the resources required to meet anticipated demand (Gellings, 1996; Siohansi, 1996). Shifting the focus from resources to the efficient provision of services represents an important move yet such strategies are still dominated by supply side perspectives. Methods of demand side management identify alternative ways of meeting service 'needs' but do not go so far as to question what constitutes ordinary consumption or consider how conventional but resource intensive habits and practices evolve.

In other words, demand side management typically focuses on just one side of demand: that is on what is seen to be the malleable, technologically manipulable demand for the resources required to provide a given level of service. The other side of demand, that is for the services themselves, remains invisible. Though consumption practices have a place in theories of demand side management, these models and the policies they inspire continue to view provision and consumption as clearly separate, well defined functions.

To summarise, once the use and relevance of electricity was established, the technologies and politics of supply dominated utility discourse. Having manufactured demand the next task was to meet it. The national grid and the large scale generation of electricity requires massive investment of financial and other resources and although networks of water supply have different technical characteristics, the common point is that existing reservoirs and power stations define the limits of the current system, and set thresholds beyond which further development is required. Quite where these thresholds or ceilings of available resources lie depends on the timing as well as the extent of demand. This is important for the need to operate within ceilings of supply or confront the costs of increasing capacity means that resource providers sometimes have an interest in managing demand and deliberately restricting consumption.

In the next section we focus on relationships between providers and consumers. What role does each play in defining demand and managing the flow of resources through the storage, transmission and efficiency devices which constitute contemporary infrastructures?

SYSTEMS OF CO-PROVISION

Though the two-part language of consumer and provider is sometimes useful, it also obscures the range of more complex relationships which sustain what amounts to a supply chain of resource management. Closer inspection of these supply chains reveals a number of curious situations in which consumer and provider roles are scrambled up or in which service provision involves the restriction or redirection of resource flows. The concept of 'co-provision' implies the active participation of both consumer and producer in the organisation of utility systems. As such it allows us to see patterns of interaction and interdependence and appreciate the extent to which resource flows are co-managed by householders and utilities. The three cases considered below explore the meaning and practice of co-provision and in the process reveal what seem to be distinctive and extraordinary features of ordinary consumption.

Infrastructures of co-provision

Energy and water consuming technologies are not neutral devices for they also help to define and re-define normal standards of domestic life. Washing machines and dishwashers are, for instance, implicated in the re-scheduling and subsequent reallocation of household tasks and the timing of resource use (Cowan, 1983). Though long range forecasts of future demand fail to make the connection explicit, such examples remind us of the extent to which consumers' expectations and practices are mediated by the actions of manufacturers and designers, and in turn anticipated by utility planners. This is a perfectly ordinary form of interdependence.

The utilities are, however, subject to a range of distinctive pressures which complicate the management of supply and demand. Consider the multiple steps and stages involved in delivering water to the home. Starting off in a reservoir (though of course water does not really 'start' here) water travels from one pumping station to another, perhaps spending some time in a utility-owned water tower before moving on to a household-owned cold water tank and flowing on from there to a basin, a toilet cistern, or into a bucket or cup. During this journey, water passes through a variety of organisational regimes. There is not one provider but many, each rather directly dependent on the actions and practices of the other. From this perspective, the householder is not just a consumer but is also the owner of an array of pipework, tanks, and containers which are literally part of the infrastructure itself.

At each step, water is stored in order to manage peaks and troughs in demand at the next point in the 'supply chain'. The size of the water tower relates to the number of houses attached and to the quantity of water stored therein. But the relationship is not all one way. When large numbers of householders reduce the volume of water used to flush their toilets (for instance by fitting hippos or other 'anti-storage' water saving devices), the effect is felt back through the rest of the system. Equally, investment in one part of the infrastructure, for instance in a new pumping station or in limiting leakage, has implications for the stresses and strains felt or alleviated elsewhere. Storage systems (cisterns, towers, tanks and reservoirs) each set localised limits or ceilings of available capacity. When thinking about the supply and demand of water, we need to recognise that there are many ceilings, and therefore many points at which demand might be managed along the supply chain of provision. Electricity is not stored and distributed in the same way but, as we argue below, the fact that there are fixed ceilings of available capacity is just as significant.

We have already noted the invention and use of devices designed to even out the daily demand for electricity. Such technologies have the further effect of binding households into networks of provision and positioning them as perhaps unwitting partners in the management of supply and demand. The example of night storage heaters illustrates the point. These devices consume cheap rate electricity during the night and help utilities match supply to demand. In rural Northumbria, the electricity company has been so successful in persuading householders to buy storage heaters (thereby transforming the pattern of peak demand which the utility has to manage) that it has created a new problem of its own making: the daily peak is now at two in the morning when all the night stores kick in! Although part of the electricity infrastructure, night store heaters belong to individual consumers and are therefore difficult to change.

This story illustrates the extent to which household technologies and practices influence the problems and opportunities open to other organisations involved at different points in the electrical supply chain. Rather than going for an all out sales pitch and consistently encouraging consumers to buy more, utility providers find themselves in the rather more complex position of managing the timing of demand and maintaining an optimal balance between consumption and non-consumption. The characteristics of this balancing act depend on the scale of provision and the location of relevant ceilings of available capacity.

Ceilings and scales of co-provision
The details of interdependence and the complexity of the supply chain of provision—both for water and electricity—depend on the scale at which generation, management, distribution, storage and usage take place. So far we have been talking about national grids and regional water supplies. The privatisation and commercial re-organisation of electricity and water promises to modify at least parts of that picture. Lovins (1996), for one, expects to see rapid decentralisation and the proliferation of small scale, localised forms of generation. We can already identify such developments. In Nottingham, Sheffield and Leicester, city councils are involved in large-scale combined heat and power schemes which provide home heating and generate surplus electricity for sale to tenants or to the grid (Hodgson, 1997; McEvoy, 1999). Localised generation is not especially new but the proliferation of novel alliances, for instance, between utilities, housing associations and local authorities suggests that what used to be the core business of established monopolies is currently being 'attacked from the margins' (Gosling, 1996). Such developments are important for they promise

to generate new ceilings of supply and hence new interests in demand management.

The DOMUS research unearthed even more radical examples of households and communities which had gone 'off grid' thereby collapsing the roles of consumer and provider into one. In these situations of extremely localised supply, ceilings of available capacity are typically low and typically unpredictable. For instance, household water resources may literally depend on recent weather patterns and total storage capacity. Similarly those who rely on local hydro power for their electricity have to adjust domestic routines to accommodate fluctuations in supply (CAT Interview, 1998).

Everything depends on how tight the balance is but consumer-providers, such as the residents of Hockerton, a sustainable housing development near Nottingham, are often involved in more or less constant monitoring of the relationship between supply and demand. Operating like mini-utilities in their own right, they adopt demand side management strategies on a daily basis, for example, being thrifty with water during hot weather, checking the many storage containers around the site and adjusting consumption to suit (Hockerton Interview, 1998). Consumer-providers manage the balance between consumption and non-consumption as a matter of course. The need to do so is obvious when the ceiling of available capacity is low and near the point-of-use but as the next case suggests, much the same sort of juggling goes on within utilities and national networks.

Consumption and negumption
We have already seen that systems of co-provision may involve the deliberate restriction of energy and water consumption at certain times of the day or year. The need to manage demand in this way relates to the scale of investment required to increase capacity and to other regulatory or environmental constraints. This leads to the perhaps surprising situation in which utilities' interest in selling more and more water or electricity is sometimes overshadowed by the more important priority of managing—and sometimes limiting—demand. Though perhaps surprising, this is not especially extraordinary. Suppliers of other goods and services may also find themselves trying to manage rather than just increase demand.

The unusual point is that some utilities have taken the further step of commodifying non-consumption, or what we might term 'negumption'. This seemingly extraordinary idea makes sense where ceilings of available capacity are fixed and where there is a constant struggle to meet peak demand. In such situations, it is in the utilities' commercial interest to even the load profile by changing the timing of demand or increasing efficiency so as to extract more service from each litre of water or from each unit of electricity.

Utilities may not have the in-house expertise required to promote non-consumption, especially since this involves reversing their normal role. In the highly fragmented electricity market of the USA a new breed of Energy Service Companies (ESCOs) is now specialising in the efficient provision of services like comfort and cleanliness rather than the sale of energy or water itself. ESCOs promise to provide services to consumers and, at the same time, deliver an agreed amount of non-consumption back to the utilities. In other words they are paid to manage consumer demand so as to produce a load profile which utilities can handle and profit from. Utility consumption of 'negawatts' is already commonplace. Looking only one step ahead, Wieman anticipates the trading of 'negamiles, negagaeons and negajunk' (1996, 51) and the development of nega-markets of negumption.

Where non-consumption is commodified the conventional roles of consumer (householder) and provider (utility) are exchanged. Non-consumption is extracted from end-consumers and sold back to the utility providers. As one commentator cryptically explains, demand side management is 'a lunch you are paid to eat' (Nadel and Geller, 1996). In other words, it is in the utilities' commercial interests to pursue the 'lunch' of energy efficiency. Though such arrangements have a longer history in the electricity sector, the development of water service companies (WSCOs) is also on the cards as the UK water industry recognises the benefits of contracting out efficiency services and as the commercial logic of negumption is put into practice (Environment Agency, 1998).

It is difficult to understand these reversed relationships if we stick to the conventional language of consumer and provider and if we think of electricity and water as mono-dimensional resources. Yet such twists and turns make sense providing we recognise that negumption is the counterpart of consumption and that utility provision routinely involves the day to day balancing of the two. Having explored ideas of co-provision, recognised that resources are important for the services they make possible, taken note of storage and ceilings of available capacity, and appreciated the balancing acts involved, we return to the question of whether the utilities represent ordinary or extraordinary forms of consumption.

ORDINARY AND EXTRAORDINARY CONSUMPTION

In the first part of this chapter we suggested that the utilities are distinctive in that they are not consumed directly (it is the services they make possible which count); that the extent and form of consumption is mediated by all sorts of domestic technologies; that patterns of use are typically inconspicuous and that householders are only dimly aware of the social and technical infrastructures of electricity and water supply.

In reviewing the dynamics of consumption and production we have argued that expectations and levels of demand reflect the routinisation of everyday practices and conventions which are both shaped and held in place by a range of now taken for granted technologies: things like washing machines, freezers and so on. This is not an especially unusual story and we might reach for similar narratives of co-evolution were we to consider the introduction and diffusion of other products and services.

Ideas of co-provision were especially useful when making sense of the flow and management of electricity and water. To give just one example, the fact that householders own the sensitive fingertips of existing infrastructures positions them, like it or not, as end consumers and as co-managers implicated in the routine functioning of the system as a whole. Of course households are also part of other systems of provision. They own pots and pans and stoves and are, in a similar sense, embedded in the infrastructure of the food system. The case of the utilities reminds us to taken note of overlapping fields of responsibility and complex supply chains of provision and in that way reminds us of issues likely to be relevant to the analysis of other sectors too.

The challenge of managing peak demand and of balancing the relationship between consumption and non-consumption takes different forms with respect to different resources, services, products and commodities. Again our discussion of co-provision and the co-management of resources within limits of available capacity touches on issues which are not unique to the utilities. The ability to store water or electricity or to stockpile other commodities influences ceilings of capacity and the methods used to manage fluctuating demand. Likewise, we might observe strategies designed to even out the peaks and troughs of consumer interest in ice cream, or new cars, or kitchen cabinets.

It is at this point that the fact that electricity and water are almost always consumed indirectly and that there are more and less efficient ways of providing those many services comes into its own. While co-provision and demand management are probably rather common, the commodification of 'negumption' is much more unusual. In the cases we have considered here, it is the ability to provide services (like comfort, or cleanliness) more efficiently which makes it possible to generate negawatts or negalitres and it is the value of deferring the financial, political or environmental cost of increasing supply which underpins the economics of negumption. In these respects the utilities do appear to represent an extreme and extraordinary case.

Mundane and inconspicuous, maybe. Boring, certainly not. In trying to pin down the characteristics of electricity and water consumption we have hit upon a number of issues, further development of which promises to extend the agenda of ordinary consumption and introduce new lines of enquiry. In conclusion we highlight three especially important themes.

In making sense of electricity and water systems we acknowledged the flow of goods and services through quite complicated supply chains—there was never just one provider or just one consumer—and we recognised the sometimes social, sometimes material, constraints on storage and the timing of supply and demand. Second, we used the concept of co-provision to describe situations in which the roles of consumer and provider overlapped, collapsed, and sometimes went into reverse. Third, by talking about the management of resources in this way, we were able to recognise the balancing of consumption and non-consumption. Though the commodification of negumption is probably rare, and perhaps unique to the utilities, the notion of looking at consumption through the lens of non-consumption is of much wider relevance. Whatever else, this chapter suggests that the utilities have their uses as generators of ideas as well as of electrons and fresh water molecules.

Note

1   DOMUS is an acronym for Domestic Consumers and Utility Services and is a project funded by the European Union's Directorate of Science, Research and Development (DGXII). The research investigates consumer involvement in utility services by focusing on cases of environmental innovation in the UK, the Netherlands and Sweden.

Chapter 4

WORKING AT CONSUMPTION: THE SECOND HOME AND DAILY LIFE

Davina Chaplin

INTRODUCTION

In a recent account of the changing role of consumption, Firat and Dholakia refer to the increasing inseparability of consumption and production at the end of the twentieth century. Citing the examples of countercultures such as New Age, punk and grunge groups, Firat and Dholakia (1998, 144) argue that consumption has been transformed and indeed *become* production for these groups, since the members of these countercultures 'construct and signify new and alternative forms of being, in and through their consumption'. Firat and Dholakia identify four dimensions to modern consumption: social relationship (individual/collective); domain of availability (private/public); level of participation (participatory/alienated); human activity (passive/active).

A manifestation of the consumption-production phenomenon is provided by empirical evidence gained through a research project to investigate the consumption of French second homes by British owners. The producing-consuming of the French rural second home contradicts to some extent the individual-private-alienated-passive trend which Firat and Dholakia maintain to be the evolving pattern of consumption of the United States over the last two centuries. It is certainly more individualised than collective (although there is some evidence of communal meals and aperitifs with neighbours), and it is of course a privatised form of consumption. However, as far as the other two dimensions are concerned, consuming second homes is participatory rather than alienated, and active, not passive, consumption. The home owners directly control and determine the products and activities consumed as well as the routines and ritual processes involved; they also interact with the house and its environment directly and actively, through Do-It-Yourself (DIY) and gardening tasks and the largely non-commodified forms of recreational pursuits adopted. The daily life of the second home is therefore one in which the participants work at consumption, simultaneously doing home and making holidays. Rather than a rigid division between production and consumption, there is a blurring at the edges; this is both the cause and the effect of active and 'productive consumption', in the manner of de Certeau (1984).

Most of the respondents spend blocks of time throughout the year at their French homes, escaping from the mundane world of unfulfilling or overly stressful work in Britain, to a world of their own creation in which they work at ordinary consumption. The context in which they do this is experienced as home away from home, exotic because of its Frenchness, its otherness, but made familiar and routine through the practices of daily life they lead there. A closer examination of the interview data reveals not only patterns of behaviour which these consumer-producers exhibit, but also the expression of shared attitudes and feelings about their homes and experiences of daily life there. After a section about the fieldwork, I deal with these behaviour patterns, coming later to a discussion of the attitudes.

FIELDWORK

A total of 30 unstructured interviews were conducted between 1995 and 1997 with couples, or with one partner of a couple, who agreed to talk about the experience of buying, restoring and using their French homes for periods from four to 20 weeks a year. The qualifying parameters were that the informants owned outright two homes, one in Britain and one in France, and that they spent less than half the year in their French property. The 30 sets of owners selected had purchased houses in two broad areas of France, around half the total relatively close to Britain in the North, across five *départements,* Pas de Calais, Somme, Aisne, Manche and Calvados, such that the homes were accessible for weekends. The second area, in contrast, was not easily accessible for short breaks and covered a total of seven *départements* in South West and Southern France, namely Haute Vienne, Corrèze, Creuse, Lot et Garonne, Tarn et Garonne, Lozère and Charente Maritime. The majority had owned their French houses for six years or less, with only two having purchased as long as 12 years ago. All but two of the houses were old properties, either already converted or renovated or in the process of being restored.

Of the 30 sets of owners, all but one were married to or in an established relationship with the co-owner of the property, which the majority had bought between three and seven years before the time of the interview. Five had retired from full-time work, but most of the respondents still had jobs in Britain; they had a wide variety of occupational backgrounds, from blacksmith, cook, mechanic, secretary, clerk, technicians, engineers to oceanographer, social workers, health service manager, careers consultant, translator, librarian, teachers, lecturers and professions such as accountancy, architecture, law and medicine. The ages of the owners ranged from early thirties to seventies, with the majority between forty and fifty-five.

WORKING ON AND IN THE HOME

There is a considerable degree of productive activity involved in the escape from British lives: some owners become so absorbed in the production process that they work at it six days a week, consuming the work as a welcome change from their occupation in Britain, as it is for an accountant ('it's totally satisfying, a total contrast to what I do for a living'), or, in the case of a lecturer and former engineer, a return to a previous form of work ('It's going back to what I started out doing, working with my hands').

Many of the home owners devise for themselves and commit to a work ethic which they apply to their stays in France, typically alternating work on the house and the land with leisure days out. This commitment to a self-imposed regime forms an act of disengagement from the paramount reality of the owners' British lives, lives in which production and consumption are far more clearly differentiated and separated. Although only about a quarter of the owners classify themselves as DIY enthusiasts, all except one (a man in his seventies) undertake some work on their French houses, around half declaring the work to be 'different' in France, while a large proportion of those for whom DIY is not an activity in Britain do carry out maintenance or decorative work on the French property. Here a man who defines himself as a DIY fanatic describes the extent of the work and his commitment to it:

'Oh, we're doing an enormous amount, yeah. It was right at the bottom end of the scale. It had walls and a roof but it didn't have much of a floor, so we're doing a lot of work. That just goes with the territory. I don't normally do any real work like that on Sundays, not because there's any significance, it's just one day off. In the summer time I'm usually doing five or six days a week, probably, to get things done. At Easter time it's pretty well all work, but it's enjoyable work.'

Conversely a single woman, for whom the purchase of the house was, on her own admission 'an impulse', uses these words to describe her lack of practical skills:

'I wasn't, you know, a DIY person, I had no skills. Well, if I'm honest, I didn't really give it any thought before I bought the house, I'm rather impulsive, I just thought I'd buy a house, I mean people say, how can you just buy a house just like that? But I'm like that in England, you know, I decide on a course of action and I carry it out! Not always wisely.'

Despite this lack of skills, this woman subsequently went on to carry out work on her French house, using paid labour instead to decorate her house in Britain:

'I haven't got time to paint a wall in Southampton, I pay people to paint walls in Southampton! That's about the only thing I do here, actually, slop paint around, I do all the inside. It's wonderful, you know, you're not trying to beat a deadline, and it seems to cover easily and quickly and it doesn't seem to be any hassle. In fact I got a friend of mine to paint my hall, stairs and landing the last time I was in France. I was paying someone to paint my house in England, while I was here painting my house in France, I've just realised that!'

Satisfaction is derived as much from the doing as from the finished result, as many of the DIYists, whether old hands or new converts, declare. This is borne out by the apparently patient acceptance of the fact that in many cases the conversion and renovation process is a very long-term project, sometimes up to ten years. Slowness, not speed, is a feature of this work, in marked contrast to the pace and pressure of work in Britain, whether occupational or domestic. Whether this is conceived of as an escape from those pressures, or a compensation for it, is unclear. Cross (1997, 115) refers to DIY in the history of suburbia as a reactive movement: 'The "do-it-yourself" (DIY) movement was a complex response to complex change: it was a creative compensation for unrewarding work as middle-class men increasingly abandoned entrepreneurship and became white-collar employees. DIY was leisure but consistent with a still powerful work ethic.'

'Compensatory leisure' is a concept which is rooted in escape from alienating work, as Rybczynski (1992, 224) observes in his account of breaks from the routine of work, *Waiting for the Weekend*: 'For many, weekend free time has become not a chance to escape work, but a chance to create work that is more meaningful—to work at recreation—in order to realize the personal satisfactions that the workplace no longer offers.'

This work is meaningful partly because it is creative and self-determined, but also for its freedom from the tyranny of the conventional work timetable, as Cross (1997, 118) points out with respect to the suburban weekend, which 'provided rich alternatives to routinized work time through cyclic and confined moments of freedom'. The work ethic side of the French owners' behaviour is present in the references many of them make to feelings of guilt on the one hand and achievement on the other:

> 'It really is in that sense kind of work-obsessive. We do take the odd after-noon off, sometimes go down to the beach... I always feel really guilty about that! I feel really guilty if I'm not working and I think I'm spending two hours here when I could have been making a bookshelf!'

'I do feel that some of those things are *my* achievements or my wife's achievements.'

The compulsive nature of this work is a shared aspect of most couples' lives in France. The men undertake the serious DIY tasks, but the women assume roles which are advisory and supervisory rather than merely supportive. The women also attempt to achieve a balance between the work and the time off, between making progress on the renovation and doing recreation. Parallels with the suburban weekend are again apparent; as Cross (1997, 118) observes,

> 'Male DIY was and is essentially a consumerist activity. It involved the acquisition of tools and work materials and the shaping of these posses-sions into self-expressions and value. But it was primarily the woman who orchestrated domestic consumption. She worked with purchased goods and transformed them into displays of status and into individual expressions of familial privacy and comfort throughout the home. Women used goods to organize those "special" times that all family members longed for at the weekends and on holidays.'

The female respondents in the French research project often talk about design, décor and style decisions, some expressing the aim to achieve (though not always successfully) 'a French look':

> 'And we put a bench in the kitchen, our friend did that, and that's all open, and we had a ladder going up the wall in this old oak. And we thought aren't we good, this is all French, we're using all the wood and as soon as French people visit us they say, isn't it lovely, it's so English! (laughs) And we've definitely tried to keep it so French!'
>
> 'I think our French friends that we've got to know think our interior is quite chic... We think it's very rustic and we've created a different style home down there, but we wanted to make it fairly uncluttered and as French as we can. Then when you go into French homes and see how, how cluttered their homes are and how big their furniture is, I can see why they find our place is very different.'

The opportunities for creative home-making which the second home provides are variously expressed by the female respondents as second chances or making another nest, or, as in the case of one woman who clearly felt controlled by her husband in Britain, as a liberating experience:

> 'How can I explain it? Well, it's... for instance, it's decorated differently, so I can... It's more fun, I can buy different things. This is very traditional, but there I can buy modern, fun things. I also feel it's a luxury whereas this is our main home, so I mean it would be something that if we needed the money I would have to sell, so in a sense it's also a luxury.'

WORKING ON THE LAND

However, working on the French home has another extremely important element, one which three quarters of the interviews contain, and which form the most substantial part of the accounts of consuming the home: working on the land. Rybczynski (1992, 209) makes the point that 'gardening is not chiefly a form of consumption, and its persistence suggests that traditional leisure may be somewhat resistant to modern influences'. Certainly, the evidence gathered from the French research project suggests that gardening is a far less commodified activity than it is in urban Britain: the number of swimming pools was surprisingly low (only four out of thirty households) and there are virtually no references to other consumer products such as water features, decked areas and garden furniture. Conversely, what Francis Bacon (quoted in Rybczynski, 1992, 199) called in 1625 'the purest of pleasures' is a key instance of consuming work, as selected interview excerpts reveal:

> 'It's such a big garden. There's always work to do in the garden. And we've tried, well I have tried, to contain nature, you know, everything that's nice, we've got loads of daisies and marguerites growing in amongst things, well, I've let them stay because I think they're nice... So I've planted things in amongst them and it's sort of controlled nature, really.'
>
> 'I mean, actually working on the garden, in inverted commas, there are bits that we try to cultivate, but other bits, it's actually creating the kind of wildness that doesn't kind of overwhelm you ... so that's what's nice. It's very easy to spend time doing not much at all really, just suddenly decide that the brambles are really impossible and therefore, getting into the kind of undergrowth, particularly right at the base, and you can spend, you know, two or three hours doing that, with not much to show for it, except later, they'll all die off and you feel quite satisfied.'

'So basically when we're there Mark's always fiddling about with chain-saw, tractor, mower or strimmer, wearing a pair of Wellington boots. [......] And then we go and do this clearing down by the river, but the terrible thing is you clear and it's wonderful and the next time you go the ferns have grown up to ten foot high and it's a jungle!'

The working and consuming sides to gardening are typically inter-woven in a rich web of narrative in which notions of retreat, bolt-hole, relaxation and role-play combine with references to the work as cre-ative and challenging, satisfying and frustrating in almost equal measure. This underlines the particular role which working on the land plays in the daily life of second home owners; experienced as a responsibility and a worry on the one hand, but deeply pleasurable and fulfilling on the other. Over half the interviews include accounts of fruit picking and bottling, chestnut, mushroom and nut gathering, and the almost sensual pleasure derived from picking wild herbs minutes before cooking with them.

There were some respondents who stretch the activities still further and actually keep animals on their land: two couples kept chickens, ducks and geese, one regularly buys sheep to graze their land and then slaughter them, whilst others allow their French neighbours to put cattle, sheep or goats on the land, sometimes in exchange for work on their gardens during their extended absences. This is constructed as a form of social reciprocity, as are the exchanges of gifts, which most families practise.

The consumption of nature which these activities illustrate, together with the widespread narratives about bird and animal watching, fishing, swimming in lakes and rivers, and rambling, is a distinctive practice, marking out the second home owners as having the cultural capital to appreciate these 'simple', uncommodified pursuits, although it may no longer define them as members of the dominant class which Bourdieu (1984, 280) describes: "Consider the new cult of nature which the fashion for second homes and the refusal of petit-bourgeois tourism have brought back into favour and which has a deep affinity with the "*vieille France*" life-style of the most "ancient" fraction among the dominant fractions.'

The contrast between the levels of capital of the second home owners (economic, cultural and educational) and their French neighbours also shows itself in differing perceptions of what is appropriate or relevant in the rural environment. There are several accounts of the reactions of local farmers to some of the gardening actions of the incomers (for example, horror at the planting of a beech sapling which would ultimately grow too large for its situation). Many second home owners admit to making prodigious efforts to sustain prolonged conversations about Limousin cattle, which are the favourite topic for discussion of their neighbours. There is also some evidence that the occupational class and the location of the British home affect the degree of involvement in gardening: the lawyers, academics, doctor and architects (all male) show commitment, enthusiasm and enjoyment of a much higher level than those in other occupations, and those who live in inner city or suburban areas in Britain are also more likely to get seriously involved in horticultural projects. Working with the hands, it appears, is attractive for its instrumental nature, especially for those whose work in their normal lives is not 'productive' in the concrete sense of the word, or whose place of residence in Britain precludes contact with the land.

The third point to be made about this activity is its appropriation, the time it takes up, a factor which has a great distinctive power, as Bourdieu (1984, 281) observes: '[...] the importance which the pursuit of distinction attaches to all those activities which [...] demand pure, pointless expenditure, especially of the rarest and most precious thing of all—particularly for those whose market value gives them least of it to waste—namely, time, time devoted to consumption...' The many references to clearing land during one visit to the house, only to find it overgrown again on the next occasion, suggest that there is both a masochistic pleasure and a cachet derived from the frustrations involved in this activity.

VOLUNTARY SIMPLICITY

There is another aspect to the daily lives of the second home owners which relates to the manner of consuming and working in the French context: the principle of 'voluntary simplicity' (Elgin, 1981). Half of the respondent couples give voice to ideals and practices which reflect this, although none use the term itself to describe their lifestyle. Much emphasis is placed by these couples on the lack of television, computing and other technological apparatus, which are all seen as being part of their British lives that they have left behind. Their French lives are often striking for doing without, the deliberate paring down to basics, a kind of self-conscious rustic minimalism. The concept of 'voluntary simplicity' defined by Elgin is an appropriate one to describe a way of life which is to a large extent not commodified.

A number of the features of voluntary simplicity are apparent in the manner of living which many of the second home owners share: an alteration of patterns of consumption towards energy-efficiency, durability and renewability, more natural, seasonal foods, smaller scale living environments, community contact, and the development of personal skills which lead to self-reliance. All of these contribute to what Elgin (1981, 165) terms 'living with balance', affecting consumption, production and interpersonal communication, and marking a shift away from the habitual, pre-programmed ways of the commodified world.

The sub-title of Elgin's book, *Toward a way of life that is outwardly simple, inwardly rich*, captures some of the desires and dreams which the owners express, particularly in relation to the accounts they give of the pressures they feel subjected to in their working lives in Britain. References abound to the relief and relaxation they experience in their homes in France, to the space and time they have to breathe, to be, often linked to accounts of natural phenomena such as the stars, the sky, and the views. To an extent there are echoes of Henry Thoreau's two years spent in his cabin in the woods in Massachusetts, recorded in *Walden* (1854). Thoreau emphasises that his time in the cabin was not a withdrawal from society, but an experiment in simple living, enabling him '*to live deep and suck out all the marrow of life*' (Thoreau, 1985, 394). Elgin's manifesto for simple living also stresses that it is not dropping out from the world, but building up a network of people with whom to share a similar intention. Emphasis is placed on conservation and frugality, not conspicuous consumption; on co-operation with others, not competition. Identity is not defined by material possessions and social position, but in the process of living.

A number of Elgin's ideas are strongly reflected in the analysed data from the French home owners' group: first, self-awareness, second, that the simplicity is aesthetic, not ascetic, and third, that there is development of skills and competence which leads to greater self-reliance. Taking each of these ideas in turn, Elgin states that it is crucial to acting voluntarily for us to be aware of ourselves as we move through life, not only of our external actions but also our inner world. The single most frequently recurring feature of the thirty interviews conducted is the level of reflection on motives and actions, which the respondents demonstrate. A striking example of this is the academic in his sixties who thinks aloud, first about his practical motivations, deep-rooted desires and finally his role-playing:

'Personally I think I was looking for somewhere which was very remote, which had a bit of land to it, which wasn't likely to involve huge amounts of structural change, and all my dealings with French builders and so on led me to be a bit cautious about embarking on something major. So something that we could more or less move into effortlessly. Which in a way reflected some of the mild residual rural idyll notions which are at the back of one's mind, and as I say somewhere with a bit of space where I could slop around and do things privately... [...] In a curious way, I expect it stems back to this sort of ludicrous myth of agriculture and rurality and the farm. I mean I had in my family quite a lot of farmers and I used to stay on this farm and if I ever had a sort of career urge when I was a child, it was to be a farmer. I never ever gardened until I was in my forties, and to an extent there is some sort of vestigial sense of my God, at last I'm a farmer, you know! (laughs) But there's enough land really to make you feel that you can make a difference, in a way that a small suburban garden of half an acre wouldn't. Here you can't do other than grow flowers, whereas when you've got an amount of land you can actually do something to change the sort of micro-landscape and to that extent, in a pathetic fashion, you feel as though you're in touch with nature and like a farmer. Rather entertaining, actually... [...] I think there's certainly an element of role-playing to it. Indeed I imagine the role-playing extends to the fact that, you know, one consciously dresses down, old clothes and holes in the sleeves or something...'

The extracts from this interview are telling for a number of reasons. First, the reflexivity of the respondent, discernible above all in his use of the words 'ludicrous' and 'pathetic' to pass judgement on his own motives, indicates the perspective he takes on his biography, a distancing of himself from his actions. Secondly, the references to 'rural idyll' and 'myth' simultaneously acknowledge his social conditioning and justify his behaviour in those terms; thirdly, the performativity of playing at being a peasant farmer is disclosed as being enjoyable on two levels, for the acting out of the role itself, and for the amusement derived from being a spectator at his own performance. This complexity of motivation and action seems to come very close to Elgin's notion of self-awareness.

Elgin's second point, that the simplicity is aesthetic, not ascetic, because it is consciously chosen, is important to gaining an understanding of the hard work involved in this lifestyle. Many owners talk about the time it takes to collect and chop wood in order to keep warm in winter; the effort as well as time invested in preparing meals is contrasted with meals in Britain; the lack of electrical and electronic equipment (as well as, at times, electricity) is also referred to as part of the simplified way of living. However, as far as the design and décor of the house are concerned, this is not what Rybczynski (1988, 198) terms 'conspicuous austerity', denoting 'a studied, refined artlessness': there is if anything a conspicuous lack of stylisation and an emphasis on 'making do', reflected in the use of furniture recycled from British houses, 'picked up' in car boot sales in England or '*brocante*' in France. Moreover, there is a sense in which the second home environment, especially in rural areas, is conducive to simplifying ways of doing things, as several of the DIYists point out:

> 'It's just that things aren't quite as perfect, surroundings wise, it is a rural community and things aren't as pristine. And you love doing it, because it's lovely doing jobs there, nothing has to be perfect, like it does in these modern houses, you know... you wouldn't dream of doing things so roughly here.' [in Britain]
>
> 'I think it's different because it's a holiday house so it doesn't have to be... nobody is going to sort of look at it and think that's your house, it's not done properly! Whereas in France, and with beams, it's just so much easier, you know, to get a lovely effect without a skilled builder doing it, I think that's the thing.'

The third of Elgin's ideas, that of skills development and self-reliance, is also strongly apparent in the respondents' stories. Leaving aside the already skilled DIYists, many of the rest not only place great emphasis, as I have described above, on the 'different' feel to undertaking jobs in France, but also value the increased competence they have acquired during the process of renovation and appropriation. One couple in their forties who view their project as long term review their progress after five years:

> 'I think we've been more realistic, haven't we? I mean when we first started in the project we were, not naïve, but we were so excited, but then we got a bit more realistic about what we can do and how fast we can do it. And certainly on the construction side of things we now know our capabilities, we know what we can do, we know we're quite willing to do certain things and learn new skills, but we have got limitations and we now accept those limitations, and I think we're not trying to do things overnight whereas when we first started we were thinking yes, three years' time, it'll all be done!'

There is, however, an element of the French owners' lives that contradicts, or at least diminishes, the simplicity to which they aspire: the more complicated and commodified English part of their lives to which they return each time. However, the fact remains that the overall practice demonstrates an in-built resistance to and critique of modern commodified life.

ROUTINES

The ways in which the unfamiliar and novel become routine and normal are also part of the story of working at consumption; just as the process of working on the house is consumed and enjoyed for its own sake, so too are the daily and weekly routines and habits. In contrast to the picture Giddens (1991, 46) gives of rituals as 'coping mechanisms', the second home owners construct their routines as sources of pleasure and feelings of authenticity. A young technician tells a story of slipping into habits of preparing, cooking and eating meals in France which he describes as 'feeling like the real life', unlike his life in London, which 'feels like a sham'. He even uses the term domestic 'ritual' to describe the change of rhythm and routine, which is a reflection of how he sees the difference between the habits of his urban British way of life and the simpler French one. Yi-Fu Tuan (1998, 23), in his book about culture as escape from nature, makes the point that escape, if it has the feel of clarity, is experienced as an encounter with the real, and that rituals can be defined in these terms: 'Participation in a ritual is participation in something serious and real; it is escape from banality and opaqueness of life into an event that clarifies life and yet preserves a sense of mystery.' Another, older, French home owner describes the early morning trips to buy bread as a 'ritual', or his 'daily fix':

> 'Yea, it's ritual, isn't it? I think it's the idea of the man going out doing the hunting... I go out every morning and nip down to C., which is about 7 kilometres, and it's just driving through the Limousin countryside, and you'll be driving past a fence, and there's a buzzard there which just watches you go past, the cows grazing, the Limousin cattle grazing in the fields, and the mist coming, oh it's just... it's my fix for the day.'

A woman with four children links familiarity and routine in her account of the happiness she feels in her French home:

> 'You can't really put your finger on quite what it is, but it is a very nice, happy atmosphere... I mean I think there is something about familiarity and everybody knowing ... and in some ways children are creatures of habit, they want the same sort of routine... aren't we going to do this?'

It seems that enjoying ordinary, simple things in a comfortable and comfortingly familiar ambience is achieved through a routine-making appropriation of the otherness of the environment, interacting with the French context in adapting elements of family life and adopting customs and practices which then become absorbed into the experience itself. Self-regulated routines are an important part of the process by and through which the consumers of the second home *make* and *do* their lives. In his account of the home as a material site for expression, Dant (1999, 72), citing the work of Michel de Certeau (1984), uses the term '*bricolage*' to denote arts of 'making do' which are 'combined with ritual practices, habits and routines out of which the shape of everyday life emerges.' For Dant, rituals are neither a matter of conscious choice nor determined by social conditioning. 'Rituals may be followed knowingly because it suits the purposes at hand but these purposes might lead to a modification of the ritual, of material objects or of skills to meet varying situations or even to bring about variations in action, experience or environment' (Dant, 1999, 72).

The consuming and producing of dwelling in second home contexts, perhaps more than in first homes (where there is less time and more social pressure to conform) amply demonstrates this kind of creative adaptation. The 'French' way of thinking or living is adopted, adapted and appropriated by the British owners and integrated into their patterns of consumption. The ceremonial and observance aspects of traditional forms of ritual are perhaps not apparent, but there is a sense in which routines and habits, lovingly repeated and carefully observed and savoured, are close to those traditions. The difference is that the actors have invented or adapted, adopted or chosen the habits for themselves, not because of any prescribed set of rules or codes. In this way, there could be said to be both a self-determined routinisation of the exotic and a re-routinisation of their lives, at least for part of the year. Changing contexts means changing gears, but also switching to appropriate forms of behaviour and practices, in a way which is constructed as profoundly different from conventional experiences of holiday places.

MEANINGS AND MEMORIES

The final part of this chapter deals with the attitudes towards and feelings generated by the daily life of second homes. One of the dominant themes of second home ownership is the duality of routine and novelty, the interplay between what is familiar and what is different. Jaakson (1986, 374) points out the possibility of recurrent novelty for second home owners: 'The meaning of second-home use suggests that serendipity can be found in nostalgia, and that there is a qualitative difference in the novelty of newness found in something familiar, compared to the novelty of newness found in something unfamiliar.' The patina acquired by the second home over the years is built up from the reliving of the past and memories associated with the house, its setting and environment. The gaps between visits merely serve to reinforce the pleasure derived from the whole experience, a mingling of anticipation and renewed acquaintance. Hetherington (1997, 193), writing about the materiality of place, refers to the role of memory in the place of home, a 'continuity of meaning that stretches over time'. The past and the future are embodied in the home as well as the present; as several of the respondents in the French group express it, the knowledge that the house is there 'gets them through the winter' in Britain.

It is, as Bachelard (1969, 62) puts it, 'a daydream of elsewhere', as well as a refuge and a retreat. Contrary to the paradox about which Bauman (1997) writes, namely that home becomes a dream once the door is shut from outside, but turns into a prison when the door is shut from the inside, Bachelard (1969, 6) argues that its chief benefit is that 'the house shelters daydreaming, the house protects the dreamer, the house allows one to dream in peace.' One woman who experiences her French house as a 'felicitous space' (Bachelard, 1969, xxxi), sums up her narrative about her love for France and memories of years spent working there:

> 'I feel very fond of it, it's very special to me, because it's in France and for what France means to me.'

However, there is one meaning of the home which is constructed by the British owners in remarkably similar terms; virtually all the interviews contain statements about the French property which reveal the normalisation which has taken place. Phrases like 'home from home' and 'like coming home' carry meanings which are clearly related to the work and time invested in the project. There is some evidence of the journey to and fro being a part of that homecoming, with different stories of overloaded Volvos and camper vans piled up with furniture or plants in one direction and with wine in the other. The moment of arrival, anticipated during the journey and relived in the interview, is another instance of repetition. It also seems to epitomise much of the emotion involved, as these three interview excerpts show:

> 'We're instantly at home, as soon as we've been there ten minutes, it feels as if we've been there weeks. So there isn't that going round, sniffing at it to see what it's like.'
>
> 'Opening the front door, opening the door, walking in and knowing, you know, where your slippers are, this sort of thing is actually quite important. It is, you know, because it's a home.'
>
> 'When we get to the house in France, we've left stuff in one place and it's still there, you know where things are, in the kitchen. So you just feel like you've been away, that's all, rather than... [Interviewer: Like coming home?] Yes, that's right! There must be a point somewhere in the middle of France where you're not leaving home, when you're actually coming home instead.'

CONCLUSION

The importance of activity and participation within consumption emerges as the *raison d'être* of this group of consumers. Evident here is what Miller (1997, 26) expresses as a second-hand relationship: consumption is 'a struggle which begins with the problem that in the modern world we increasingly live with institutions and objects that we do not see ourselves as having created'. What Miller refers to as 'appropriation' in these circumstances is about taking over, singularising, and using cultural goods and services for our own purposes and in our own contexts. One of the 'myths of consumption' which Miller (1995) identifies is that consumption is opposed to authenticity, and more particularly that the rise in mass consumption is necessarily opposed to involvement in production. As Miller (1995, 27) states, 'consumption, so far from being opposed to production, increasingly involves production at those points when the consumer prefers to be involved in creative labour'. Whether the labour is associated with home-brewing, car-care or gardening, the creative and productive elements are clear, certainly to those who participate in the activities; home owners involved in renovation, DIY or decoration express in almost equal terms the work and leisure aspects to the chosen projects. In their appropriation of the French properties, the owners are clearly working as well as playing; integrating work into their consumption of holiday time; actively consuming the process of making the house their home; transforming object and self through routines and labour. In contrast to their British work, the work is autonomous, not heteronomous (Gorz, 1985, 50), just as the consumption is self-determined and enjoyed for its own sake; both are interrelated and form an integrated and satisfying whole. As one middle-aged couple expressed it:

> 'It makes the holiday, doing things. Yeah, we enjoy doing things. We enjoyed holidays before, didn't we? Sightseeing, sitting reading, but it's just so much more satisfying when there's something to show for your four weeks off work.'

Chapter 5

EXTRA-ORDINARY AND ORDINARY CONSUMPTION: MAKING SENSE OF ACQUISITION IN MODERN TAIWAN

Shou-Cheng Lai

The rising dominance of modern consumption and its social consequences is a concern of many social scientists. Many social theorists, such as Bauman, Beck, Giddens (see Warde, 1994a) and, to some extent, Bourdieu, believe the resources derived from social networks have gravely declined, if not disappeared. They believe that modern consumption has led to a high level of individualisation. Bauman's assertion is particularly characteristic of this position.

> 'The activity of consumption is a natural enemy of all coordination and integration. It is also immune to their influence, rending all efforts of bonding impotent in overcoming the endemic loneliness of the consuming act. Consumers are alone even when they act together.' (Bauman, 1998, 30)

Bourdieu's framework is more sophisticated. He argues that the ambitious middle classes, constrained by their limited resources, will abandon their network connections to concentrate their energy on improving their social positions, with the consequence that the importance of social capital will be reduced in a modern differentiated Western society.

> 'It is in the area of sociability and the corresponding satisfactions that the petit bourgeois makes the greatest, if not the most obvious, sacrifices. He is convinced that he owes his position solely to his merit, and that for his salvation he only has himself to rely on ... For the petit bourgeois, kinship and friendship can no longer be an insurance against misfortune and disaster ... They are merely hindrances, which have to be removed whatever the cost, because the gratitude, the mutual aid, the solidarity and the material and the symbolic satisfactions they give, in the short or long term, are among the forbidden luxuries.' (Bourdieu, 1984, 337)

Thus, according to Bourdieu's argument, for the rising middle class, social capital will not have a significant function in the universes of consumption in differentiated societies. I want to challenge such a simplified argument and suggest that this is not the case in a society characterised by swift transition such as Taiwan. Nevertheless, Bourdieu's conceptualisation of social capital is still one of the best instruments to explore the role of social networks in modern consumption.

> 'Social capital is the aggregate of the actual or potential resources which are linked to possession of a durable network of more or less institutionalized relationships of mutual acquaintance and recognition—or in other words, to membership in a group—which provides each of its members with the backing of the collectivity-owned capital.' (Bourdieu, 1986, 248–249)

His definition emphasises the crucial importance of recognition in the dynamic functioning of social capital because the reproduction of social capital presupposes a continuous series of exchanges in which recognition is endlessly affirmed and reaffirmed.

Contrary to the explanatory formulations of major social theorists working in Euro-American contexts, the resource derived from family members and interpersonal connections still plays a significant role in modern consumption. This tendency is particularly obvious and pervasive in contemporary Taiwan. In order to explore the concrete mechanism of social capital mobilisation in the process of consumption and to have a more comprehensive understanding of consumption processes in different social contexts, I shall put forward a better framework which seeks to explain the critical convertibility of social capital in a different mode of consumption.

Consumption in the Taiwanese context

In the last forty years Taiwan has been radically and quickly transformed from an agricultural to an industrialised society. Thirty years ago, with regard to consumption, Taiwan was different in almost every important respect from most Western industrialised societies. Before the 1960s Taiwan was a relatively poor country predominantly based on an agricultural economy and haunted by political and economic insecurity. Thus, social capital had a more significant and pervasive role to play as a source of reliable support and protection. Consequently, most of the current elder generation (aged over 50) have their primary experiences of socialisation based in traditional social processes. Their dispositions and their model of social relations will not be easily changed and therefore they tend to maintain a traditional model of consumption practice, even though their wealth has greatly increased.

Not everything in Taiwan was revolutionised by the region's fast and dramatic industrialisation. The fuzzy integration of rural and urban life within the same families and the strategic importance of social networks provided the safety net to protect against the shock waves of fast industrialisation on the one hand, and the social-control mechanisms to facilitate or discourage most social activities on the other (see Castells, 1998, 254–276). Social bonds had a double function for members of a network: protection and control. In the sphere of consumption, the elder representatives of an integrated social group (family or kinship), traditionally not only had authority over the delegation of tasks, the control of expenditure and the group's external relations, but also had the capacity to manipulate individual aspirations, channel members' 'speciality', and to orient their expectations of consumption. This social process also implies the unequal distribution of the symbolic profit derived from consumption practices.

The pervasive influence of Confucianism reinforces the central importance of social capital in social relations and daily lives. Its central axiom is based on the symbolic significance of the hierarchy of social relations (especially in family and kinship relationships), a form of relationship that effectively supports the dominant cultural values in Taiwan. In contemporary Taiwan many people still believe their social lives are based more on human feelings, instead of automatic abstract 'laws', 'principles', 'institutions' or 'structures'.

In the 1980s Taiwanese people experienced the arrival of modern consumption. During the same period, Taiwan became disliked by many multinational corporations for its well-known 'pirating' capacity in international markets (Teng, 1997). The situation is in fact even more confused in domestic consumer markets. A huge number of similar goods emerged through pirating, counterfeiting, imitation, unauthorised production, parallel exports, OEM (Original Equipment Manufacturer), etc., making consumer markets extremely chaotic and risky.

Moreover, before the mid-1980s, the authoritarian Kuomintang regime was more interested in economic development than in protecting the consumer. It was only in 1980 that Taiwan acquired its first institution to protect consumers' interests when the Consumers Foundation, which was modelled on similar American organisations, was formed by a number of active civic groups. However, as a non-governmental foundation, and therefore without the substantial power afforded by state sanction, its influence remains relatively limited and mainly lies in giving advice and providing consumer education. Its position has been further weakened by a recent financial crisis in the organisation (Hsieh, 1998). Official consumer protection takes the form of the Consumer Protection Law which was only passed in 1994.

The extent to which this is actually implemented is still in doubt. It would be no surprise to discover that in Taiwan most companies tend to cheat the consumer through a variety of strategies. In short, compared with many Western societies, consumer protection in Taiwan is underdeveloped and, many companies, national and multinational, tend to take advantages of this low level of consumer protection. The extent of the problem is borne out by the fact even the Taiwanese branch of the leading American bank, Citibank, has been accused of cheating consumers in their promotional activities in the mid-1990s (Hsien, 1998).

Taking both factors into consideration, it is understandable that in general Taiwanese consumers have more trust in interpersonal relationships rather than institutional 'experts' from markets of consumption. From the perspective of network membership, universal 'experts' from markets of consumption are outside-'strangers', dangerous, biased and unreliable. It is particularly important to observe that because the market is risky and unpredictable, nearly all the strategies of consumers are aimed at limiting the insecurity accompanying that unpredictability, by transforming the impersonal, instantaneous relations of the commercial transaction into durable relations of reciprocity through recourse to guarantors and mediators (Bourdieu, 1990, 121–134). They achieve this through the mobilisation of social capital.

Research method

A national survey in 1996 (see Table 1), demonstrates very well the significance of social capital in the universe of consumption. In the survey consumers revealed that, across a diverse array of products, from the expensive item to the cheap one and from the high-tech product to the common one, though to a different degree, the 'channel of information' that they trust most is the 'family and friends'. Family and friends constitute the paradigmatic model of the dominant social network and most Taiwanese people believe the opinions, messages and judgements derived from it.

During 1997–1998 I conducted 31 interviews, addressing some of the themes of this survey. These interviews, ranging from 50 minutes to 90 minutes in length, were with 14 male and 17 female consumers. The ages of the participants ranged from 23 to 45 years and most of them (over 70%) were between 25 and 35 years old. The questions were about which kind of channels, and how, consumers acquire different kind of products, including cars, TV sets, shampoo, tissue paper, restaurants, clothing, computers and mini-stereos. Most of these interviewees are

Table 1: If you do buy some items, which channels of information do you trust most?* (N = 941) (percentage by row)

Item/Channel	Television adverts	News-papers adverts	Magazines adverts	Family and friends	Sales-person
Cars	7.3	2.3	7.3	78.9	4.2
TV Sets	17.5	3.4	4.4	66.8	8.0
Shampoo	40.1	3.5	4.2	49.4	2.8
Tissue Paper	40.2	3.5	2.6	51.1	2.6

* Source: Guo, 1996, 88.

relatively affluent members of the upper middle class with higher cultural capital (over 80 % have college degrees). I focus especially on the cultured middle classes—social groups supposed to be most interested in Western life-style— because, if one tries to examine the transforming consequences of modern consumption on social relations in Taiwan, the manifestations of transformative impacts on the Taiwanese should be most obvious in these groups. In the following sections I analyse how social capital facilitates and orients the agent's strategies in different types of consumption processes.

MODE OF CONSUMPTION PROCESS AND MOBILISATION OF SOCIAL CAPITAL

'Sense of consumption investment' and consumption processes

Consumption is far from being merely a moment of shopping for something or using it up. Rather, consumption, for both individual and collective agents, is one of the stakes of social struggle and also an instrument of social investment (Bourdieu, 1984). Like modern consumption in many countries, in Taiwan, superior social positions are to a certain degree defined by consumption of distinctive goods or services; at the same time, consumption of 'superior' goods or services itself is a set of instruments to achieve better positions. In this sense, consumption could be better understood as a form of transformative and reproductive investment, not only in economic and cultural dimensions but also in social and symbolic dimensions. Investments imply a recognition in the stakes of struggle and difference in return of profit. Not everything possesses equal value in the fields of consumption at a given time in a given social space. Most importantly, this practical sense of perception and evaluation will classify every consumer good or service into categories of ordinary or extra-ordinary, and then activate different kind of strategies of resources mobilisation which are supposed to be appropriate to the specific good or service in question. Thus, in terms of return rate (which is seldom explicit and codified), investment in certain goods or services—with their acquisition and appropriation—has more strategic importance in maintaining or improving one's position than others.

Through this 'sense of consumption investment', we can make a distinction between extra-ordinary consumption and ordinary consumption which is appropriate to a more integrated and more comprehensive explanatory model of consumption processes. However, we should never forget that the sense of consumption investment varies with the consumer's position and is also the site of competitive struggles between different groups of consumers to impose on the social world their taste as most legitimate (Bourdieu, 1989). Therefore the distinction between extra-ordinary and ordinary consumption is always contested and items will often be re-classified as a result.

Extra-ordinary consumption: Maximising returns on consumption investment

In terms of the framework outlined above, the series of practices which is concerned with the acquisition and appropriation of those distinctive goods or services such as new cars could be identified as the process of 'extra-ordinary' consumption. Relationally, extra-ordinary consumption is characterised by two central qualities: it is both culturally *hazardous* and socially *prestigious*. By 'culturally hazardous', I mean that due to relatively limited cultural capacity, which is unavoidable in an unfamiliar specialised field of consumption, one is inclined to worry about 'misconception' or 'misjudgement' in the process of acquisition. 'Socially prestigious' refers to the perception that most members of one's networks of relationships recognise that, by acquiring the specific goods or services, one is able to greatly improve one's position in social space. These extra-ordinary goods or services are 'expensive', 'difficult to judge', 'seriously important', 'highly concerned by family or good friends', and, thus, potentially may cause 'a massive loss' and 'have grave consequences', as various interviewees said.

The acquisition of those economic and symbolic goods perceived as extra-ordinary is very special in the time and space parameters within the social universe and those parameters vary with different groups of consumers in different social positions. Compared to other common or ordinary goods, they tend to be purchased only rarely, especially on 'great occasions'. Their serious magnitude and the high stakes attached make them like a diplomatic manoeuvre, something highly ritualised, and there is a tendency to abandon ordinary improvised dispositions. Higher returns and higher risk usually go hand in hand, and the world of consumption is no exception. The heavy stakes of extra-ordinary consumption make for their remarkable significance and the grave consequence of error is widely recognised among members of collective units. That, in turn, provides the basis for strategies of collective action.

Ordinary consumption process: Minimising the cost of consumption investment

Ordinary consumption could also be characterised by two major social qualities: it is culturally *common* and socially *taken-for-granted*. One of the main reasons for people to perceive these goods as common and trivial is that the acquisition and appropriation of these goods or services only has a low or limited stake in the multi-dimensional struggles for winning a better position in the modern social world. It seems that they have no other function than the simple reproduction of the social networks and the everyday maintenance of social relations that make them possible. Or one can say that in one's everyday social struggle, ordinary consumption is easy to have and thus easy to match. Ordinariness provides another important social characteristic of ordinary consumption; that is, taken-for-grantedness. Ordinary goods, like toilet papers, and the associated routine purchasing processes, occur so often that they tend to pass unnoticed and consumers habitually have almost nothing to say about them, i.e., they tend to be taken-for-granted.

The insignificant value associated with certain goods or services in the sphere of consumption implies an inarticulate secret usually hidden behind the 'pure' economic dimension. That is, due to its low return, investing too much 'social' energy—the 'expenditure' of time and effort—in ordinary consumption will be wasteful. In the process of ordinary consumption, much acquisition of common goods or services will, if possible, be delegated to the weaker agents, those in dominated positions within a social network, though the items will be later appropriated by the stronger agents in dominant positions.

Mobilisation of social capital

In reality, social agents are inclined to have a multi-dimensional appropriateness in different modes of consumption process. To account comprehensively for the concrete practices of consumption process in a society characterised by the significance of social capital, such as Taiwan, in addition to field-specific cultural capital (Bourdieu,

1984; Holt, 1997), we must take social capital—with its selective convertibility—into consideration. One can identify two forms of social capital which are fundamental to its exercise and conversion in different fields of consumption: trustworthy information and proxy labour-time.

Timely trustworthy information: K'ou-Pei

The first form is a kind of practical or theoretical knowledge cultivated principally from personal experiences of goods or a specialised knowledge of goods. In the socio-cultural context of modern Taiwan, people name this informational form of social capital *K'ou-Pei*. In Taiwan *K'ou-Pei* generally is understood as: *Many people with whom I am acquainted say good or bad words for the 'X'* (goods, services, brands, things, persons, etc.). It refers especially to the expressions of 'authentic' information or 'genuine' judgement derived from personal experience. These acquaintances might be friends or 'local' experts in your social network and consequently their information or judgement should be both competent and trustworthy. Furthermore, critically, the condition of interpersonal connection with the person places this person under a moral obligation to share his or her personal experience with you in a sincere way. In this sense, *K'ou-Pei* is opposed to distorted, manipulated or misleading communications, especially those with 'interested' motives such as advertising or salespersons. It also involves one of the most crucial things in the world of consumption—judgement or classification. The classifications and judgement produced by these acquaintances owe their effectiveness to the fact that they are 'practical', amenable to mutually shared understanding and that just enough information for the needs of practical behaviour is introduced, neither too much nor too little, since otherwise mutual communication would then become impossible.

Therefore it is not so surprising that, in order to have a quick and reliable grasp of the information regarding the goods or services in question, most people will launch advice-obtaining operations through their networks of relationships. For example,

> 'Last month, a friend of mine from Japan visited me ... I planned to treat her to a dinner, so I ask my aunt for advice about where I could have an appropriate dinner with my friend. Because I suppose that she is more familiar with restaurants of traditional Taiwanese cuisine and it's easier and faster for me to get such information from her.' (Female, 29)

Social capital increases the efficiency of consumption practices. One of the most valuable sorts of information derived from established social capital is practical or theoretical knowledge of the fluctuations of the market for various (distinguished) goods and services. Such knowledge, thus, enables one to get the best return on the economic and cultural capital mix in those different markets. In the fields of consumption, this is, consciously or unconsciously, achieved by knowing the right moment to pull out of devalued categories of products (ranges, brands, models, types, styles, specifications, etc.), by sensing the right time to change out of unprofitable channels of acquisition (supermarkets, conventional markets, night markets, stall vendors, relatives and friends, friends of friends, etc.) and then to switch into those with profitable potential. Both of these strategies help to direct agents towards securing the highest material and symbolic profit in the current state of the market. In brief, networks of relationships increase the efficiency and reliability of information diffusion specific to fields of consumption through min-imising uncontrollable redundancy, reducing costly and time-consuming monitoring, and diminishing worrying opportunism (Nahapiet and Ghoshal, 1998).

Proxy labour-time: Pang-Mang (doing favours)
The second form is proxy labour-time: due to mutual recognition or trust, a person's labour-time may be authorised to act as a substitute for another's. In the Taiwanese context, this labour form of social capital is called *Pang-Mang*, literally meaning jointly together to accomplish more painlessly an onerous and pressing task, i.e., come close to do a favour. This is not an easy, simple task. In fact, a host of cultural capacity (linguistic, cognitive, aesthetic, etc.) and social com-petences (manners, etiquette, sociality, etc.) are vital to the smooth and successful performance of substitution. In this sense, *Pang-Mang* implies the mobilisation of another person's labour-time by proxy. A typical example:

> 'My first new computer was purchased through the "invisible" assistance of my father's employee (and also friend). He is the technician in charge of computerised machines in my father's factory. At that time I had a very limited knowledge of personal computers and my father did not know very much either. He suggested that we can buy this personal computer through his friend's help. So I just told my father what kind of function I need ... and then as an intermediary my father passed my messages to his friend. (That is, he took charge of everything in purchasing the computer). Three weeks later, my father delivered this personal computer by car to my resi-dence in Taichuan [a city in the middle of Taiwan] from Tainai [a city in southern Taiwan].' (Male, 28)

On the one hand, proxy labour always takes time, one of the most precious resources in modern world, and on the other hand, it is an embodied form of cultural competence, which presupposes the prior investment of the other person's time. Hence, some members of networks, through the mobilisation of proxy labour-time, save an enormous amount of time and effort by not needing to accumulate cultural capital specific to an unfamiliar field of consumption.

STRATEGIES OF MOBILISATION OF SOCIAL CAPITAL AND THE TRANSFORMING CONSEQUENCES OF MODERN CONSUMPTION

Extra-ordinary consumption and amplified mobilisation of social capital

With regard to the social process of consumption, amplification of social capital could be achieved mainly in two directions: extensive mobilisation and intensive mobilisation. The extensive mobilisation of social capital will lead to enlarged connections of network relationships and the intensive mobilisation of social capital will give rise to a division of labour in the consumption process.

One of the characteristic features which makes social capital powerful and dynamic is the capacity of connection enlargement and execution substitution. This makes possible the amplified mobilisation of social capital in the extra-ordinary consumption process. The key function for such extensive mobilisation of social capital is to reach people in different social spheres familiar with the field of consumption in question. The larger one's social network, and the more diverse one's social connections with people of different positions, the better one's general manoeuvrability in social space and the greater the capability to obtain resources and opportunities (Yang, 1994). There is a certain cumulative effect in extending a social network. This could be illustrated by the following typical example.

> 'In 1994, when I was in my second year of postgraduate study, I was under pressure to have my own personal computer... . In a casual telephone conversation with my classmate, she told me that her junior brother ... was intent on buying a computer for himself and his two friends... She recommended that I join them in order to browse and shop around for my computer together with them. I then thought that's very great! So she arranged a meeting time and place for me to meet with her brother, because I was not acquainted with her brother and hadn't met him before. Several days later I joined them and shopped around for my computer during the period of a commercial exhibition.' (Female, 29)

As illustrated in this case, the work of broadening one's networks of connection frequently depends on a go-between or intermediary making an introduction to a new 'friendly' stranger. A general principle in long chains of connection involving go-betweens is that such chains are composed of a series of dyadic relations in which each person will help the next person in the chain on account of their direct personal relationship and not necessarily with the intention of helping the stranger who made the original request (Yang, 1994, 124–5). The intermediary is implicitly a guarantor in the process of extra-ordinary consumption.

Another approach is to organise a temporary division of labour, a task force for extra-ordinary consumption. This is a high density mobilisation directed to the core network of relationships. By organising a unit specially for extra-ordinary consumption, the collective actors could profit more from the efficiency and specialisation—which is critical to the successful conversion of social capital into a specific field of consumption—derived from the provisionally intensive collaborative operation. This could be highlighted by the following description.

'In the course of searching for our second-hand car, we [his father, his brother and himself] had a quite interesting division of purchasing labour. My father, who will pay the money in the form of a gift to his mature son who is going to begin his own career, pays attention to the price and its value; my elder brother, who has a lot of technological knowledge and experience of the car, is in charge of car testing; and I, a new adult in my family, am preparing to learn how to drive this car from my home to my work place safely.' (Male, 26)

This division of labour could take place on different levels and at different occasions in every series of the consumption process. As a relatively stable organisation, the network of relationships has the capacity to co-ordinate individual members and groups to which they are linked, carrying out different but integrated activities so as to maximise the return, especially in the process of extra-ordinary consumption.

As regards social relations, these strategies of amplified mobilisation of social capital associated with processes of extra-ordinary consumption (if they succeed), lead to two outcomes. First, by launching an extensive mobilisation, new social connections could be created or old social bonds might be reinforced. Second, by exercising an intensive mobilisation and then achieving a successful result, the 'local experts' authorised by social networks will be endowed with superior symbolic profits and their leading positions within networks will be enhanced.

ORDINARY CONSUMPTION AND IMPLICIT APPROPRIATION OF SOCIAL CAPITAL

Routinisation of the division of 'expertise' in consumption

The continuous and naturalised process of ordinary consumption does not make the mobilisation of social capital disappear. Rather, it takes a more indiscernible form. To minimise the cost of investment in ordinary consumption, two subtle strategies are employed. The first is routinisation of the division of 'expertise' in consumption. The second is the improvisation of proxy labour-time.

With the unspoken intention of reducing the expense of the recurrent activities of ordinary consumption, by conventionalising the sense of consumption investment linked with specific ordinary goods or services, the division of 'expertise' in ordinary consumption is transformed into a somewhat standardised procedure. A prescribed, detailed course of action to be followed regularly emerges and, hence, the processes of ordinary consumption are made simple and easy. That is, collectively different 'skills' associated with ordinary consumption become common and routinely tend to pass unnoticed. The following experience told by a man from traditional family with high education capital is illuminating:

> 'In my childhood, I suppose most of the time the toilet papers were purchased by my grandmother in corner shops nearby (because my mother had an office job). But I didn't really know the exact process. For me, toilet papers were always there and I never concerned myself with that kind of thing… I cannot remember very much about the details of my purchases of the toilet papers in my college years… However, a friend has ever reminded me that at that time I often 'borrowed' them from the friends of the same flat since we were very close friends and shared many common things (e.g., cookers, appliances, clothes, etc.) among ourselves.' (Male, 28)

By appropriating the collectivity-owned resources derived from membership in a group, some individuals can mobilise by proxy the resources of a network and escape from the routine continuous and less prestigious tasks related to ordinary consumption. Oriented by the economy of perpetuating the existence of a united body, the mobilisation of specialised 'expertise' in ordinary consumption is naturally routinised and thus becomes indiscernible and imperceptible in the continuous daily social process.

At the same time, the countless practices of ordinary consumption are parts of the endless efforts at establishing or maintaining biological and social relationships. This is mainly because the processes of ordinary consumption also involve a series of continuous ordinary exchanges—exchanges of words, information, judgement, attentions, services, assistance, devotion—which not only reproduce the daily existence of networks but also endow each member of a network with a 'network feeling' (Bourdieu, 1986; Yang, 1994). It is important to emphasise that the existence of a network of connection—even the most 'natural' ones like the family and kinship—is not a natural given, or even a social given, constituted once and for all by an initial act of institution. Rather, it is the product of an endless effort at creation and re-production (Bourdieu, 1986). In Taiwan this work, traditionally and characteristically, takes up a higher proportion of women's time and effort. Other members habitually use these commonly shared ordinary goods or services provided by them without paying much attention. This could be subtly illustrated by the explanation—which originated from the intention to expand on the blurry account cited above—provided by the interviewee's female partner:

> 'In fact, I always have to keep vigilant and alert over whether the toilet paper supplies are nearly running out or not. If this is the case, then, I have got to remind him that a hurried purchase of toilet paper is necessary.' (Female, 28)

A series of practices in regard to ordinary consumption cannot be appropriately accounted for without considering the structure of the power relations among the members of the network. And this structure is always at stake in the struggles within the network.

Improvisation of proxy labour-time

The conventionalisation in the sense of consumption investment also leads to the standardisation and substitutability of consumption practices that make possible the improvisation of proxy labour-time in the process of ordinary consumption. Many ordinary consumer goods and services such as tissue paper are so common, familiar and accustomed that they are 'stereotyped', 'standardised', normalised, and naturalised in the eyes of most members of the same network. Therefore, it is natural to suppose that the acts of acquisition could be easily accomplished by another member of this network by proxy. That is to say, the channels or routes of execution of ordinary consumption are relatively flexible and unstable and therefore are highly dependent upon practical contingency and the state of the network configuration.

My interviews show that in Taiwan tissue paper might be purchased periodically by a mother who is 'normally' supposed to be in charge of providing domestic consumables for the family. It might also be unexpectedly bought by sisters who accidentally happened upon a big sale. Sometimes it would be a father who was delegated by a mother to acquire it because she is too busy. It might even be a free offer (promotional gifts) provided by some companies. Network members commonly share these 'facts' and take them for granted. Everyone is supposed to know where, when, and how to buy such obviously common ordinary goods and thus any qualified member could take those responsibilities without difficulty.

So, unexpected sales discovered by accident can result in unplanned purchases, because 'it can always be used and "save" more'. Sometimes this kind of improvised proxy purchasing labour brings forth unanticipated consequences. As an office worker said, 'sometimes an obviously over-excessive volume of tissue papers will stock up in my house.' Such an 'unexpected' consequence in fact is not a trivial phenomenon; rather, it reflects the depth of ordinary consumption and its role in perpetuating households and wider networks through mundane and taken-for-granted activities.

The new division of 'expertise' in modern consumption

Most of the time, the pattern of behaviour within a network organisation which performs particular practices of ordinary consumption tends to be recurrent. This, of course, reduces the necessary effort essential to the reproduction of social networks. However, the highly competitive and fast changing market makes the process of ordinary consumption more complex and variable. Sometimes, agents in different positions within a social network may, unexpectedly, take advantage of surprising market situations, perform common practices of ordinary consumption, and therefore contribute to the reduction of the cost of consumption investment. In these circumstances, two vital consequences surface. First, in order to reduce the cost of labour-time investments in ordinary consumption, networks tend to normalise the division of 'expertise' in consumption, thus stabilising the hierarchical social relations. Second, the traditional model of social ethics are undermined. In traditional Taiwan, that elder and senior persons should be respected and served by the younger and junior is a dominant cultural value strongly supported by traditional family ethics and Confucianism. However, with a view to taking advantage of unexpected market conditions, contrary to the traditional pattern of ordinary consumption, other categories of consumers, such as male adults and members of the older generations, are encouraged by the sense of collective feelings and obligations to equip themselves with the common competences to acquire ordinary goods. Thereby, the traditional patterns of social relations are destabilised. An interviewee said:

> 'In order to find real "functional" valid toilet papers for my whole domestic unit, my grandmother tends to buy them from street hawkers because she believes that the rougher quality of toilet paper can have real utility for toilet cleaning; these type of toilet papers, however, are not very popular in modern supermarkets.' (Female, 26)

New structuring forces arising from modern consumption are emerging. For the whole network of relationships in modern Taiwan, the arrangement of division of 'expertise' in the process of ordinary consumption is now more flexible, and the configuration of social networks, thus, is more dynamic and changeable.

THE RELATIONSHIP BETWEEN EXTRA-ORDINARY AND ORDINARY CONSUMPTION

Ordinary consumption as enduring micro-support

Although smooth interpersonal relationships facilitate the process of extra-ordinary consumption and move the whole series of related tasks forward safely and efficiently, it takes time and effort to build or maintain such relationships. One of the most important, if not the most visible, mechanisms which create or reinforce particular connections is the multitude of minute and continual acts of ordinary consumption i.e., material or symbolic exchanges among network members. This could be usefully highlighted by the principle of eating out suggested by an informant:

> 'Most of the time, I don't have any personal taste principle in eating out with my friends or my classmates. I always accept their tastes and their favourite choices to avoid hurting the feelings and relations between us in the long terms, because we always need help from other people sooner or later.' (Female, 26)

Similarly, corporations and institutions increasingly use many ordinary goods or services as 'free offers' or 'small gifts' to create or maintain harmonious relations between consumers and themselves, hoping thereby to lay a solid foundation for forthcoming extra-ordinary consumption. However, in Taiwan, 'good' gifts tend to have timely material or symbolic utilities. The report below is not uncharacteristic:

'It seldom occurs to us to buy shampoos or casual wear, because there are always so many there. These things include soaps, towels, shampoos, tissue papers, drinks, etc...There are free "gifts" from a numerous events, festivals, elections or promotional "offers" from a lot of companies... To be honest, sometimes these things are too many to be used up.' (Female, 38)

One of the most 'effective' strategies for accumulating social capital, and hence potentially to enable success in extra-ordinary consumption, is through small and continuous co-operations in ordinary consumption.

Extra-ordinary consumption as symbolic redemption

Agents in better positions within social networks tend to appropriate the symbolic profits that accrue from commanding the extra-ordinary consumption processes and to disassociate themselves from the continuous, common process of ordinary consumption. In many instances, within networks, extra-ordinary consumption is constituted as special gifts with higher symbolic value to balance the daily asymmetry of profits associated with ordinary consumption. From this perspective, it is easier to understand that along with the trend towards a less rigid network structure, extra-ordinary consumption events such as Mother's Day, birthdays, the Chinese New Year, have an increasingly irreplaceable significance in maintaining the balanced relationship between prestigious extra-ordinary consumption and common ordinary consumption. In talking about extra-ordinary banqueting, a female interviewee noted:

'Mother's Day we [my family] always have a sumptuous dinner in a quality restaurant to reward my mother. It is a very very important day and cannot be ignored (otherwise there will be "horrible" consequences)... Nevertheless, a family dinner is not enough! Every family members must prepare gifts and have cards for my mother.' (Female, 29)

Consumption does not necessarily directly individualise consumers, especially in the social context of a country like Taiwan, where the processes of consumption produce and reproduce networks of relationships with associated sentiments of solidarity.

CONCLUSION

Contrary to the popular belief that social connections are annulled in the world of modern consumption, the network of social relations is a key determinant of consumption processes in Taiwan. Evidence concerning the rise of modern consumption in Taiwan suggests that the transformative consequences of modern consumption for social relations are more complex and subtle than many social theorists assert. Modern consumption matters to symbolic struggles in a national social space because consumption continues to serve as a strategic field for the reproduction of social position (Bourdieu, 1984). Differences associated with different social positions are not only expressed by the consumption of goods or services but also constructed through the practices of consumption. To claim that a highly institutionalised individualisation has emerged and liberated consumers, who then become dependent on fully established market, is both distorted and inaccurate. What does seem highly probable is that more sophisticated strategies of competitive struggle focused on consumption are flourishing and at the same time a more adaptable configuration of social networks is emerging.

Chapter 6

TAMED HEDONISM: CHOICE, DESIRES AND DEVIANT PLEASURES

Roberta Sassatelli

"For these words of Good, Evill, and Contemptible, are ever used with relation to the person that useth them: There being nothing simply and absolutely so; nor any common Rule of Good and Evil to be taken from the nature of the objects themselves; but from the Person of the man."

Thomas Hobbes

While the Frankfurt School considers all consumption as potentially dangerous, in everyday life we tend to discriminate good consumer practices from bad ones. As the sociology of deviance has recognized, we may all deviate in different degrees from the normative expectations of our culture and from the assorted expectations of different groups within it. In the classical interactionist approach, deviance is understood as a process of adjustment between rule-breaking and rule-enforcement whose heterogeneity depends on the nature of rule-enforcement and on the strength of commitment to those rules by those infringing them (Becker, 1963; see also Goffman, 1963a, and Matza, 1969). On these grounds, the notion that we are all consumers is as important as the notion that we all consume differently. So, the social regulation of consumption—with its many levels of entrenchment ranging from implicit routines, to institutionally enforced manners, to highly formalized rules and the implementation of social policy—is based now, as in the past, on the moral classification of different goods, different spaces of consumption and different types of consumer.

This chapter sketches a social-theoretical account of what can be described as the 'frame' for such classification.[1] I will work on the idea that there exists an over-arching rhetoric which operates in contemporary society as a framework for the different local moral norms deployed to evaluate consumer practices, their worth and propriety. This will emerge from exploration of the notion of consumer choice. As I shall show, far from having the status of a pure descriptive concept, choice exists as a normative claim. Choice relies on complex anthropological presuppositions: invited to think of themselves as choosers, individuals are asked to promote their desires and pleasures as the ultimate source of value while keeping mastery over them. This solicits a particular picture of normality, whereby the consumer is sovereign of the market in so far as he or she is sovereign of him or herself. Consumer hedonism must thereby be tamed by forms of detachment which stress the self in order to work as the organizing principle for the legitimation of contemporary consumer practices.

Drawing on a variety of concrete examples, I will examine how desires and control are articulated within different social contexts to establish the moral adequacy of consumer practices. I will look at the way goods as diverse as cosmetics, fitness and drugs can be framed as normal or deviant. As we shall see, the normalization of pleasure is crucial both in the commercial promotion of ordinary items and in the legitimatory strategies of more equivocal and marginal goods.

THE AMBIVALENCE OF CHOICE

As it is well known, the term consumer society was contrived after the Second World War to grasp the fact that consumption had become a central mode of modern life and is based on the assumption that the movement towards mass consumption in the inter-war period was accompanied by a general reorganization of everyday experience. However, historians and historically informed studies have shown that already in the late 17th and in the early 18th century, both in everyday routine and in public discourse, consumer practices had become central together with the liberal notion of choice. Indeed, innumerable commentators have observed that consumer culture typically refers to the liberal ideal of individual choice (Slater, 1997). Today, among mundane consumerist discourses and institutions, even very diverse phenomena such as advertising and consumer protection organizations are based on a rhetoric of choice (Aldridge, 1994; Pinto, 1990; Sassatelli, 1995). The analysis of situated consumer practices—of how people actually come to learn how to consume and to attribute value to goods—does not deny the idea of choice. On the contrary, it underlines the necessity to consider its ambivalence.

We may fix an image of the ambivalence of choice by qualifying its status. Choice is better understood as a normative claim rather than a fully realized practice. On the one hand, the idea of individual and rational choice does not correspond to the practical modalities by which subjects learn how to consume. On the other hand, it constitutes the normative frame for such processes and a structuring principle for the institutions where they take place.

Whether we look at health centres, discos, pubs, theme parks, restaurants, or supermarkets we can see that, as a practice, choice is realized through an interactive learning process. A good example comes from the sociology of dining out (Warde, 1997). Only through practice do people learn that they want certain foods, learn to want them in appropriate ways, and learn to make sense of them beyond the immediacy of their enjoyment. Choice of certain foods and restaurants entails a process of learning which is locally sustained by a series of specific and highly codified manners and whose significance goes well beyond the context of consumption, being appropriated as knowledge to be used in different social contexts. Even when we shop, choice of a particular item is shaped by the organization of space, time and interaction. Our choices in the cathedrals of immediate satisfaction, the supermarket and the shopping mall, are rooted in daily rituals marking human relationships and will acquire much of their meaning in subsequent, again specifically situated, display and use (Miller et al., 1998).

The recognition that consumption is, in practice, a situated process of learning is vital. Yet, like all other social action, consumption must also be felt as valuable. We should not forget that the subject which consumer practices demand is modelled on the notion of choice. Ideal as it may be, it is an autonomous, self-sufficient subject with particular objectives, who strives towards them and who believes that the best way to do so is to act on the basis of a goal-specific, instrumental rationality, following the advice of experts or resorting to specialized agencies. As a category of action, choice relies on a distinctive anthropology: invited to think of themselves as choosers, individuals are asked to make themselves calculable and foreseeable, while promoting themselves as the ultimate and non-substitutable source of value. This requires individuals who are sovereigns of themselves, who have become, as Friedrich Nietzsche would say, the owners of their will (see also Foucault, 1976 and 1983).

Choice is ambivalent because it is the normative model for consumer culture yet, in practice, it dissolves into a myriad of situated learning processes entrenching rituals and routines. Moreover the way we get some assurance that we have voluntarily chosen a particular good is rather paradoxical. In other words, what counts as confirmation of choice is as ambivalent as its status. It is the possibility to choose *not to choose* a particular good which—in line with the prominent place assigned to negative freedom by liberalism—functions as a warranty that we have actually voluntarily chosen it. Individuals who are sovereigns of themselves and of their will, have not only the capacity to continue willing what they once chose when that corresponded to their desires. They can also exit that choice, should the conditions of choice be altered or the initial wants remain unsatisfied.

To explore this issue we may come back to Albert O. Hirschman's well-known essay *Exit, Voice and Loyalty* (1979). Hirschman conceived of product-exit as a fundamental structural device within the modern consumption sphere. When close substitutes for an insatisfactory product are available, as in current markets, consumers may well safe-guard their interests, at least in the short term, without resorting to any interest articulation or 'voice'. Exit however is much more than a 'market failure recuperation mechanism', more than 'the operative instrument through which competition should work' (Hirschman, 1979, 30). It also defines the framework within which consumer practices obtain value: it is a key component of the narratives used in contempo-rary society to legitimize consumer practices, evaluating their worth and propriety. Such narratives in fact typically require that customers *can* renounce any specific item they may once have wanted, and even that they *can* abandon the idea of choosing any commodity within the relevant product category.

Paradoxically, therefore, we understand that it is because people can give them up that goods are responsive to their true desires, to their will. Choosing things just for a try or just for fun, for present physical enjoyment or for sophisticated aesthetic pleasure is fine so long as it is the self who is playing the game. The self is to be portrayed as being in charge of his or her desires: he or she has, in a word, to possess his or her own desires, for only then will he or she be autonomous.[2] Even the fact that our desires may discover different objects, that these objects are continuously changing, helps sustain the game of having a self-possessed self. The development of the so-called post-Fordist economy may be seen in this light: the ceaseless innovation of consumer goods, the continuously superseded fashions, the endless combination of styles appear to grant consumers a continuous liberation from the specific objects which they have chosen.

THE NORMATIVE RHETORIC OF THE CONSUMER SOCIETY

Once we assign choice such a paradoxical character, we can better appreciate the continuity between the contemporary and the early modern discourse on consumption. In the 18th century new, modern patterns of consumption emerged and underwent difficult legitimation processes (Appleby, 1978; Boltanski and Thévenot, 1991; Hirschman,

1977; Pocock, 1985). The legitimation of modern consumer practices took off from the new possibility of social and political order that they promised to guarantee. The pursuit of personal gratification through goods may still have been dangerous for the individual body, but it was becoming beneficial for the body politic (Hundert, 1994; Sassatelli, 1997). It was appreciated as an unintended path toward common wealth and welfare. Still, the socializing passions and desires which were associated with consumption—envy, imitation, pride, etc.—did not stand at all as a guarantee that public welfare was going to feed back into private life. This was at odds with the liberal ideal of individual autonomy which was so important for the development of the new political order.

With Adam Smith, however, not only political order, but also personal order became possible through consumption. This happened not just because individuals' desires for pleasure and acquisition were deemed to be socially positive, but also because the subject of desires became a rational actor. Modelled onto production, consumption was tamed into a rational, self-interested, long-term pursuit of personal gratification: the drive towards pleasure was tempered by the 'uniform, constant and uninterrupted effort of each man of bettering his condition' (Smith, 1776: 325). Smith portrayed the marketplace as an institution where subjects develop the capacity to reflect upon themselves as social actors, to excel by the pursuit of a decent, commodious and well-ordered life (Muller, 1993). Merchants—as we all become under market conditions—are not pictured as ascetic monks, they do not disdain the decencies of life; they are indeed good, well-behaved, rational consumers as opposed to the immoral, irrational, whimsical wasters impersonated by the old, declining nobility. Under these conditions, the consumer-merchant becomes the foundation of a new social and political order: the sovereign whose desires the market shall respond to and the sovereign of his/her own desires.

That the cult of self-control is crucial in the development of consumer culture may be found in the way alcohol consumption has been discussed under the rubric of diseases of the will since Locke's famous example of the drunkard (Sedgewick, 1992; Valverde, 1998). Addiction remains one of the most powerful stigmatizing strategies against a variety of consumer practices. Likewise, the consumer's double-edged sovereignty remains the driving force of our discourses about consumption. As the individual becomes the source of value, his or her desires and pleasures become the foundational horizon for commercial culture. Still, the satisfaction of desires is viable so long as desires do not come into conflict with individual autonomy and the self retains its hold on them. Likewise, while pleasure testifies to the realization of individual desires, it cannot guarantee that the desires which are so obviously satisfied are actually true to the self. Hedonism thus works as a theory of correspondence between individual desires and commodities. Yet, alone, it cannot deliver a self-possessed self. There is the crucial need for some management of desires through forms of detachment which suggest convincing images of self. Pleasures have to be both supported and neutralized: well-behaved consumers must enjoy their lot and still find that their deepest selves lie somewhere behind these pleasures, so that they can still govern their desires. The rhetoric deployed to support and regulate consumer practices in contemporary society thus relies on what may be called tamed hedonism: consumers must be after pleasure only when pleasure is after them.[3]

I can see at least two major ways for the realization of such normative rhetoric: immediate pleasures must be either reasonable from the wider perspective of self-realization or insignificant to the deep structure of the self. The first option is close to the old Smithian plot. Immediate pleasures are echoed by and ultimately anchored to long-term projects of well-being. Reference to these may be found in a number of discourses which re-classify the repeated use of a good as part of an overall design, a promise of the self to the self, corresponding to an original and autonomous will, to get certain positive states of happiness, prosperity, welfare, etc. Routines and repeated purchases are very important in everyday life. To be sure, we do not need to address the nature of many of our consumption habits. Entrenched consumption habits are part of a taken-for-granted background and may not even be experienced as existing within the domain of choice or described as consumption. In most cases they are certainly not questioned. Yet in the face of a fast-changing market and with the increasing fragmentation of society some of these routines may lose their self-evident character. Discourses on regime, regulation and nature directly associated with visions of both personal and social order become important to provide a legitimation for not-so-entrenched routine practices. Especially when a repeated practice no longer bears the sign of choice (understood as the possibility not to choose this very practice) the suggestion that it anyway corresponds to a wider project of well-being helps in the playing of the fundamental game of having a self-possessed self.

The second option is prevalent for the justification of novelties and extraordinary practices. In contemporary culture even intoxication, so long as it does not last too long, so long as it is confined to certain spaces such as the rave party, or to certain phases of life such as youth, may be accepted. Indeed, we discover in such confined practices a legitimatory style which has gained increasing importance, namely self-experimentation. Probably thanks to romantic teachings, the primacy of well-cultivated feelings and the pursuit of oneself through originality and novelty have become part of consumer culture (Campbell, 1987; Williams, 1982). The image of individuals as dandies committed to an ironic heroicization of the present may well be included in the picture (Featherstone, 1991; Frisby, 1985). Self-experimentation can thus be described as a discursive tool enabling subjects to produce a strong self-narrative which provides them with a measure of distance from both desires and pleasures. In its own terms, reference to self-experimentation makes consumer pleasures, if not reasonable, at least innocent. The pursuit of sensation and excitement are no longer conducive to addiction when they are classified under the rubric of that *blasé* detachment which firmly alludes to a space for the self. Again, under these conditions, the self is the master of his or her pleasures, so much so that he or she can indulge in them without really giving in.

Reference to self-experimentation or to projects of well-being operates as a promise that pleasures in consumption conform to individual autonomy, and thereby are just and normal. The normal-pathological distinction is crucial.[4] For a self-evident property of these discourses is their normative quality, their capacity to discriminate between right and wrong, between normal and deviant practices. If we consider how and when consumer practices can be stigmatized as deviant and corrupting, it is patent that this happens mostly through the denunciation of excess. Such denunciation is nothing but a suspicion of the inability of the self to gain distance from his or her desires and—stretching the point—to get along without them. In so far as untamed hedonism is deemed to be deviant we may have isolated a framework which—reinterpreted in different ways in different contexts—works in everyday life as the normative rhetoric of consumer society. In the following section I will thereby look at a number of different contemporary practices in order to show how consumer pleasures are normalized.

THE NORMALIZATION OF PLEASURE

As we shall see, a variety of consumer practices may be considered, to different degrees, as deviant and dangerous or normal and innocuous according to whether or not they openly challenge the anthropological prescriptions inherent in the notion of choice. In most cases, deviant consumers are identified by their indulgence in pleasures which appear excessive, irrational and uncontrolled. Normal consumption instead typically relies on tamed hedonism. In particular, reference to long-term projects of well-being and to self-experimentation are, if differently, deployed to normalize pleasure. I will firstly deal with goods that are now widely held to be normal. I will then look at practices of consumption which are still ambiguous and are more often caught in a struggle over normalization. In both cases I will show that consumer practices may be considered normal not only because they are imbued with individual meanings, nor simply because participants get pleasure from them, but also because these meanings and pleasures are articulated with narratives which ultimately testify to the autonomy of the self.

In contemporary western culture the 18th century emphasis on the corrosive nature of consumption has been dissolved in the ever longer list of dietetics, or natural products which guarantee pleasure without excess. Indeed, the development of a market for body maintenance and transformation provides excellent examples of how immediate gratifications and longer-term projects of well-being are normatively articulated in contemporary culture. The marketing strategies of products as diverse as low-fat foods, organic fabrics or natural cosmetics rely on immediate enjoyment as much as on long-term narratives of personal welfare and of political and social responsibility (Weil, 1993).

A recent advertising campaign of The Body Shop points to this direction. The campaign was launched by the publication of The Body Shop's magazine *Full Voice* which openly challenged conventional cosmetics advertising and its use of glamorous images of femininity. The magazine asks consumers not to surrender to desire. Rather, they are asked to be in control of their wants and of the images of the body which advertising is said to use to elicit desire. The subsequent billboards and press adverts have emphasized the immediate physical pleasures to be gained from the use of cosmetics and have relied on themes such as authenticity and naturalness which neutralize such pleasures by suggesting that they correspond to a real project of self-realization. Being overtly opposed to dominant body ideals and proposing beautified pictures of the fleshy and plump body, The Body Shop's campaign suggests a consumer who is solidly positioned on her own grounds, so detached from social pressures and so conscious of herself as to get some immediate pleasures while respecting her own authenticity. Also, with images of a multiethnic and working body, and with the claim that the products on sale are the result of fair trading and ecological awareness, self-realization becomes part of a wider vision of social order and morality. Finally, even in The Body Shop's last shot, its handbook *The Body Shop Book of Wellbeing* (Blanks, 1998), we get a compendium of individual pleasures, political correctness and green activism. All in all, ethical considerations, nature and authenticity are marshalled for assuring that the immediate pleasures obtained through consumption are part of an overall project of well-being which the self is ultimately engaged to promote.

We find that a similar version of tamed hedonism is articulated not only in representation and text, but also in institutions. Fitness gyms have often been understood under the rubric of asceticism and deferred gratification responding to an ideology of healthism (White et al., 1995). However, when one gets inside the gym and listens to the voices of the clients a different picture emerges (Sassatelli, 1999). Physical activities within the gym are locally organized as coherent domains of action where involvement in the procedure of exercising is sustained. Involvement is described by regular participants as 'fun' and works as experiential confirmation for the work-out scene: managing to get involved in the focus of attention prescribed by training, clients feel sure about the reality which they sustain, they feel natural and at ease. Training may thus be experienced as an inherently meaningful and compelling present. Such an enjoyable present is still fundamental for the self who has good reasons to train, as the wealth of underutilized home equipment for fitness testifies. Although without a time which is organized for them as a present they find it very difficult to stick to their projects, participants in fitness understand themselves as actors who organize their present so as to master their future. While the reality of training rests on a body-mind involvement in the present, the value of training rests on the creation of a calculating self who bestows value on his or her practices, and who reconstructs his or her training story as a project of well-being and a promise of self-determination. Regular clients in particular find themselves in a position to understand their gym routines as a well-balanced mix of both immediate and wider rewards. They arrive at the conclusion that fitness is 'right' because it is 'good' for them, but that this would 'not be right' if they did not 'enjoy' the process.

In other, less undisputed domains of consumption we find that the domestication of pleasure is invoked, possibly more urgently, to neutralize the dreadful suspicion that the consumer is no longer an autonomous chooser as a result of his or her practices. Goods which are still equivocal, marginal or deviant, such as alcohol and drugs, which may be stigmatized by reference to addiction, may come to be justified by seizing some moral boundary stressing the strength, the authenticity and even the rationality of the choosing self. Doubtful as it may appear to the moralist, reference to a project of well-being is often implicated in the way cannabis consumption is advocated. Despite a number of diverse legal restrictions, in many European countries the consumption of home-produced cannabis appears to be on the increase. *Weedworld*—a magazine for the self-producer initiated nearly a decade ago in the Netherlands and available in the UK to anyone above the age of 16—opens with the hope 'to educate the world's population as to the many and varied uses of Cannabis Hemp and teach how it can be used to save our increasingly unstable environment'. Its pages, together with factual advertising for seeds and growing paraphernalia and detailed farming tips, feature editorials and reader's letters on issues such as marijuana and AIDS, the disinformation about hemp, support networks for misuse, etc. The emerging picture is that cannabis, when grown at home for self-consumption, is to be understood as a well-managed pleasure: it is politically correct as it does not finance mafia, it is a social activity with its rhythms dictated by growing and harvesting and facilitating occasions for sharing, and it favours personal wellness by being absolutely natural.

Ambiguous consumer practices like using drugs or alcohol are quite often justified by other means too. In particular we may see that pleasure is fine so long as it remains fun—an unserious, inconsequential involvement in the present which does not jeopardize the self and his or her capacity to choose. This may be achieved by referring to self-experimentation, as it is evident in some recent films which offer a sophisticated picture of drug use. In *Trainspotting*, for example, the leading character is the champion of an ironic presentism which entails that he is not stuck with the drugs, thus normalizing the pleasures he gets from them. On the contrary, his friends, portrayed as the 'real' deviants, produce very serious and encompassing narratives about their drug habits and cannot detach themselves from immediate pleasures. In the end, the leading character can and will choose a wholly different set of pleasures and the spectators are invited to like him precisely when they witness the sarcastic and disengaged mood that once again accompanies his new preferences.

Similar legitimatory styles are not confined to pictures. Recent research stresses that a substantial proportion of young consumers consider drug or alcohol consumption as something harmless, even normal, something related to a particular phase of their life (Lenson, 1995; Preston, 1996; South, 1998). After their youth they will put an end to the bracketing of serious pursuits that drugs and alcohol imply for them, they will start a more conventional life—a family and a job—which is recognized as incompatible with these practices. Whether or not this will actually happen, when young people present these ambiguous pleasures with carelessness and themselves as self-possessed choosers, they are grasping their chance not to be excluded from the wider culture, even if this may result in a lower status within their peer-group. In any case, what is involved in this understanding is not so much a rebellious, heroic youth. It is rather a protected period of pleasure and fun, where the necessity of a long-term rationality is suspended, but at the same time recognized as relevant through the very idea that what one is living is a particular, anti-structural but ultimately limited, stage of life.

The social organization of alcohol and drug consumption is itself directly implicated in the domestication of pleasures. The farther we move from representation and the closer we get to situated activities, the more we see that drug taking and alcohol consumption are socially regulated in very different ways, if only for their different legal status. Yet, in practice both alcohol and drugs are tolerated if they are confined to specialized spaces which are specifically carved out for their consumption. To be sure, the more these spaces appear as controlled and regulated, the easier it is to refer to them as innocuous. Still, in general, the very provision of spaces which organize—shape and contain—experiences of fun and involvement helps combine present enjoyment with narratives of self. The modern separation of relatively different and discrete spheres of life makes room for what Goffman called the 'bureaucratization of the spirit': the subject can play the game of having an autonomous self provided his or her desires are not out of place, and provided that he or she is able to switch to appropriate moods, manners and habits whenever required. Under these conditions no pleasure or desire can contain the self. The self is still governing him or herself by appropriately governing his or her conduct.

Although they all have their own specificity, rave parties, discos and pubs are spaces where participants can, and indeed must, follow certain manners and demonstrate their motivations in order to participate in consumption in locally appropriate ways. Immediate involvement and present enjoyment are fostered as part of a meaningful reality where what is relevant in everyday life is temporarily suspended. Here individuals are supposed to abstract from their normal duties and everyday social roles to take part in a contained domain of 'ordered disorder' where practices which would be embarrassing or even dangerous elsewhere can and must be enjoyed (Elias and Dunning, 1986; Shields, 1991; Turner, 1969; Urry, 1995). In this view, the pub provides a space where drinking is confined and controlled by a set of rules and manners. These manners and rules bear, as it were, the conditions for narratives of well-being as sociability and emotional release to be deployed with some success (Alasuutari, 1992; Partanen, 1991, 217–235; Selden, 1962, 87–88; Sulkunen et al., 1997). To the extent that raves are much less strictly and formally regulated, similar legitimatory styles may be less convincing with respect to drugs. Yet, even here, drug-taking is inserted in a whole universe of meanings and marked by an overt discontinuity with normality. Indeed, recent ethnographic work shows that going to the rave party means taking 'time-off' from everyday reality, experimenting with a feeling of being in another world and having the possibility of communicating in a manner out of keeping with one's own role and character (Corsten, 1999; Malbon, 1997). All these experiences are clearly constructed and valued as a world apart. As such, drug-taking may be framed as a normal abnormality. Participants may thereby find ways of presenting their pleasures as somehow controlled and confined to otherwise meaningful contexts which suspend, but do not abolish, the importance of self-control.

CONCLUDING REMARKS

Despite differentiation and fragmentation, and because of its role in the consolidation of the infinite local normativity of consumption, tamed hedonism appears as powerful practical metaphysics. Rooted in the ideal of the self-possessed chooser and entrenched through the history of modernity, it amounts to a frame of classification which works as the normative rhetoric of the consumer society, not because every one deploys it in the same way, but because it is both deeply rooted in the liberal vocabulary and sufficiently abstract to function as the default basis for the political and ethical problematization of consumption. The issues of legitimation and normalization often go unnoticed in the sociology of consumption. The notion of choice, ambivalent and utopian as it is, has provided the starting point to individuate the coordinates for the discrimination of consumer practices as corrupting or innocent. Practices considered as normal are viewed as both the realization of desires and their containment: they are presented and regulated as moral worlds responding to ethical, autonomous and self-possessed selves. While deviant pleasures seem to master the self, discourses and contexts for the domestication of pleasures are also deployed to legitimize a host of practices at the fringes of consumer culture.

The overearching quality of tamed hedonism would remain sterile if not complemented by the minutiae of cultural embeddedness. Indeed, without the depth of culture, the ordinariness of place and the contingency of practice, many of the examples provided would not have made sense. It is in the contextual, concrete details that we find the conditions for the development of different norms and discourses, and it is there that we may see under which conditions the deployment of tamed hedonism is both possible and convincing. If fitness is more easily asserted to be a legitimate pleasure and a project of well-being than, say, cosmetic surgery, this is because of the way it can be associated with a long-standing tradition which praises body transformation through work and asceticism. Similarly, as the materialization of gourmand restraint, low-fat foods are more defensible than alcoholic drinks which, in many cultures, are associated with a disorderly life and addiction. Institutional contexts themselves work as conditions of assertability. Thus, it is especially when drugs get out of the contained anti-structure of the rave party and the disco with their appeal to self-experimentation, when alcoholic drinks get out of the formality of the dinner party with its possibility of a sophisticated rhetoric of well-being, that they may much more easily become a problem. It is especially when drugs and drinks get out of these places—and their locally specific worlds—that they become (for the wider public as well as for the users) deviant and corrupting. To a degree, affording an articulation of pleasures and longer-term neutralizing narratives, places like these respond to the normative requirements of contemporary consumer culture and help normalize ambiguous practices.

Notes

1   The notion of 'frame' is inspired by Goffman's work *Frame Analysis*: frame is a 'context of understanding' which orientates our perceptions, a set of 'organizational premises—sustained both in mind and in activity' (Goffman, 1974, 39 and 247). For a critical discussion of the uses of such notion in different contexts see Deborah Tannen (1993).

2 Of course, I am not arguing for an essentialist view of the self, nor for a rational model of action. The subject who represents him or herself in such terms can best be seen as a Weberian dominant *'menschlicher Typus'* (Weber, 1917), a concept-tool not of consumer actions *tout court*, but of the modalities of rationalization and self-constitution with respect to one's own consumer practices that subjects are urged to adopt in every day life.

3 A number of commentators have indicated some form of tamed hedonism as a crucial dimension of contemporary consumer culture. Campbell (1987) has argued that the 18th century cult of polished emotions and 'sentimental hedonism' has given way to modern hedonism in which pleasure is separated from physical satisfaction and pursued in daydreaming and imagination, a longing which results in the ceaseless consumption of novelty. Following Bourdieu's observations on the new middle-class, Featherstone (1991) talks of a reflexive cultivation of pleasure close to the aestheticization of experience which is typical of the artistic avant-garde and associates this with contemporary Yuppies portrayed as 'perfect', 'narcissistic', and 'calculating hedonists'. However, while in the former hedonism is a basic endowment of human nature, in the latter its strong moral tones are underplayed. In both cases, the links between hedonism and the ideal of choice remain unexplored.

4 Again, this is to be taken in its constructivist version. Especially within the interactionist perspective deviance has been defined as a negative departure from the social expectations held within a particular social situation or culture (Goffman, 1963). In this view, deviance or abnormality only makes sense in relation to normality; it works when and if deviants understand themselves as such; and it is practically realized as the impossibility of continuing a smooth, taken-for-grated interaction.

Chapter 7

MOBILE COMMUNICATION AS A WAY OF URBAN LIFE

Pasi Mäenpää

The mobile telephone is rapidly becoming a necessity in everyday life. This has happened already in Finland where 80 % of households had a mobile phone in autumn 1999, and the figure is still rising. In Finland most mobile phone calls are concerned with pleasure rather than business, and the bills are paid by callers themselves—or their parents. Teenagers are heavy and inventive users of text messages in particular, and the youngest regular carriers of mobile phones have not seen their tenth birthday yet. Public debate on mobile yuppies, disturbing behaviour, or the artificial need to call has faded, and virtually the only places where the use of mobile phones is banned are churches, hospitals and aeroplanes. A frequent topic of Finnish newspaper's life-style columns today is whether one can still survive a week without a mobile phone.

Why Finland has become the leading country is not the issue here, but let us note that the world's leading cell phone manufacturer Nokia is a Finnish company and that in Finland the prices of mobile phone calls are the cheapest in the world. All this is not just a coincidence, of course, but it seems that there are no fundamental differences between the cultures of Finland and the rest of Europe, which would lead us to consider the phenomenon characteristically Finnish (cf. Roos, 1999; 1993). It is reasonable to assume that Finland, among other Nordic countries, is a forerunner, rather than a special case, and that in the long run everyday telecommunication will turn wire-less in the rest of the world, too. Thus, to observe Finland today is to foresee the probable future of mobile communication world wide.

This chapter offers observations and interpretations of the mobile phone's effects on the organisation of people's everyday lives and social relationships. The subject has not been previously studied, apparently due to the novelty of the phenomenon, although the mobile phone is both an interesting example of new technological consumption and a significant part of digitalising everyday life. The mobile phone—or just 'mobile'—does not merely replace the traditional telephone or move the calls into another place and time. The underlying argument is that the mobile creates its own user-culture which in turn produces new urban culture and new ways of life. The study is aimed at locating the most intense areas of present-day 'mobile culture', areas which crystallise the mobile phone's significance in its users' lives, but where the social interaction also takes new forms. These intensities are regarded as the opening of a large-scale mobile remote communication of the future. Most of the analyses derive from listening to and observing 20–40 year olds, because their relationship to their phone is more intensive and their uses of it are more frequent and meaningful to them than is the case with older people.

Thus this chapter does not aim to describe mobile culture as a whole, but rather tries to analyse its most probable effects on modes of social intercourse. The framework for these interpretations consists mainly of the sociology of urban interaction, because public places, meaning something between private spheres of home, work, etc. are the sites of mobile communication. At the most general level a question for the research is what kind of a social connection is formed around interaction and how is way of life mediated by the mobile phone? It is not so much a question of what changes as what kinds of shapes and contents this change contains.[1]

THE INTENSIFICATION OF INTERACTION

What type of intercourse characterises use of the mobile, and which types does it promote? Everyday thinking leads us to suspect that the mobile is bound to replace face-to-face meetings. This would also seem natural according to the principles of technological determinism. It seems natural to think that the mobile—like the traditional telephone—was created in order to avoid unnecessary travelling in a situation where a person wished to convey a message; thus travelling and conveying messages face-to-face would first become unnecessary, in time even a nuisance. Yet this does not seem to be happening in practice. The interviewees particularly denied any decrease in their face-to-face contacts after buying a mobile—on the contrary, many swear that the mobile has increased the amount of their face-to-face contacts.

This claim seems to be supported by observations of the most commonplace call from a mobile phone: 'Hi! I'm on my way.' Another typical form of phone call is one in which a future meeting is planned, and places and times are set. The interviews also included several discussions concerning the mobile in conjunction with meetings. The mobile is used for contacting people whom one plans to meet or is just about to see. Therefore it seems to promote face-to-face meetings, since it makes meeting people easier for those who live a mobile life. Calling on the mobile phone is often about organising and fixing future meetings, particularly among people between 20–30 years of age, whose lifestyle is mobile and whose spare time is oriented outside the home.

Although the amount of face-to-face meetings may generally increase because of the mobile phone, there are some relationships which are prone to be left on the level of mere calls. In this respect the mobile theoretically adds nothing new compared to the traditional telephone, although in practice things might be different. Many of the younger interviewees had acquired relationships which are maintained solely by the mobile, such as old school or army friends or other acquaintances who have grown remote with time. These relationships have survived as 'mobile phone relationships' because calling on the mobile is easier than calling on an ordinary telephone, which in turn is based on the mobility of the mobile phone. One calls with the mobile while on the way to somewhere, while doing something else, while waiting etc., which makes the call less charged since it does not need a particular reason and since one does not have to go deeply into the other person's personal life. A mobile call is expected to be short, even superficial, and it is easy to make since the recipient also understands it to be short. Another option the mobile offers is text messaging (SMS), which is widely and frequently used among youth and young adults. It is sometimes found more suitable than a call, because it is more anonymous and distant, and as such resembles e-mail messaging. But sometimes it is used for the most intimate communication between best friends and lovers, because it is considered an alternative and more favourable way of sharing emotions or enacting humoresque sociability.

Therefore we can expect mobile remote communication to bring about an intensification and enrichment of intercourse, rather than its decline or replacement with virtual worlds. The visions of digital intercourse seem more familiar and less dangerous when observed as they are manifested in the mobile phone rather than in conjunction with computers and nets, since using the mobile always includes a corporeal relationship with the spatio-temporal reality. The user of a computer is static within a familiar space and prone to get drawn into a visually conveyed mock reality which knows no time and place. The user of a mobile, on the other hand, is generally assumed to be physically on the move and within the public rhythm of social life. This way the mobile makes the digitalisation of social reality more visible in society, by bringing it into social life. Yet at the same time it enters the sphere of social control, for public space always acts as a kind of reversed Panopticon, in which everyone is a potential object for everyone else's observation (Mäenpää 1993). In this respect one could claim that the mobile phone and urban publicity have a common historical mission to take in the strangeness of artificial digital reality and mould it into a part of the familiar social world and its modes of interaction.

When regarded as leisure-oriented lounging and dealings between individuals, one could say that the mobile shifts urban culture into a new gear. The mobile seems to promote spending one's spare time 'out' rather than at home: 'Yet another reason not to go home' (male, 23 years). Urban lounging and partying get a new promoter and accelerator in the mobile. Directing one's spare time into the urban environment becomes an increasingly available option. At the same time its quality also increases, since the mobile makes it is easier to bring together larger groups of friends for a Friday night. Abundant meetings and larger groups as such do not bring about any qualitative change in urban culture, but do the forms and contents of these meetings and flockings exhibit new traits?

LIVING IN TWO PLACES—LIVING IN A COMMON RHYTHM

One of the visions by Nicholas Negroponte, a guru of the digital society, is that of the 'asynchronous world' which, according to him, is brought about by e-mail and answering machines (1996, 167). For Negroponte, being asynchronous refers to the way concerned parties are freed from the necessity of being simultaneously present in interaction. The mobile phone users' culture, however, refers to a 'synchronous world' in which life is lived spatially in different places while setting a shared pace or rhythm with others. This is one of the several instances in which the mobile seems to be going against the current in the development of the digital society.

One of the young interviewees says that she spends up to six hours a day in a café. During that time she and her friend call each other every half an hour. Sometimes, she says, these calls come close to being 'terrorism' when the friend calls late at night: 'Hi, what are you doing, I'm off to bed now.' This is an exceptional case within the material, one which caused amazement and bursts of laughter among the group of interviewees. Yet it is an understandable, if extreme, example of something more general. Spontaneous contacts, which especially the younger interviewees make 'ex tempore', tend to be these 'where are you' and 'watcha doing' -calls. Such chatting hardly resembles real exchange of information or even intercourse, as much as merely sharing one's life with others in real time. It is a question of living in the same rhythm or wave with one's closest friends, the feeling of a continuously shared life.

There can hardly be many such people; usually one shares one's life with one or two good friends, but through them it is possible for an individual to be a link in a longer chain, or a network of people. Living within such a network is not, however, characterised by the diversity of contacts or their exploitability as a network of specialists, such as is commonly referred to in conjunction with institutions of the business world or occupation. The central characteristic of such a network of friends is living in real time, i.e. things are shared when they take place. It is a question of a shared feeling of living lives together, a feeling maintained by the mobile phone. Another aspect of this feeling is one of worry: something bad might happen to the other, which is also eased by continuous contact. This is typical of young adult's relations with their parents. As a student girl puts it, 'mother stays calmer than before'.

The mobile also enables real-time control over the modern, dispersed and illocal networks of human relationships. Or more generally, it gives its user a sense of 'where it's at', which is analogous with the 'global village' united by the media (cf. McLuhan and Powers, 1989). The inhabitants of the 'global village' routinely and repeatedly update their knowledge of current affairs, for example by watching the evening news every night. The real-time network maintained by the mobile can be regarded as an intimate equivalent of living in the flux of public mass media information. The mobile does not convey news of the world but information on the lives of friends and acquaintances. From media culture's point of view it offers a personal, custom-made 'reality-TV'. A media supply based on everyone's individual needs is expected to become the revolutionary benefit offered by digital media (Negroponte, 1996, for example). One of its effects may also be a transformation of media consumption into communalising mechanisms which create separate social worlds (cf. Becker and McCall, 1990). Living in a shared rhythm, wave or flow may be characteristic of a new sense of community. The societal rhythmics promoted by the mobile point towards the self-sufficient communities that have been described by Michel Maffesoli (1996), in which a constant sharing of one's life with others from afar gains a specific enchanting quality as a social form. The societal utopia of the 'mobile phone society' could consist of the urban communities floating upon remote communications, communities that are born under networks resembling mailing lists. But what type of a community is essentially defined by simultaneously experiencing things while far away from one another?

LIVING IN TWO PLACES—OVERLAPPING LIVES

In addition to the 'I'll be there in a minute' -talk, another famous phrase on the mobile goes: 'Where are you?' It is part of the etiquette of mobile communication, intended for creating a world-in-common and informing the caller of how long and to what degree of concentration or intimacy the receiver can converse (cf. the reply 'I'm on the bus'). But do place and location bear some internal meaning in remote mobile communication? In the early days of the telephone 'long distance calling' was a special experience caused by the mere distance between the speakers. Since then the long distance call has become an everyday matter. Now the mobile phone enables not just the remote, but *any* place to be present in phone sociability.

The disappearance of place or its meaning is one of the big themes of the digital society. For Graham and Marvin, for example, the definition of the aims of telecommunications is to minimise time in order to erase the limitations set by place (Graham and Marvin, 1996, 114–115). Again the everyday usage of mobile phones seems to point to the opposite direction. A student calls up a friend for a cup of coffee after work, assuming her to be studying in the library nearby. A 30 year old man moving around the city remembers a friend living nearby. A middle-aged salesman driving past a town decides to call up an old friend to say that he is just driving past his hometown. The common denominator for these calls is, besides pure sociability, the fact that the impulse to call is caused by the caller's location. In other words it is a question of the geographical proximity between the caller and the receiver.

Since one may speak from any place, the place becomes the object of a new kind of reflection. A mobile caller must always *choose* a place from which he or she talks. Therefore the place is always charged with meaning. One calls from a place either because he or she wants to discuss it or because it is suitable for calling. Place thus becomes significant either in the relationship between the speakers or in the relationship between a speaker and his or her surroundings—or both. Taking this line of thought a step further, the illocality of the mobile phone actually reverts to 'neo-locality'. When people call from specific places to specific people, intercourse conveyed by the mobile gives new meaning to the place. The ability to communicate wherever and whenever does not imply randomness or arbitrariness of place and time as much as the opportunity to choose the right place and time. According to the stronger interpretation, the place and time practically pick out themselves, or dictate where and with whom one has dealings with at any given time. The mobile offers a possibility of spontaneous contacts, but this spontaneity is not random: the calls acquire repetitive or ritualistic traits, in other words contacts are made at specific times and in specific places. Thus instead of the *postlocal community* we move towards the *mobile local society*.

Already the next generation in the evolution of mobile phones gives us reason to expect increasing digital neolocality. In 2002 the market will open to dataphones, and their producers are already in the business of 'anticipatory marketing', offering image transfer as the most tempting new capacity. Transferring images, for its part, gets marketed mainly as visual calls and digital postcards. The idea of a postcard contrasts with the spontaneous neolocal mobile-calls, in that postcard-writing is not encouraged by geographical proximity as much as distance. The more remote and exotic a place one visits, the more reason to send a postcard home. 'Guess where I'm calling from' probably acts as the motive for many calls today as well.

Therefore a second, and more far-reaching aspect of this new sense of place deals with the way a mobile phone not only opens up one's own place but another place as well. Friends living in a shared rhythm must also live 'overlapping' lives since they enter each other's lives. Repetitive communications by phone are not merely an exchange of information, they also open another world of experience beside, or instead of, the one presently inhabited. The development of technology is prone to increase the building-blocks of this other world by making the experience available to other senses as well. Thus the theme of living in two places at the same time enters the discussion about a virtual reality and its relationship with the ordinary one.

MOBILE VIRTUALITY AS AN ALTERNATIVE PLACE

Using the mobile is not commonly considered a form of virtual reality. Yet it does exhibit traces of a separate reality of its own, one which the speakers create as an alternative to the surrounding physical reality. It is exactly the motive of 'being somewhere else' that one can claim to be behind those calls which are made just on the impulse to call someone. When nothing happens or attracts the attention in this world, when idling, a person can create another and more stimulating world by making a call. According to the interviewees, being idle was the primary reason for picking up the mobile. Worlds are also prone to stimulate each other, which is actually an aspect of every impulsive call, since the call is brought about by one's own feeling—a feeling that is, for its part, anchored in one's relationship with the surrounding reality. This means that a mobile phone call is not very strong virtuality, meaning that it is only partly detached and independent of the real reality.

Looking into the future, the mobile phone's virtuality can be expected to increase, as many of its functions develop into things that take up more and more of one's attention. The development of the user's interfaces particularly points towards stronger virtuality. The development in display technology has already brought to the designer's table a mobile which requires 'dataglasses'. From a display built into such glasses one can view texts and pictures by scanning them through with a hand-held control. Meanwhile one can see the surrounding reality through them just as with ordinary sunglasses. The overlapping of common and virtual reality is, of course, more evident in conjunction with visual perception than with hearing, since the visual world is more dominant in our perception of reality. In addition to the user's interfaces, the developments in content are also prone to virtualise the use of mobile phones. As the internet connections and user's interfaces evolve, scanning through www-websites will probably become a common pastime and utility wherever people go. In the final analysis it seems that all of the virtual reality presently and prospectively represented by the computer will be transferred into the mobile, the implement of information and communication which we carry with us.

HOW PRIVATE INTERMINGLES WITH PUBLIC

What is the mobile's effect on urban culture? How does it alter the culture of public intercourse? As an implement which promotes private mobility, the mobile phone responds to the needs of urban culture rather than altering it. It is not prone to change the social order of public spaces. The user of a mobile phone takes advantage of the state of privateness which the avoidance-based public order offers to every city-dweller. It is exactly this private peace that the people who are opposed to the mobile feel they lose when other people call. Those who find mobile phones odd think that mobile-users are withdrawn and act autistically. By this they refer to closing off other people or being absent in regard to one's surroundings. Researchers who study the use of personal stereos as a cultural phenomenon have also expressed their worry over the withdrawal or atomisation of people (du Gay et al., 1997). When moving around in the human currents of urban centres one is constantly required to take other people into account—something the mobile-users seem oblivious to. In public spaces they cannot withdraw altogether from the surrounding social situation into the shared other world of the phone call, but are forced to develop skills and means to adjust to the public order of things. You do not shout out whatever you feel like on a bus and then afterwards sit down as if nothing happened. Someone of course might do exactly that, but it would be inappropriate norm-breaking and not a novel mode of public behaviour. Therefore the mobile represents a new tendency in urban behaviour. Yet it does not change the rules, but rather adapts to them.

A famous claim by Richard Sennett is that the public space of the cities as a place where people meet each other is in a state of decline (1977). According to Sennett, the 19th century and romanticism brought the 'tyranny of intimacy', to the streets, which used to be places where opinions were exchanged and politics discussed freely among strangers. Does the mobile bring back such genuine urban publicity or does it take away even what is left? It does make people say out loud that which would otherwise remain unsaid in public. Thus it acts as a social invention which revitalises public communication. However, at the same time it also strengthens the line drawn between familiar and unfamiliar people, those you talk to and those you do not. Actually the mobile is a public statement of the segregation between intimate and public life. The freedom to communicate personally wherever and whenever, brought about by the mobile phone, merely expands the sphere of the intimate society at the expense of the public. It also, in a way, folds these spheres within each other, or at least the intimate into the public.

Although conversations are held on the streets again, it does not implicate a return to a public political state such as *agora*, in which public opinion would be formed by conversations held on the streets. The mobile increases the liveliness of public space by increasing the amount of things taking place on the streets and making urban life more sprightly, which today is considered an important characteristic of a comfortable city. Yet although public life increases in amount, the public sphere is narrowed down as people bring their private lives inside it. The mobile and its public use cannot overcome the urban public norm of ignoring other people and avoiding personal contact.

The interviewed users of mobile phones reached their strongest agreement when the discussion came to regard the mobile as something to show off with or its use as a social act. The emphasised norm was that one should not 'display' the mobile but keep it hidden and only take it up if necessary. At the same time, the mobile's display value was also denied with equal vehemence because so many people have them nowadays. Thus attitudes towards using the mobile as a social act were quite ambivalent: it both is and is not an act for showing off or self-assertion. The reason why using the mobile cannot get rid of the stigma of showing off is that using it in public means bringing forth the personal level in a situation where it is against the basic norm. The social order of urban publicity is based on avoidance, i.e. strangers respect each others' privacy even when forced into close contact. In such a social situation any digressive behaviour is interpreted as a personal offence against the norm of impersonality, and consequently using the mobile is self-assertion (cf. Simmel, 1950; Goffman, 1972; Mäenpää, 1993).

BLENDING WORK AND LEISURE

The mobile's ability to fold or intertwine different social worlds is also visible on the boundaries of work and leisure. According to the interviewees, its function is to 'ease' everyday life by 'freeing' one from the shackles of the workplace and working hours. Yet this freedom did not seem to mean that the amount of work as such would grow any less or that being able to take care of one's affairs more swiftly would give one more spare time. On the contrary, the intensification of work usually signifies an increase in the amount of work. Therefore it is rather a question of the experience of neatly handling one's work-related affairs, or a sense of being able to create the time to take care of these. In this sense spare time, time of one's own, can be brought within office hours since it is possible to take care of one's work while walking through the city centre.

On the other hand, work also seemed prone to enter people's spare time. One often has to answer work-related calls even after work. It is difficult to tell the boss or a customer you have left work when there are none of the transitory rituals of passing time or changing places to support this. When the employee is under unlimited, and in this sense constant, potential control, this might give birth to a kind of digital

Panopticon which he or she cannot escape (cf. Bentham in Foucault, 1979). One of the most famous technological nightmares ever created is George Orwell's 'telescreen', a solid interactive device resembling a TV (Orwell, 1955). The mobile, for its part, remains constantly with you, which on the one hand implies a more intimate control, but on the other hand frees you to move and choose the place where you want to be. The employer who calls you at your summer cottage was the interviewees' worst example of such deprivation of leisure. It is obvious that the mobile increases one's working hours and thus also the workload, but in the meantime the increasing sense of freedom, independence and efficiency compensate for and even surpass the associated inconvenience. Although work was able to penetrate their spare time, it was not considered bad because they nevertheless felt in control of their own time and lives. The mobile is regarded as a device of everyday control, one which gives control to the one in possession of the device.

The interviewees often found it difficult to answer whether the mobile is a thing related to work or leisure, since it commonly had both aspects. The older ones (45–60 years) were prone to label their mobiles strictly as tools, which especially emphasised its serious and rational uses as opposed to young people's 'toy-usage' and 'tinkering'. Yet in practice they also made personal calls. On the other hand even intense use of the mobile during hours of work did not stop them from regarding it as an accessory related to leisure. One of the interviewees (male, 36 years) said that he usually started to make personal calls in the car park outside his workplace. For a single parent (female, 34 years) driving home from work offered the best chance of the day for talking with her friends. The journey passed almost unnoticed. Cars were generally seen as one of the best places to make calls from—particularly when you are driving alone. In everyday routines, driving a car forms a quiet moment with the time and space for one's own affairs and social relationships. The car is also a kind of a safety bubble amidst the public, and for this reason also a suitable place for using the mobile. But these reasons do not explain all of it, for making phone calls while walking or travelling in some other way also seems to hold a special attraction, which cannot be explained away merely by the urge to call.

It seems that movement simply promotes calling. The interviewees also like to make phone calls when they have nothing particular to do. So it seems that both movement and immobility inspire them to make calls. A further specification is that moving marks just such a lack of anything to do, i.e. a state that is easily directed into conversing with others. One possible interpretation would be that movement simply multiplies the immediately surrounding stimuli, which might increase one's desire to share the experience. If we were to combine this observation concerning movement and phone calls with that of to whom and to what purpose are the most typical mobile calls made, we will return to the theme of overlapping lives in a new way. The mobile not only signifies simultaneous living in two places, it also means living in two times, the present and the future. It is essentially connected with the rhythms of life; life's rapid and quiet moments.

But why does movement urge us to make phone calls? Paul Virilio thinks moving does not refer to getting from one place to another as much as to anticipating that which is yet to come (Virilio, 1994, 25–26). Now it can be argued that remote communication is an alternative mode of arriving, seeing the future sooner than it is bound to actually happen. The same idea can be applied to the urge to hold discussions from a distance. This applies especially to calls made from mobile phones, since they typically deal with future meetings and events. The mobile doubles the speed in which the traffic (transport) carries the 'arrivee' towards people. Thus the mobile call rarely replaces journeys from one place to another, although one of the ecological high hopes for the digital society has been a radical reduction of unnecessary traffic. But instead of this, mobile phone culture is constructed along with the traffic as another way to accelerate the future's approach.

CONSTANT AND FLEXIBLE LIFE IN THE FUTURE

As a device which increases mobility, the mobile phone responds to the needs of urban life rather than altering them. Mobility means that contacts can be made while moving, i.e. from a space in time, whereas with the traditional telephone contacts were always tied to a place. In the urban environment movement becomes a series of temporal spaces from which one keeps up contacts and runs affairs 'on the move'. As I have tried to show, the mobile is not used for conversation as much as for making future conversations possible. Its user is not forced to plan and organise his or her doings and meetings in advance. In the mobile culture one lives with the other foot permanently planted in the future, using the mobile to administer and manage future meetings and affairs. Places and times are not planned in advance, rather people agree (or just understand without further explanation) to call 'when they get there'. This makes life less bound, since it is possible to arrange each day according to the events it brings about.

The mobile maintains a readiness for flexible meetings and for arranging them as befits the day. This change can be described in terms of warfare, as a shift from strategies of life-management to tactics. The mobile blurs the previously organised everyday structure and shifts it in a more flexible direction. This brings about a change in our perception of time, so that the notion of a previously produced, organised future is replaced by a sliding sense of time which is constantly tilted towards the future. The future is no longer conceived as something consisting of exact moments as much as approximate places-in-time which are open to negotiation according to the situation. In this sense the mobile replaces the almanac, both as a concrete organiser of the future and as a model which gives shape to one's own life, a paradigm for anticipating the future. The near future condenses into increasingly numerous open possibilities; the mobile is used for prioritising, organising and actualising these, and as these functions gain significance in everyday life, so does the mobile.

THE INTENSIFICATION OF PRIVATE, AUTONOMOUS LIFE-MANAGEMENT

The need which makes one use the mobile—or the need created by using the mobile—is not just a need for social contacts, but also for the ability to be in control of one's own life, a need to extend the sphere of such control both spatially and temporally. This is the mobile's most significant function. It can also be regarded as the direction into which technological development is being guided by the mobile users' culture. With the mobile one increases the possibilities and simultaneously lessens the feeling of missing something.

The new meanings attached to the mobile along the way from the engineer's table and through the marketer's fingers to finally become a consumer's utility are portrayed in Finnish mobile phone-related terminology. While the term 'mobile phone' describes a device used for making or receiving phone calls while you are out of town or on the move, the more widely adopted Finnish term 'kännykkä', i.e. 'handy', is a made-up diminutive word that refers to an extension of the child's hand. The hand is the most important part of our bodies when we manipulate our physical surroundings, whereas the mouth is an instrument of the culturally more significant symbolic control, i.e. speech. The Finnish terminology applied by users themselves seems to support the interpretation that the basic meaning of the mobile phone is tied to life-management, rather than communication. Further, the term's familiarity, even tenderness presents the gadget as intimate, close and private, contrasted to the otherness of the outside world. The mobile phone, the 'handy', is an extension of intimate space, which is used for a symbolic manipulation of the surrounding world in order to bring it to us in a controlled and ordered form.

The mobile, both as a thing and as a being, signifies the way its owner's selfhood opens up to others. The mobile can be described as a part of an extended selfhood, which makes it significant not only in relation to the self, but also in relation to the world. When observed from such a point of view, the dimension of social appearances or enacting roles, so central to the mobile phone culture, becomes understood in a new way. In Finland using the mobile as a social performance is no longer a way to advance one's status; it does not signify wealth, nor does its constant use indicate the user's high social status. Appearing with a mobile has, instead, to do with the user's sovereignty concerning the space required by individual selfhood. Those who go about their business with a mobile pressed against the ear are merely suggesting that they are taking care of their own lot in the constantly moving society in which one's land or home is always present in his or her own personality. By talking to the mobile people show that they have their own personal areas, into which they do not invite just anybody, only the chosen and select important people. Thus they do not just mark out their territories, but also show their capability in taking care of it and the people within it. By acting out themselves while using the mobile, people display and reproduce the intactness of their selfhood in conjunction with the outside world. One shows that one has one's own personality and a world organised by personal relationships attached to it, which one aptly controls.

The mobile-mediated mode of acting in the world is markedly two-directional. On the one hand the mobile is a projector projecting an unlimited amount of possibilities into the world. When observed through the mobile, the surrounding world is organised from possibilities that have not yet been singled out, a world in which all the doors are open constantly and simultaneously. On the other hand the mobile is also a receiver, through which the world's possibilities are singled out and actualised. It develops a role in sorting out, prioritising and organising the world. Using the mobile, and living by the mobile, signify a concretisation of social exchange or reciprocity, or giving and taking, into one technological device. By exteriorising it into a device outside the human body the reciprocity becomes technical by nature, which can signify the hubris-like feeling that the social exchange or the personal relationship with the world is not handed down from above (pre-modern) or by society (the modern project), but rather by one's own hand.

The mobile is both a funnel, used for straining the world into a world of one's own, and also an accelerator with which one speeds up, controls and organises the world's approach. With it one gets more, gives up less and stretches one's own selfhood ever further. While striving to establish an ability to anticipate and embrace the world, the mobile expands the sphere reserved for selfhood in the world, but can meanwhile also build a higher wall between a world of one's own and the rest of the social world. The interactive world transmitted via mobile phones does not seem to point towards a new civil society, which is one of the utopian hopes people connect with the digital society, since the mobile's democracy rather prefers separate social worlds than one common society. Instead of this, it builds a social world of its own in a way which might leave others even stranger than before. In such a case it is prone to create a counterpart for the world that is familiar and controllable; an increasingly uncontrollable and chaotic general area that acts as a clean slate for projections of uncertainty, fear and scourge, images of evil.

NEW TECHNOLOGY OF THE EVERYDAY

It should be emphasised that in this interpretation autonomous, subjective life-management is not seen as a consequence of the supposed way of life today, one with a set pace and fragmented everyday, something the mobile as a device would accustom and socialise us to. The interview material does not support such an interpretation of the mobile being a mere adjustment to constraints of the everyday. Neither does the interpretation offered by technological determinism—that the mobile would have created the need to control one's life—seem plausible. Rather it seems that individual life-management is about a higher ethos. This has not been the mobile phone industry's conscious aim, although the industry's input in creating our culture and needs is considerable. The relationship between technology and society is more complex. The introduction of technological inventions and their application is both connected to social structures (i.e. corresponds to them) and further constructs them (cf. Pantzar, 1996). A mobile and private phone responds to a social structure based on individual life-control and further changes this structure towards an increased ability to control one's life and produce the everyday.

What separates the mobile from the traditional telephone is that it is constantly carried along and kept ready to receive communications, which means an uninterrupted control over the stream of information concerning oneself. There is, however, another technical function of the mobile that is central to administering one's life, and it has nothing to do with the mobile's mobility—which is why it is easily left unnoticed without empirical observation. Because of the display on the mobile, the person in possession of it knows not only whether someone calls or has called or not, but also who calls or has called. The younger interviewees especially, for whom the mobile meant new possibilities for social interaction in general, considered this characteristic particularly important. It signifies another form of control over the surrounding world, the chance to choose and select.

Everyday communications become increasingly optional when the mobile is used as the most important device for guiding social exchange. In principle people do not need to have dealings with anybody, since they get to choose not only the time and place of communicating, but also the person they allow themselves to verbally interact with. The optionality of intercourse with others means selecting, organising and prioritising one's human relationships. This also situates the mobile phone culture into a continuum, rather than an interruption, of urban life, since selecting whom one chooses to have dealings with is characteristic of the illocal urban life of the big cities.

The mobile is also used for organising and classifying one's own social networks. Product development has already offered the chance to classify this network into work relationships, friends and relatives, for whom the mobile either rings differently or only lets through communications of a specific category. The mobile becomes a device one uses to control whom he or she wishes to 'let in' at a given time. In this respect the mobile phone culture resembles consumer culture, in which selecting the symbolic material one accepts as part of oneself according to one's own taste forms a central part of the meaning of consuming (cf. for example Falk, 1992; Gronow, 1997; Lehtonen and Mäenpää, 1997). From a point of view of cultural critique sceptical of technology, the objectification of people and the instrumentalisation of human relationships could come under discussion in a new way.

So far the main moral critique of using a mobile has been the claimed artificiality of the need to make mobile calls. Next, we may turn to the critique of human relationships becoming increasingly mediated and organised. In mobile phone culture other people are considered but as a part of the organisable world or media flow, and the approach to this is what individuals wish to administer. In the near future the overall flux of mobile information and people within its reach will be multiplied. The third generation of mobile phones will be launched around the year 2002 with access to the internet and VCR's, for example. As this chapter is being written in November 1999, new WAP-applications are already paving the way among Finnish consumers for expanding uses of the gadget we today associate with the telephone, but which may soon remind us more of a pocket computer, a mobile multimedia giving access to systems supporting our everyday lives.

A hundred years ago Georg Simmel described the modern city-dweller's relations to each other as intellectual and calculating (Simmel, 1950). For Simmel the domination of objective over subjective culture signified more superficial and instrumental human relationships. In the mobile phone culture people are not used as instruments, but are subordinate objects of instrumentalist attitudes. For the mobile-phone urbanite other people as such are an end in themselves, but the process of other people coming in contact with him or her becomes increasingly instrumental. Simmel's city-dwellers were rationalists in their attitudes towards each other. In the mobile phone culture the objective and subjective sphere become merged in such a way that in the final analysis it is the feeling of whom does one want to be with right now that guides one's dealings. At the same time it is also a question of in what kind of a world does one want to live one's life at this moment?

Notes

1   This article is based on an ethnographic study carried out in co-operation with PhD Timo Kopomaa. During summer 1997 we carried out five group interviews for the study. We interviewed altogether 30 users of mobile phones, who represented different age (20–60 years) and socioeconomic groups, as well as three opponents of mobile phones. In addition we observed the uses of the mobile phone in the public spaces of central Helsinki, capital of Finland. The method of the qualitative analysis was utilizing one set of data to fertilize, question and verify the observations and findings on the other, and vice versa. As complementary material we used photographs and videotaping as well as published and unpublished Letters to the Editor sent to the *Helsingin Sanomat*, the leading newspaper in Finland. The material was collected mainly in 1997. The research was done in the departments of Sociology and Social Policy in the University of Helsinki, and it was funded by Nokia Mobile Phones and Telecom Finland (later Sonera).

Chapter 8

ORDINARY CONSUMPTION AND PERSONAL IDENTITY:
RADIO AND THE MIDDLE CLASSES IN THE NORTH WEST
OF ENGLAND

Brian Longhurst, Gaynor Bagnall and Mike Savage

INTRODUCTION

It is clear that the work of Pierre Bourdieu (especially, 1984) has set an agenda for research on relationship between social class, cultural forms and the consumption practices of everyday life.[1] His development of the concepts of cultural capital and habitus has been critical to the progression of the understanding of the changing nature of cultural consumption. Despite the theoretical points that can be made against Bourdieu (see Longhurst and Savage, 1996; Bagnall, Longhurst and Savage, 1997), his work has prompted a significant level of empirical investigation of class and culture, especially in the USA and Canada. Building on this North American literature (specifically, Peterson and Kern, 1996; Bryson, 1996, and Erickson, 1996, see also Peterson, 1992; Peterson 1997; Bryson, 1997), Warde, Martens and Olsen (1999, 107) suggest that a critical issue exercising contemporary research is the extent and manner in which class and consumption have been affected by the 'variegation of cultural items in circulation'. They find evidence from survey data on dining out in Britain to suggest that there has been an expansion in consumption of a variety of cultural genres. While their data do not allow them to explore the meaning of this for consumers, they suggest that this evidence should be explored for the opportunities it provides to the middle classes for 'personal assurance, for demonstrating social competence and for staking claims to social exclusivity' (120). This reinforces the importance of distinguishing 'two rather different types of consumption action, that geared towards impressing others and that directed at reassuring oneself' (Longhurst and Savage, 1996, 294). However, it is far from clear that the types of data used by Bourdieu, in the North American literature, or by Warde, Martens and Olsen are fully adequate to examine these sorts of issues (Holt, 1997a, 1997b, 1998, see also Longhurst and Savage, 1996; Bagnall, Longhurst and Savage, 1997).

We suggest that analysis of the meaning of consumption requires paying more attention to the narratives mobilised by consumers to discuss practices than this literature has so far recognised (see Somers, 1994; Longhurst and Savage, 1996; Lieblich et al., 1998). Exploration of these narratives enables us to comment on the extent to which consumption practices are concerned with 'personal assurance', 'social competence' and 'social exclusivity' as suggested by Warde, Martens and Olsen (1999). Further, it facilitates consideration of the ways in which consumption action is geared towards impressing others and reassuring oneself.

In this paper we will explore these issues through a study of the consumption of radio, using data from a recent study of the middle classes in the north west of England. We have chosen this medium for several reasons. First, radio is a significant part of the everyday lives of our respondents: nearly everyone listens to it. However, it is less ubiquitous than television, which is watched by everyone. Second, as radio is an inexpensive consumer item, its consumption is relatively unaffected by issues of cost and availability. As Murroni, Irvine and King (1998, 61) point out using Radio Advertising Bureau data:

> 'Every year, 12 million new radio sets are sold in the UK: portable receivers, car stereos and stackable hi-fi tuners. On average, a good portable radio receiver costs around £30 and each British household has five to seven of them.'

Third, a wide variety of genres and types of programme are available through the radio, simply by turning it on and tuning in. There are no extra subscription costs. In these respects radio provides a good example of ordinary consumption, while potentially allowing examination of preferences in, and meanings of, media choice within such contexts.

To explore these issues, we will first explain the study that we have carried out. Second, we will examine the patterns of radio listening identified. This will lead us to a discussion of the social contexts of radio listening, followed by an exploration of how radio is used in the construction of narratives of personal identity. We conclude by suggesting that this mode of consumption and its meaning illustrate some broader cultural changes and their interaction with identity.

OUR STUDY

Our research, which was funded by ESRC between 1997 and 1999, is entitled *Lifestyles and Social Integration: A Study of Middle Class Culture in Manchester*.[2] It has examined the social and cultural activities undertaken by residents of differing middle class areas of Manchester to explore how they either facilitate or forestall the social integration of their residents. We have been concerned to consider whether it is possible to distinguish the development of new forms of middle class sociation, and to consider whether everyday interaction tends to lead to compartmentalised, discrete, middle class lifestyles, or whether, by contrast, patterns of sociation tend to link otherwise diverse populations in 'communities' of different types.

We conducted interviews in four areas in or close to Manchester, each potentially exemplifying different kinds of middle-class 'habitus' and 'cultural capital'. Interviewees were selected randomly from the electoral roll in each place. Cheadle was selected as a traditional lower middle class suburb, located six miles south of Manchester. Our interviews took place on a relatively self-contained estate of 1930s semi-detached houses, mostly valued between £50,000–£65,000. Respondents were a mixture of older working class households, younger households of self-employed or affluent workers, older lower professionals and younger professional households who were entering the housing market. Wilmslow was in direct contrast to Cheadle, in that it represents one of the most affluent areas in the North of England. Based around an exclusive Victorian suburb, we interviewed in two areas of detached housing, where properties were valued at between £250,000 and £750,000. Residents were almost exclusively managers and professionals, with a mixture of long-term residents alongside some 'spiralists' who had moved into the area to work. Ramsbottom was selected as an example of an old industrial mill village, located close to the traditional Lancashire textile belt between Rochdale and Bury. Although traditionally a working class mill town, it has experienced rural gentrification in recent years following the development of a steam railway, because of the proximity of attractive countryside, and the development of new suburban housing targeted at commuters who wish to be near the motorway circuit. For these reasons our sample in Ramsbottom was mixed. We interviewed a significant number of long time residents as well as a larger number of largely professional and managerial employees living in new suburban estates built within the last ten years. Finally, Chorlton was selected, as an area of urban gentrification, close to, but not in, the city centre. We interviewed in a series of older, mostly terraced houses around a street that has seen the development of a 'café culture' in recent years. Some residents were long stay working class members, but most were part of a young, middle class grouping, mainly working in the public sector or in the media and arts.

Our sample was drawn from the electoral roll in selected districts of the four areas, with one in five addresses being sampled, and with an attempt to alternate male and female names drawn from the electoral roll. Response rates varied slightly between areas with an overall figure of 34%. The class position of respondents in the four areas matches closely our rationale for selecting them. Our Wilmslow sample is overwhelmingly affluent with respondents (or their partners) being located in the upper service class. Cheadle, by contrast, is socially more mixed, with a considerable number of manual workers. It is important to note that our decision to sample on the basis of residence meant that it is possible that respondents in non middle-class occupations may be selected. Respondents from Ramsbottom and Chorlton proved to be intermediate between Wilmslow and Cheadle.

We carried out in total 200 interviews (50 in each place) between 1997 and 1999, all of which were tape-recorded and have been or are being transcribed. The interviews took between 40 minutes and two hours (the average was approximately one hour) and covered the following topics in this order: social life in the neighbourhood and locality; social life, kinship and family; activity in voluntary associations; leisure enthusiasms and interests; social life around work and employment; and finally a set of questions about socio-economic position. Our interviews have been numbered and are referenced by letter (C—Cheadle, D—Chorlton, R—Ramsbottom, W—Wilmslow) and number.

PATTERNS OF LISTENING

We begin our discussion with a consideration of our respondents articulated listening preferences. As with other previous research (for a summary see Crisell, 1994, 204) we found that our respondents tended to talk about radio preferences in terms of stations rather than programmes or genres, though there were, as we shall note below, some significant exceptions. These preferences are summarised in Table 1.

For each area studied we have categorised each individual's listening habits. Perhaps the most salient point is the strength of commitment to BBC radio. In Chorlton and Ramsbottom this is overwhelmingly the most significant type of radio listened to. It is also very important in Wilmslow and Cheadle. Moreover, when combined with those in the category that said that they listened to BBC radio and commercial stations, in each area this totals to the majority of the sample. Of course, BBC radio covers a range of material. There are five main national BBC stations with an overall share of listening of 38.9%

Table 1: 'Simple' Taste Cultures

	(1) BBC	(2) BBC & Commercial	Classic FM	Jazz FM	(3) 'Pop' Radio	(4) Mix of stations	(5) Local or mainly local	No specific station	Not listened to	Not asked/ no ref
Cheadle (38)	9	10	1	0	4	0	1	5	6	2
100.1%	23.7	26.3	2.6	0	10.6	0	2.6	13.2	15.8	5.3
Chorlton (41)	20	4	2	2	2	3	1	3	1	3
100%	48.8	9.8	4.9	4.9	4.9	7.3	2.4	7.3	2.4	7.3
Rams'btm (43)	15	6	0	0	5	6	0	4	4	3
99.9%	34.9	13.9	0	0	11.6	13.9	0	9.3	9.3	7

Table 1: 'Simple' Taste Cultures – *continued*

	(1) BBC	(2) BBC & Commercial	Classic FM	Jazz FM	(3) 'Pop' Radio	(4) Mix of stations	(5) Local or mainly local	No specific station	Not listened to	Not asked/ no ref
Wilmslow (38)	12	12	1	0	1	2	2	3	1	4
100%	31.6	31.6	2.6	0	2.6	5.3	5.3	7.9	2.6	10.5
ALL 160	56	32	4	2	12	11	4	15	12	12
100.1%	35	20	2.5	1.3	7.5	6.9	2.5	9.4	7.5	7.5

55%

NOTES

1. All BBC stations including local.
2. BBC station(s) plus any commercial station.
3. Clear preference for commercial 'pop' stations, including Atlantic 252, Red Rose Rock FM, Key 103, Virgin.
4. Clear mix of stations of different types.
5. Local commercial stations or mix dominated by local.

(RAJAR, 1999a). Radio 1 programmes pop music of top 40 type during the day and more diverse contemporary pop, rock and dance in the evenings and through the night. Its share of the audience is 10.6%. Radio 2 covers popular music for an older age group, it has a 12.2% share of the audience. Radio 3 focuses on classical music with a 1.2% share of the audience. Radio 4 features current affairs, documentary and general interest and attracts a 10.6% share. Radio 5 is the newest national network station, which focuses on sport and news. It currently has a 4.2% share of the audience. In all cases share is 'the percentage of all radio listening hours that a station accounts for within its transmission area' (RAJAR, 1999a). In addition the BBC operates regional stations such as BBC Greater Manchester Radio (GMR) and Radio Lancashire, which have a mix of programming. GMR attracts a share of 5.6% and Radio Lancashire a share of 10.2% (RAJAR, 1999a). Table 2 identifies the patterns in BBC listening for our sample.

This shows the overwhelming importance of Radio 4 and Radio 5 in our sample as a whole. Thus, of those who identify BBC preferences, 53.6% say they listen only to Radio 4 or Radio 5 or a combination of these stations. BBC local radio is very little listened to. Only three cases overall concentrated only on BBC local stations and in only five cases were these combined with national stations. All these cases occurred in Cheadle and Ramsbottom. The BBC patterns in Chorlton and Wilmslow were completely national (with the exception of one case of a focus on the World Service and another where BBC radio was combined with French Radio). Radios 1 and 2 are also very rarely the single focus of listening and Radio 3 never is. Indeed Radio 3 only figures in three cases as part of BBC patterns at all, always in combination with another station.

In each of our areas a taste pattern represented by BBC stations in combination with commercial stations was also common. Within this type there is a broad range of combinations with the exception of Wilmslow. In Wilmslow there is a very clear pattern of combination of BBC stations with Classic FM. This relatively new station, which has been broadcasting since 1992, concentrates on 'classical' music, but in a less 'highbrow' mode than the 'serious' BBC Radio 3. Its share of the audience is 4.1% (RAJAR 1999a). As Murroni, Irvine and King (1998, 41) point out, 'Classic FM has proven that classical music broadcasting can be commercially successful, RAJAR figures for 1998/3 show Classic FM's share of listeners (3.4 million) at over 2.5

Table 2: BBC Patterns

	N	R1	R2	R3	R4	R5	GMR	4/5	2/4	2/GMR 2/Lancs	4/1 (+ Fr)	4/1/5	4/3/5	4/2/1	World	4/3	4/ GMR 3	2/ 3	4/3
Cheadle	9	1			1	2	2	1	1	1									
%					11.1														
Chorlton	20		2		6	2		3			3	2			1	1			
%					30														
Ramsbottom	15				4	2	1	2	1	2							2		1
%					26.7														
Wilmslow	12		2		5	2							1	1			1		
%					41.6														
TOTAL	N=56	1	4	0	16	8	3	6	2	3	3	2	1	1	1	1	2	1	1
%					28.6	14.3		10.7											

times that of Radio 3 (1.3 million)'. In our sample, Classic FM is even more popular than this.

Those who mentioned listening only to commercial pop music type stations were rare, as were those who listened only to commercial local stations. There was a group of listeners who did not articulate a station preference, but who simply talked of listening to the radio. There was also a group who did not listen to the radio at all. In a small number of cases, mostly from our earlier interviews, discussion of this specific topic was missed.

So far we have tended to focus on the nature of our overall sample, making brief comment about the differences between the areas. However, as Table 1 shows, there are clear differences between the areas. In the context of the patterns already identified, it is possible to sketch a profile of radio listening in each area. In Cheadle, BBC listening alone is as likely as BBC listening in combination with commercial stations and there is wide variation in the patterns of these BBC and BBC plus commercial station combinations (each case of the latter represents a different combination). Pop radio is relatively strong compared with the other areas (with the exception of Ramsbottom). This area has more listeners to local radio (both BBC and commercial stations) but numbers are still very small. It has the largest percentages of those who do not listen to any particular station and who do not listen at all. Chorlton residents express strong preferences for BBC stations and tend to combine the BBC with commercial stations less than do those living in the other areas. There is little local listening and only one person who do not listen to the radio. Ramsbottom exhibits the widest variation in taste in general across the categories. This is also indicated by the largest percentage that articulated that they listened to a mix of stations. Wilmslow has the strongest patterns of BBC and BBC plus Classic FM listening and relatively little BBC and commercial listening. Pop music is not popular and there is little mixing of stations of diverse types.

What can be said about consumption on the basis of this discussion so far? We find very little evidence of highbrow snobbery here (Peterson, 1997). One significant indicator of this would be the existence of a clear Radio 3 taste pattern. However, as we have seen, Radio 3 is very rarely listened to at all. The expression of a preference for BBC stations might suggest that respondents were seeking to display high status through their public service broadcasting connotations. The salience of Radio 4 among this pattern, especially in Wilmslow (the most high status area) would offer some evidence for this. But counter evidence also exists in the increasing popularity of Radio 5 as a kind of mid-market station akin to daily newspapers like the *Daily Mail* and the *Daily Express* rather than the 'quality' press associations of Radio 4, especially in its news coverage and in the popularity of the 'middle brow' classical station—Classic FM. For example, 'I like Classic FM. I used to listen to Radio 3 but then Classic FM came along and it suits me because I have an odd half-hour here and there' (D70), 'Yes I do listen to Classic FM. I suppose classical music is something that I've discovered and Classic FM, although I suppose you could argue it's like the *Readers Digest*, it is good for me because not knowing much about classical music it's a nice entrée into it. The day will come I suppose when I will listen to Radio 3, but I haven't quite got there yet' (D98). Further counter evidence to elitist status seeking can be found in the diversity of tastes found in Ramsbottom. However, there is little evidence of a mix and match where, for example, Radio 3 is combined with Atlantic 252 (a commercial top 40 pop station, with a 0.9% share, RAJAR 1999).

In summary, there is little elitism of a 'pure' kind, but BBC stations are still resonant, especially Radio 4. Furthermore, despite tendencies to a pluralism of listening, especially in some places, there tends to be relatively less boundary breaking than might be expected if cultural pluralism was as advanced as some versions of postmodernism might suggest. Our data have already allowed us to comment on the complexities of taste in this area. However, we have so far tended to use our data in a relatively quantitative fashion. It is therefore important first to examine how respondents located radio in their everyday lives. We will follow this with a consideration of how it is located in narratives concerning and constructing identity.

RADIO IN SOCIAL CONTEXT

The most common ways of talking about radio involved use in the car and at a particular time of the day. Radio was a significant part of the experience of driving or being in a car. Hence 'I listen to it in the morning coming into work and in the evening going home' (W 23), 'only when I am driving' (D23), 'Driving is so boring anyway. You're listening to one thing and watching the road' (C70). Such boredom, combined with the desire for information, is found when radio is linked to the drawbacks of car travel, 'I occasionally listen to Classic FM, especially if I'm sat in a big traffic jam and very very occasionally GMR, but that's only if I'm sat in a traffic jam and I want to find out what's going on' (R81). Comments about using the radio came from all our areas, but they were most common in Ramsbottom, perhaps the area with most commuting by car. This significance of in-car listening could clearly be the result of our focus on the 'better off' in broad terms. As RAJAR (1999b: 4) explain, 'a key group which spends a disproportionate amount of radio listening time in-car is AB men aged 25–44'.

Radio was often connected to a time of day, involving particular uses and tasks. 'I normally listen to it first thing in the morning' (C57), 'It is on during the day' (R104), 'in the evenings at 7pm' (W82), 'only in the middle of the night when I can't sleep' (W73). It is sometimes a weekend only activity, 'we do at the weekends, we always have cooked breakfasts on a Saturday and Sunday so that usually goes on' (C51),

Radio is also part of the everyday routines of domestic life, forming part of the background for washing up, ironing and so on. Hence, 'I have it on in the background' (W33), 'Well, I do if I'm ironing out in the kitchen, some of the afternoon programmes are very nice' (C120). This can become a stereotype to be discounted, as for example, 'I don't really listen to the radio, which my husband and girls find funny really because when you're ironing the housewife usually has the radio on, I probably have the television on, I like noise but I don't parti-cularly put the radio on very much' (C100). The uses and contexts identified so far are often combined, 'I only ever listen to two pro-grammes, Radio 5 or Radio 4. I do a lot of mileage in the car and I'd rather have a voice than music. I would never dream of putting Radio 1, 2 or 3 on, although I do sometimes listen to classical, but mainly Radio 5, I'm a news addict, I go to bed listening to the radio, I wake up listening to the radio' (C13).

Radio was less frequently used as background at work, though there were a small number of discussions of this: 'Through the day, yes, when I'm at work' (C102), 'When I'm at work all day long' (R48), 'I have a radio in my surgery and I keep it to Radio 2 because that's something that everyone can listen to' (W99).

In some ways our discussion of radio in social context so far could seemingly be located within a rather conventional uses and gratifications approach to media use. This approach emphasises '(1) the social and psychological origins of (2) needs, which generate (3) expectations of (4) the mass media or other sources, which lead to (5) differential patterns of media exposure (or engagement in other activities), resulting in (6) need gratifications and (7) other consequences, perhaps mostly unintended ones' (Katz et al., 1974, 20). It has long been suggested that this perspective is overly mentalistic and individualistic in approach (see, for example, Elliott, 1974). Moreover, Crisell (1994, 211) offers an important critique of this approach when applied to radio:

> 'If uses and gratifications theory is applicable to other media, if it is indeed true that in pursuit of our various gratifications we select a particular medium rather than particular content, it will be especially true of radio. However much we may adapt then to our psychological needs the other media first require an adjustment from us, in the sense that we must suspend most other activities in order to attend to their messages. But radio, being non-visual, is different. Locked into some primary activity such as driving or cooking, we resort to the medium almost irrespective of its content because there is no other medium we can attend to. Consequently we adapt radio to our physical circumstances and requirements in the way uses and gratifications theory argues that we adapt all the media to suit our psychological circumstances and requirements.'

Our data have confirmed this approach, however the identification of taste cultures which are contextualised by the routine use of radio at certain times of the day and in particular social context, does not exhaust the examination of the meaning of radio in consumption. In recent years a number of audience studies have identified the way in which routine media is used as resource in the construction of narratives of personal meaning that are not captured by concepts such as personal need (Abercrombie and Longhurst, 1998). For example, drawing on Hermes' (1995, 144) argument that 'women's magazines offer material that may help you imagine a sense of control over your life by feeling prepared for tragedy, or a more perfect vision of yourself by supposing that you would be able to answer any question regarding the difficult choices someone else might ask', it is possible to suggest that 'clipping recipes from a magazine may be an aspect of the imaginative construction of the self as a better 'home-maker', even if the recipes are never actually used' (Abercrombie and Longhurst, 1998, 109). Therefore, fully to understand radio consumption it is necessary to identify the way in which it features in narratives produced by respondents that can be seen as constructing identity.

NARRATIVES OF SELF

Earlier we pointed to the importance of narrative and narrative location to the understanding of talk about consumption practices. Up to this point we have included a number of rather short quotations to illustrate our findings. We now consider two longer narratives containing comments on radio use. We shall argue that this shows that the patterns we have identified so far should be seen as part of other narratives that construct a personal identity. Both are from Wilmslow and are chosen to exemplify the sort of narratives that recurred in our interviews. The first extract comes from W21.

EXTRACT 1: W21

Q Have you ever belonged to a PTA?

A In the junior school when I was in the south, I did but I started work when I came up here. That might have cut out some of the contact. My husband did at orchestra, he used to go and do things.

Q Do you have any particular interests or hobbies?

A Knitting, it has been cut down quite a lot. A little sewing, embroidery, I like reading.

Q What kind of things do you read?

A Historical novels. Novels about areas like Liverpool and this friend from Worthing he put me onto stories about the war, fiction. It does bring back the things you thought you had forgotten and the library here is quite well stocked and I do like reading about the Northeast, Manchester. I am interested in historical things. I did say to a friend I would like to delve back into the history of Wilmslow. I haven't done it up to now.

Q Do you listen to the radio?

A Yes. I like to listen to plays. With the television it does lapse a bit. When we go away the radio becomes our companion and it takes you back, Friday night is music night, that kind of thing and the plays that we like to listen to.

Q Gardening?

A We have never been keen gardeners. I can't do much now. I do like to see it tidy. I can't sit out in the garden if the grass isn't cut nicely. I like to potter, I suppose you could say we have an interest.

Q Do you use the telephone much?

A I used to take turns ringing my daughter, one weekend I would ring her and she rang me the next weekend and I was always on the phone for at least an hour. We totted it up one time and it was quite expensive but I think it's cheaper now. I ring my sister-in-law in the Northeast and my nephew occasionally. If we have got any news we do keep in touch. I ring a friend in Bristol. We have reached the age when my friends are growing short. My cousin he died just this year, so they were down in Cornwall. I have a friend down in Cornwall, mainly she rings me, perhaps twice a year and we have a friend, my husband's boss I was very friendly with his wife because when we were at Cranfield College we were very friendly. This last year she died.

What is significant about this is the location of radio in particular places of time and space. The respondent exhibits nostalgia for a past mode of radio listening, which has been replaced by television.

However, this extract, like the rest of the interview, is layered with comments about the meaning of old age and the loss of friends and family. Moreover, place is very important as this narrative about ageing is connected to present and past locations of people. Hence, the discussion of radio is only part of a wider consideration of ageing and social change. The performance in the interview of a narrative of ageing identity is very clear. Radio is located in different ways in Extract 2 from W35.

EXTRACT 2: W35

Q   You haven't got a video recorder, have you got satellite or cable?
A   I've got a small portable with video player in it, but that's predominantly for the OU.
Q   What about your daughter?
A   Yes, she sometimes watches the cartoons. *Mary Poppins*, that kind of thing.
Q   What about the radio?
A   All the time.
Q   What sort of things?
A   I have it permanently tuned to Radio 4.
Q   In the home?
A   Yes.
Q. In the car?
A   I would do in the car, but its [mumble].
Q   So what sort of things do you listen to if it's on permanently?
A   *Today* in the morning, again in the afternoon.
Q   But at other times during the evening?
A   Yes, if I am washing up. I like the 6.30 slot usually a comedy or a play and Saturdays I like because....., No it's on whenever I'm in the kitchen. When I get through the door the first thing I do is switch the radio on. That's my Dad, my Dad always listened to the radio that's where I get it from. G's [daughter] the same she listens rather than watching. Comedy programmes, *I'm Sorry I Haven't a Clue, Desert Island Discs*.

Here, radio is located in the context of an ongoing narrative about family life. The respondent, who was in the process of a divorce at the time of the interview, locates radio in her own busy schedule, which involved being the head teacher of a primary school, care of a young daughter and an Open University course. She forms links between her own tastes and practices and those of her father and daughter. In this case it is not age that is important *per se*, but the development of family life over time. At a time of potentially very significant life change, the respondent is concerned to construct a narrative of personal continuity. At other points in the interview she pointed to the differences in class origins between herself and her husband. It is therefore significant that she locates her daughter's identity as close to that of herself and her father.

What is particularly significant for us here is the way in which the consumption practices around radio are part of a narrative that developed through the course of the research interview. This structure is partially generated by the order and nature of the questions posed by the interviewer, but the respondent has great space in which to develop their own themes (Lieblich et al., 1998). In the two examples given, interviewees use radio in construction of narratives that represent and construct identities. The first is a narrative about old age and nostalgia, where geographic separation of individuals has become an important issue. The second respondent develops continuity in identity that connects together different members of the family at a point where, due to the process of divorce from her husband, this may be a particularly salient issue and where her own working class roots were distinguished from the middle class background of her husband.

These narratives locate radio use, but the discussion of radio also provides a resource for the respondents to develop their own 'grand narratives' of self. What these respondents are 'doing, therefore, is drawing from the endless media stream that passes them by a set of diverse elements out of which they can construct imaginative worlds that suit them' (Abercrombie and Longhurst, 1998, 107; see also Bagnall, 1996 and 1998). These imaginative worlds provide communities within taste cultures 'where community defines an abode marking people's ways of belonging within the structured mobilities of contemporary life' (Grossberg, 1996, 105). Hence, we suggest that the taste cultures found within our data may be understood first in the patterns of the routine nature of ordinary life (driving, cooking, ironing and so on), but also in the context of the rather less ordinary narratives of personal identity. We shall explore why this is the case in the final section.

CONCLUSION: RADIO, ORDINARY EVERYDAY LIFE AND NARRATIVES OF PERSONAL IDENTITY

Our use of qualitative data enables us to comment on the meanings of the consumption practices that we have identified. We find little evidence for highbrow snobbery or for extreme diversity of taste. The reality seems to lie in a middle ground, where BBC stations prevail, but are increasingly listened to in combination with commercial stations. The trend to increased listening to stations like Classic FM is perhaps of most significance. This enables a range of groups to 'meet in the middle' of the middle class. Hence, previous Radio 3 listeners may find that they prefer the lighter approach of Classic FM and new-comers may use Classic FM to educate themselves in areas of culture that they previously knew rather little about. The result is that most people know more about a greater range of things, but are less expert in each of them than more bounded individuals might be. A common way to conceptualise this process is in the idea of 'dumbing down'. We think that this misconceives what is actually happening. A key organising theme here is ordinariness.

We have found in analysis of other parts of our data (Savage, Bagnall and Longhurst, 1999, see also Carrabine and Longhurst, 1999) that claims to 'ordinariness' are a common 'refrain' among different middle class groups. For example, people either resist or (less often) adopt class identifiers as part of a desire to appear ordinary. Therefore, whereas Bourdieu would direct attention to the multiple strategies used to display and construct cultural distinction of one type or another, nearly our entire sample chose to play down any cultural distinction they may be able to claim and intead to play up their ordinariness. This does not fit well with narrow interpretations of Bourdieu's work. Why should ordinariness be seized upon? We suggest that ordinariness as discourse allows people to retreat from social fixing. By being ordinary, people can claim just to be themselves, and not socially determined people. In this way they can claim to be real people. The ordinary consumption of radio as part of everyday life reinforces these ordinariness claims. However, once this ordinariness has been established, identity can be revealed, or partially constructed, through the kind of wider narratives that we have identified in the longer extracts and discussion above. If society is perceived to be changing rapidly, then the desire to be ordinary and to consume ordinarily can be seen as part of a process of protection from these changes or for reassurance in the face of them. This new type of ordinary 'community' is inclusive in that it incorporates those from groups with previously diverse tastes and backgrounds. It offers a certain comfort. Radio offers many opportunities to facilitate this process, in both its programming and its location in routines. However, once ordinariness has been established, or while it is being constructed, the individual may feel the need to differentiate themselves from the rest of the ordinary community. It is significant that this is done in personal narratives, rather than terms of wider social groupings. One way of thinking about this is to argue that these are narratives of extraordinary personal identity. The individual is not necessarily extraordinary, but the resources for the construction of this identity are part of the individual's *own* biography and life. These narratives of self are constructed from social resources, especially as we have discussed in terms of family life, but are not then described in wider social terms.

The middle classes increasingly seem to want to appear ordinary and radio is ordinary consumption. We therefore suggest that consumption in this field has relatively little to do with the impressing of others in demonstrations of social exclusivity. It is concerned with the need to exhibit the social competence of ordinariness. It is about inclusion, rather than the marking of the boundaries of exclusion. However, within such a context, radio has clear potential in the construction of narratives of personal assurance in social terms. We suggest that being ordinary and consuming in ordinary ways is reassuring in precisely these ways, but that the longer narratives offer evidence for the integration of radio into wider, more personal accounts of self. In these senses radio exemplifies the ways in which ordinary consumption responds to wider social changes in a media saturated society and the ways in which these social changes are being dealt with in personal lives.

Notes

1   Thanks to the editors of this volume for their very helpful comments on an earlier draft.
2   Award Number R000236929. We are very pleased to acknowledge this support.

Chapter 9

BY CAR: CARRYING MODERN SOCIETY

Tim Dant and Peter J. Martin

INTRODUCTION

The proliferation of the 'private car' as a mass medium of transportation has been one of the most momentous developments of the twentieth century. In bringing a previously unimagined degree of personal auto-mobility to the populations of industrialised societies, the car is a highly distinctive mode of transport. Over the last hundred years the motor car has developed from being an unreliable and extremely expensive hobby for the rich to being part of the normal equipment for modern living in industrialised societies—it has become an ordinary object that is consumed through routine and often daily use. During the last fifty years it has facilitated and encouraged the creation of a mass culture increasingly organised around large-scale physical mobility, with enormous social consequences. The degree of mobility which is now taken for granted in the developed world is quite unprecedented in human history, yet in contrast to other culturally-transforming technologies, notably mass television and electronic information processing, the apparently irresistible rise of the car has gone virtually unnoticed by sociologists. No longer is being the owner of a car a sign of status or of special interest. Like televisions, telephones, central heating and inside toilets, cars are just part of the equipment of modern living that is more noticeable when absent than when present.

The aims of the present paper, then, are quite simply to highlight the disturbing lack of attention which has up until now been paid to cars and their consequences by academic sociologists, and to raise some pertinent issues which arise from the consideration of a culture increasingly shaped by the presupposition of automobility. We want to begin to approach the question of how the car become so deeply entrenched in our society.

CARS AS SEDUCTION AND REPULSION

Driving cars is clearly more than transporting the human body from here to there. As Urry points out, '[m]ost car journeys now made were never made by public transport' (1999, 29). This means that other means of transport cannot simply substitute for cars. Baudrillard reminds us that:

'Travel is a necessity, and speed is a pleasure... Movement alone is the basis of a sort of happiness but the mechanical euphoria associated with speed is something else altogether, grounded for the imagination in the miracle of motion. Effortless mobility entails a kind of pleasure that is unrealistic, a kind of suspension of existence, a kind of absence of responsibility.' (Baudrillard, 1996, 66)

The pleasure in driving cars, even being driven in them, is not only to do with functionality as transport but also with what interaction with that particular object can do. Speed can be enjoyed as a mystical experience, as competition and as overcoming natural and machinic forces (Macnaghten and Urry, 1998, 208–210). It is a pleasure that can even be enhanced by interaction with other cars in traffic, it is certainly a pleasure that can be enhanced by having others observe one's pleasure. Looked at this way, it is not difficult to understand the 'joyrider' who steals another person's car and then drives it recklessly, often with passengers, often through their own community. Showing off, gaining status through identification with a status object may be partial motivations. Challenging those distinctions based on class, locality, ownership and possession may be influences. But above all, the seductive pleasure of driving a car is what 'joyriding' is about. O'Connell (1998) reminds us that joyriders were originally young men who 'borrowed' cars without permission to gain 'respect' and to attract the attention of young women.[1] Because the cars were later abandoned and recovered they were not technically 'stolen' and those who took them could avoid prosecution until the offence of 'taking and driving away' was introduced in the 1930 Road Traffic Act. It did little to discourage offenders. Pleasure in the car was not only in the driving but in the seductive power it gave to those who possessed it.[2]

The technological development of the car can be understood as to do with its *seduction* (Baudrillard, 1990, 119–120). The history of car production is linked to the difficulties of reproducing the quality of the hand-built car on mass production lines (see for example Forty 1990) but the basic structure and capacity of the car has changed little in the last hundred years. What has happened is a series of incremental improvements to aspects of the basic vehicle such that each new 'model' is slightly more attractive than previous models. Manufacturers are constantly trying to anticipate what will make their cars more seductive than others—but there is never a sure thing. Initial improvements were largely mechanical, reducing noise, increasing speed. Then changes to the body work became far more significant in seducing potential owners (see Gartman, 1994, for a detailed history of styling and design). In recent years 'functional features' have become more important, including the safety of occupants in the event of a crash and the recycleability of the components and fuel efficiency of the engine. The fading of the importance of the aesthetic appearance of cars suggests that they are no longer objects from which there is much social status to be derived. Seduction is much more likely to be through a blend of subtle styling, manufacturing precision, internal comfort and reliable and powerful engineering. Modern cars that make a special claim to aesthetic appeal often do so by referring back to previous designs from a time when aesthetics were more important. So, for example, the BMW Z3 recreates many design features of the classic two seater sports car, including many BMWs from an earlier era; soft top, long low body, bonnet extending in front of the driver, distinctive grills, wire wheels, curving lines.[3]

As well as being seductive the car can repel. In its early days it was recognised by those not seduced by its charms as dirty, dusty and noisy as well as dangerous to people and livestock. It damaged roads covered with gravel for horses and carts and forced pedestrians onto pavements. Its more recently identified offences include polluting the air with lead, carbon monoxide, particulates and other carcinogens, and polluting the landscape and cityscape through the building of roads and facilities designed for the car (suburbs, out of town malls, industrial estates). Concerns about health and environmental risks began to replace earlier fears about the volume of road accidents (Altshuler et al., 1984; Liniado, 1996, 47–72) to sustain an 'ambivalence' about the car (Macnaghten and Urry, 1998, 237–238). The result is the delivery of too many people to certain places and, as Sachs argues, it begins to bring about a disenchantment with the car:

> 'What most damages the automobile's attractiveness is its success. Mass motorization itself is responsible for bringing experiences in tow that undermine enthusiasm for the automobile.' (Sachs, 1992, 175)

The beauty spot loses some of its appeal when it becomes crowded and the open road that promises freedom becomes a nightmare when it becomes unavailable for driving through repair works or simply too much traffic.

THE CAR AND MASS CONSUMPTION

In Britain, it was the inter-war period which initiated the 'first era of mass motoring', with the numbers of private cars rising from 100,000 in 1918 to over two million in 1939 (O'Connell, 1998, 19). By the 1960s having a car was commonplace and no longer itself a mark of social status although the *type* of car driven continued to be an indicator of distinction and social identity (Shove, 1998, 3–4). Since then the UK population increased moderately from 52.9m in 1961 to 59m in 1997 (*Social Trends*, **29**, 30), but the number of cars licensed in the same period almost quadrupled from 6.1m to 22.8m annually (*Social Trends*, **13**, 124; **29**, 198). Fewer than one in three households (31%) had regular use of a car in 1961; by 1997 this had risen to 70%, with a quarter of all households having two or more cars.

By the late 1980s the car had come to occupy a central place in everyday social life and expenditure on motoring had become the third largest item of household expenditure. No other category of household expenditure exceeds 10% of the total and the proportion spent on motoring continues to rise relative to housing and food.

Table 1: Expenditure on commodities or services as % of total expenditure

	1987	1997-8
Food	19.0	17.0
Housing	16.1	15.1
Motoring expenditure	12.6	14.2

(Source: *Social Trends*, 29, 129)

However well-intentioned, proposals to reduce car usage often neglect the effect on employment and the extent to which the car has become an integral part of the national as well as the household economy. The manufacture of cars requires materials, services, and labour but local economies are also heavily dependent on the sale, maintenance, repair and decoration of cars (Graves Brown calculates that car related activity accounts for over 10% of businesses listed in *Yellow Pages*, 1997, 67). The provision of roads and ancillary services—such as mandatory accident insurance—create work in both the public and private sectors (Shove, 1998, 8–9). Even the huge volumes of crime associated with cars and the consequent police investigations and legal proceedings, or the deaths (more than 70 each week in the UK in 1997) and serious injuries arising from accidents are, 'social facts' (Durkheim, 1964) of considerable sociological and economic significance. Such facts shape the development of institutions (such as the police, health care, and the law) and generate a huge demand for goods and services.

SOCIOLOGY AND THE CAR

The social and political problems caused by mass car use are unlikely to be alleviated swiftly or simply (the category 'car users' now includes the vast majority of the electorate, and so cannot be easily demonised or antagonised). In 1986, Hawkins concluded that in America sociologists had generally ignored the impact of the automobile (1986, 61). Since then, unlike broadcast and information technologies, the private car has been almost completely neglected in the sociological literature on both sides of the Atlantic. In general, sociologists displayed what Hawkins called a 'pedestrian approach' (Hawkins, 1986, 66) condemning the car as a machine which could only accelerate the decline of community and the decay of social solidarity, both facilitating and symbolising 'the North American flight into privacy' (John O'Neill quoted in Hawkins, 1986, 63). Hawkins points out that the lack of academic interest in the car led to its history initially being written largely by and for enthusiasts, but more recently cultural historians have begun to examine the rise of the car (Flink, 1988; Sachs, 1992; O'Connell, 1998). The traditional account of 'car culture' focusing on the impressive and rapid development of car production in terms of techniques, organisations and marketing (e.g. Flink, 1975) has more recently been supplemented by studies such as Gartman's (1994) account of the cultural impact of the developing symbolic form of the car. In a different vein, Bert Moorhouse's (1991) study of 'hot rod' car culture charts the enthusiasm for building, racing and showing hot rod cars that brings a sense of pride, identity and fulfilment that is largely unavailable in industrial employment. However, it is the industrial production of cars that has attracted the most sociological interest, although it has been the autoworker rather than the automobile that has been the focus. Beynon (1973) explored the working life of those who were employed 'on the line'. For Chinoy (1955; see also Moorhouse, 1983), the lives of automobile workers exemplified the ways in which industrial work corrodes 'the American dream', and it was a British car plant—Vauxhall (now General Motors), in Luton,— which provided the setting for the studies by Goldthorpe et al. (1968)

of 'affluent workers' and their increasingly privatised lifestyles. In sociology, car production has often been viewed both as characteristic of production generally in modern societies—Fordism—and indicative of the change to post-modern—or post-Fordist—societies (e.g Harvey, 1989; Crook et al., 1992).

THE DIALECTIC OF CAR CULTURE

The sides in political disputes about the benefits and disadvantages of cars map onto other social divisions of class, gender, rural and urban dwellers, and, of course, users and non-users. From a more specifically sociological perspective, John Urry has emphasised the impact of 'automobility' which:

> '... reconfigures civil society, involving distinct ways of dwelling, travelling and socialising in, and through, an automobilised time-space.' (Urry, 1999, 6)

Urry identifies six components of automobility, or the 'social and technical system of the car': manufactured object, individual consumption, machinic complex, quasi-private mobility, culture, and environmental resource-use (Urry, 1999, 3). He emphasises the extent to which car culture is fuelling tendencies towards globalisation but concludes that there is little evidence to suggest that 'virtual' or 'weightless' mobility via television or the internet will replace the demand for real, corporeal, travel[4]. Ultimately though, Urry's position rests on a value judgement that everyone, even those who do not or cannot use cars, is forced to live their lives according to the dictates of automobility, which:

> '... coerces people into an intense flexibility. It forces people to juggle tiny fragments of time so as to deal with the temporal and spatial constraints that it generates. It is perhaps the best example within the social world of how systematic unintended consequences are produced as a consequence of individual or household desires, in this case for flexibility and freedom.' (Urry, 1999, 13)

This doom-mongering sees the car as trapping people in congestion and a privatised environment with dire consequences for late modernity, including: separating workplace from home, home from shopping and leisure, family members and friends from each other (Urry, 1999, 13). But these are processes more deeply embedded with the development of the capitalist mode of production; they are not simply *caused* by the car and they cannot be unravelled by abandoning the car even if that were a possibility. This rather one-sided view of car use argues that the car reduces 'choice' but it is not clear with what this list of consequences can be compared or what state of affairs would have maintained or expanded choice. Our fundamental point is that as the automobile has become integrated into the lives of most modern people, it has become an ordinary object. Even for those who do not own or have continuous access to one, 'the car' as an object continually shapes our lives through its pervasive and multi-faceted effect on our culture. Moreover, not the least of the car's attractions is its capacity to empower, and to have a positive impact on sociality. It has become a key feature of modern culture because of what it can do for people.

SOCIALITY WITH THE CAR

Karin Knorr Cetina calls for 'an expanded conception of sociality and social relations' such that 'individualization then intertwines with objectualization—with an increasing orientation towards objects as sources of the self, of relational intimacy, of shared subjectivity and of social integration' (Knorr Cetina, 1997, 9). Unusually for a sociologist she is arguing that individuals are not simply embedded in social relations with other human beings but that their identities are at least partially sustained by relationships with objects. Human interaction with objects is not just physical; objects are also appropriated at the level of knowledge of their properties and limitations and how they will meet human wants (Knorr Cetina, 1997, 12). Knorr Cetina's examples are from the history and sociology of science but we can understand the car as a technical device with a material form and as a knowledge object.

Knowledge about a given car or type of car will include the wants the car will satisfy but also what it lacks; how fast, quiet, safe, efficient, cheap, long lasting and so on it might be. Our knowledge of the object establishes a social relationship with it and a context that will shape any subsequent physical interaction with it. The structure of users' wants will vary according to social and historical circumstances and in relation to the inadequacies of an existing series of objects.[5] Expert knowledge will also respond to expressed wants and the perceived deficiencies in objects to produce new, 'better' objects. However the major features of sociality with objects are not to do with ideal wants and lacks. The flow of everyday relationships between users and objects such as motor cars is rather more pragmatic; that a particular car falls short of what I *want* does not stop me driving it—if it gets me to the shops and back.

Our routine collaborative action with complex objects like cars can lead to a sense of 'solidarity' (Knorr Cetina, 1997, 18) with them which may take the form of giving the car a name, talking fondly about its 'behaviour'—even talking directly to it and feeling proud of or disgusted with it. For most people though, any affection for cars will come behind that for children, lovers, partners, friends and pets. Knorr Cetina suggests that sociality of this sort is 'somehow linked to knowing the objects' (1997, 20). As with a human being, the way we know a complex object like a car may be through both its familiar characteristics and its unpredictability—sometimes it seems to have a 'will of its own'. Nonetheless, cars are ordinary and unremarkable objects for most people and what is distinctive about the place of cars in modern society is their impact on sociality between human beings. What is sociologically interesting about material objects such as cars is how they become embedded in the flow of social life, enabling us to do what we do.

SOCIALITY THROUGH THE CAR

Cars are often desired, it is claimed, because they emphasise the individuality and self-mastery of their owners, freeing them from the constraints of social means of transport (Sachs, 1992, 92–101). This anti-social relationship with the car is reinforced by its polluting effects which are always a disbenefit for the rest of society (Altshuler et al., 1984, 47–59; Liniado, 1996, 47–72; Macnaghten and Urry, 1998, 238). It is not surprising then that the car is seen as a 'Frankenstein-monster' that extends individual freedoms always at a social cost (Shove, 1998, 9; Urry, 1999, 14). But cars in modern society are not merely an indulgence, toys or playthings that in a utilitarian perspective could be done without, neither do they in any simple sense lead to privatisation of the individual. Different types of activity involve different groups of people who are in different places; cars extend sociality precisely by allowing us to organise the continuity between these different loci of sociality. When cars are no longer used for 'sport' or 'recreation', as they were when driving was seen as good for one's health and wellbeing (Sachs, 1992, 5), then they extend sociality by bringing individuals together in groups that would otherwise occur much less frequently if at all. Distances between people are shrunk and the time taken for communications to be made are reduced (Sachs, 1992, 183–187). The contemporary location of shops, schools, places of work, leisure facilities and other services in relation to where people live, often makes using the car much more convenient if not inevitable—especially if babies, shopping or other items are to be carried (Shove, 1998, 6–7). Cars allow the complicated scheduling of daily family routines that often involve both partners being employed. Without the car(s), the pattern of many modern lifestyles would be impractical.

There are of course a number of different vehicles that could link physically separated social contexts (foot, horse, bicycle, bus, tram, train, aeroplane). But the car is an exceedingly flexible vehicle and despite frustrating delays is usually quicker than alternatives for door-to-door mobility. The driver chooses when to depart and the pace of travel and can therefore modulate the time of arrival. If the context involves sociality with a large number of people who are unknown to each other (a shopping centre, the seaside, a concert), the car enables participants to come from very different locations, setting off at different times to be co-present at exactly the same time (the concert) or in a sequence of arrivals and departures around a core time of co-presence (the shopping centre, the seaside). The car promotes sociality through flexibly mixing people from one social context to another but can also increase sociality in transit. This can of course also be seen as promoting private time, time out of sociality in which the driver need not consider their appearance and sustain a 'front'.[6] For the solitary driver, the time in the car can be time to think, including talking out loud, to explore emotions (a car is a good place to grieve privately without fear of arousing the sympathy of others), to daydream or fantasise. The car, unlike public forms of transport, provides an outer clothing or mini-environment for 'downtime' from the flow of sociality in peopled contexts (which for many of us include our homes and workplaces). This downtime prepares us to re-enter a social scene when we arrive, refreshed and ready to engage with interactive sociality anew. Public transport (trains, buses etc.) on the other hand has a strict schedule that *requires* continuous co-presence in transit. What is co-experienced beyond the success or failure of public transport to meet its schedule is a sociality of 'civil inattention' (Goffman, 1963, 84) characteristic of being in public.

The private space of the car can be an ideal situation for intimate sociality (O'Connell, 1998, 94; Shove, 1998, 2–3). Lovers, couples, friends, families, parents and children can talk in close proximity while the car is in motion. The driver must give some attention to the road and handling the car but the 'surplus attention' of driver and passengers can be given to social interaction. This can even help keep the driver awake or alert because there are relatively few outlets for this attention; the driver cannot engage in hand-eye work other than driving and the vehicle's movement makes activities like reading or writing difficult for passengers. It is difficult to maintain eye contact in a car because everyone faces in the same direction—although the occasional glance may thereby gain more significance—but the close physical co-presence allows body movements and gestures to cue conversation. Even above the noise of the engine, road wheels and wind, a wide range of vocal variation (volume, tone, timbre) can be heard. The intimacy is closer than in most living rooms and is also sustained—one cannot simply walk out on a difficult conversation while the car is moving! Even without conversation, the simple experience of close and continuous co-presence can have an emotional tone—the pleasure or discomfort of being together—which does not have to be excused or explained by any other specific activity. Strangers sharing a car (giving a lift, hitch-hiking) have to manage the intimacy with care, although it may lead to getting to know someone much more quickly than in other 'social' contexts where such a meeting might have originated (at a party, at a club, at work). Unlike public transport both driver and passenger in the private car choose who, if anyone, to share the space with.

A final level of sociality achieved through the car is via mediated forms of communication. The surplus attention of driver and passengers can be given to the radio or to recordings on tape or CD. The aural environment can be excellent, enabling 'in-car-entertainment' that can be pleasurable and absorbing. The unpleasant sounds of the car and traffic can be overlaid with sounds that are socially produced and chosen. The mediated cultural exchange, like the exchange over a mobile 'phone, provides the car user with a form of sociality, albeit not one that involves physical co-presence. Whether it's the news or popular music the car user is engaged with the flow of information and ideas that constitute the culture of their society.

INTERACTION WITH THE CAR

We can begin to translate these various forms of sociality with and through the car into potentially researchable forms by exploring how we *interact* with and through the car. The object of the car is external to the human agent who is driver or passenger—although part of the fantasy of J. G. Ballard's *Crash* is precisely about interaction in which car and body leave their marks on each other (Ballard, 1995). Driving a car involves interaction between human and machine through the physical movement of limbs which bring about steering, braking, acceleration and gear changing[7]. These movements 'instruct' the car to 'act' in certain ways. The driver in turn responds to information from not only his or her sight of the road, but also the information felt through the vehicle and through the components of the vehicle (steering wheel, brake pedal, accelerator pedal, gear lever). The action of the human subject (driver) affects the action of the object (vehicle) and the action of the object feeds back to the subject who responds continuously to bring about the sort of driving that he or she intends (speed, direction, position on the road). For example, the forward inertia of the human body during breaking provides the driver with information about the rate of braking which is in turn modulated by the pressure of his or her foot on the brake pedal (see Dant, 1999, 120–127, for a fuller discussion of interaction with objects).

The human subject has a physical relationship with the object of the car to do with manipulation and operation. But the car that we interact with can become almost like an 'extension' of our body[8]:

'The expert driver when parallel parking needs very little by way of visual clues to back himself into the small place—he 'feels' the very extension of himself through the car as the car becomes a symbiotic extension of his own embodiedness.' (Ihde, 1974, 272)

Ihde also points out that we experience the world as a continuation of our interaction with certain types of objects—the blackboard is felt at the end of a piece of chalk, the world of the blind-man at the end of his cane. Interaction with the car forms the sensory experience of its driver and its passengers such that the perceived nature of the world outside the car is transformed. The pothole feels much deeper through poor suspension than it does when stepped over, noise is modulated, air temperature is different, dust, dirt, wind and rain are removed and so on. The world becomes framed and flattened by the shape of the car window, presaging the view of the world through a television screen and related to that other tourist gaze through a camera lens. In the early years of the automobile, this was clearly a great attraction to users who experienced unusual places, the countryside and other sites/sights as images at the windows of cars (see O'Connell, 1998; Sachs, 1992, 150–160).

INTERACTION THROUGH THE CAR

As the car becomes embodied in the way Ihde describes, it becomes an object *through* which we interact with each other—this is the sphere of action we normally call 'traffic'. Pedestrian traffic has been famously analysed by Goffman using motor traffic as an exemplar of the way such complex interaction is ordered through 'traffic codes' (Goffman, 1971b, 5–18). In modern cities there are some pedestrian-only areas but generally foot traffic has to follow and cross roads dominated by cars whose power and mass is physically superior to that of the most powerful and massive human being. The passenger, whether in a car or a bus, is in an intermediary position, not dominating but enjoying the privileges of domination. There are very few people in western industrialised societies who are *always* pedestrians and most of us board a bus or climb into a car and frequently exchange the roles of dominator and dominated. There is a much finer status of power and distinction between automotive road users which is continuously negotiated—although white vans and large lorries do seem to get their own way more often.

The car needs the human agency of a driver to become a danger rather than merely an obstacle but there has been a massive increase in the volume, density and speed of traffic which has brought its own risks (Sachs, 1992, 25–31). Nonetheless, what is most remarkable about cars being driven in the presence of other cars is how infrequently they collide. Even as volumes of traffic flow increase and the speed of vehicles increases, there is a continuing reduction in the proportion of collisions and deaths[9]. Drivers in general sustain a very high level of skill in driving even when in other respects they will undoubtedly have very variable skills. The co-ordination of limbs to control the car must become unconscious, reading the road and the skill of interacting with traffic must be learnt. But like learning a language, just about every mature human, who has no handicap, can learn to drive a car. Birds and fish are able to fly and swim in large numbers in very close proximity without colliding—in cars of course, everything happens much more quickly and the consequences of error are rather more far reaching. While the ability to co-ordinate movement in animals is innate to their species, the human ability evolves according to changing contexts; the building of cities, the development of technologies such as the car, the increase in traffic volume.

Norbert Elias explores the relationship between the progressive reduction in deaths by driving and the civilizing process, the 'acquired self-regulation that is imperative of a human being' (1995, 9). Technization, such as the introduction of the automobile, brings a new, decivilizing, dimension into social life and the members of that society have to learn how to live with it. As Elias points out, this learning is in part due to learning how to design and make cars and roads but is also about drivers learning not just how to drive but how to interact with other vehicles:

> 'Controlling the car (including maintaining it) is nothing but an extension of the driver's self-control or self regulation. The pattern of self-regulation by a driver at the wheel of his car, however, is determined to a large extent by the social standard that society in every country has developed for the individual self-regulation of the men and women who drive cars.' (Elias, 1995, 25)

Society responds to the decivilizing effects of new technology that causes death and injury by introducing laws to regulate usage—for example those to do with licensing drivers and limiting alcohol consumption. But such standard rules and practices become a habit for drivers and 'in the end relate to the individual self-regulation by the driver' (Elias, 1995, 25). He identifies a parallel between the care taken in steering the car, and so avoiding killing people, and steering the *self* through society (1995, 28). Using annual statistics of road deaths and car registrations, Elias argues that the interaction of technization and civilization reduces road deaths but at a different rate in different countries that have different cultures and a different place in the evolving process of civilisation. The decline in deaths on the road with the development of the civilising process is not simply to do with technical improvements in roads and cars but also to do with the willingness of drivers to regulate their own driving in the light of others' driving so as to achieve an integrated co-operation.

As well as responding to the presence of other road users and the physical form of the road, the car driver must respond to the signs which have been placed to give information about the road and how it should be used. As Clay McShane points out, traffic lights are systems that 'attempt to impose a strong social control over the most fundamental of human behaviors, whether to move or be still' (McShane, 1999, 370). Such systems are not 'natural' but have a history and politics and one of the most noteworthy features of traffic lights is the speed with which they have become a global system, used on roads in very different cultures. Traffic lights developed from the policeman directing traffic at junctions, via a mechanical semaphore system. The first permanent traffic lights, which of course saved on the human labour of stopping and starting traffic, were installed in Cleveland, Ohio in 1914 and the system that included red, yellow and green lights was introduced in 1920. By 1931 much of the United States and the UK had adopted automatic lights and similar systems were being introduced in Stockholm, Tokyo, Spain, Paris and Berlin with encouragement from the League of Nations. It was realised as early as 1923 that 10% of the US population was colour blind and could not adequately distinguish between red and green but it seems that standardisation was more important than technical superiority. Blue and yellow would have been easier for a larger proportion of the population to distinguish but red and green (derived from maritime signals) remained the standard system (McShane, 1999, 382).

Driving in busy traffic involves a large numbers of interactions with other vehicles, all of whom are looking to maximise their chances to make progress within the context of traffic lights and other regulatory systems. Most interactions more or less smoothly follow a set of learnt behaviours to do with rights to proceed and safety margins for road users. Drivers manage more complex interactions, such as letting each other in, by flashing headlights, waving and gesturing and even mouthing words through the windscreen at each other. Similar means of communication are used to express dissatisfaction with another person's driving behaviour—usually to do with them getting in the way or not following the conventions. The car itself provides an *expressive* extension of the driver's body to communicate emotion and anger; hooting the horn, flashing headlights, revving the engine noisily. The tyres can be made to squeal and the movements of the car made jerky and exaggerated, often involving driving faster and closer to the offending car than would normally be recognised as appropriate. The body within the car may also be used; facial expressions, gesticulations, one or two raised fingers and finally, the window may be wound down so that verbal abuse may be hurled.

CONCLUSIONS

Writing in 1984 on the 'Future of automobility', the report of a four year, seven-nation study from the Massachusetts Institute of Technology, the authors argued that for the next twenty years there were no serious challenges to automobility. The threats from consumption of finite resources and atmospheric pollution were problems that they predicted technological sophistication could keep pace with. Other means of transport and communication alternatives to transport would continue to be developed but without threatening the car:

'... there is no evidence of a shift in mode share away from automobiles in any of the developed countries, and for the longer period under consideration in this study we have found no convincing arguments that probable improvements in service and reductions in costs for competing modes will have any noticeable effect on the purchase and use of automobiles.' (Altshuler et al., 1984, 61)

While their period of projection is only three-quarters of the way through, their prediction seems to be well justified. Even as it changes and develops by becoming smaller, more efficient, using other fuel sources, banned from certain parts of society, the car will remain for the foreseeable future the model of personal mobility in modern societies. Recognition by sociologists of the importance of the car is long overdue; a thoroughgoing sociological analysis of the way that the car is reshaping the society we live in will enhance our capacity to adapt to the changes and steer them rather than be led by the pull of technology or the push of political expediency.

Notes

1 '... the pre-1939 joyrider's chosen vehicles do not appear to have been systematically damaged by excessive speeding or dangerous driving as is frequently the case today' (O'Connell, 1998, 103).

2 In Finland, there is a culture of poor young men whose lives become entwined with old cars that they renovate, live in and for, and drive, often drunk and dangerously. Research on this phenomena is currently being undertaken by Heli Vaaranen (personal communication 23.10.99).

3 BMW's brochure traces the development of the 'roadster' from the 1936 BMW 328, through the 1956 BMW 507 to the 1988 Z1 which it calls the 'father' of the 1995 Z3. See Dant, 1999, 158–161, on aesthetics and objects including the BMW Z3.

4 Confirming a rather earlier analysis by MIT's International Automobile Program (Aultshuler et al., 1984, 61).

5 There is of course a whole 'material discourse' that helps to specify knowledge objects, from engineers' drawings and specifications, through advertisements and images, to test reports, consumer surveys and the object in the showroom (see Dant, 1999, 107, 126–127, 158–160).

6 Goffman, 1971a, 32—except of course in stationary traffic when 'offstage' behaviour (nose-picking, exaggerated facial expressions, talking aloud, singing and so on) may be inadvertently revealed to others.

7 Urry refers to the car/driver as a 'hybrid' (1999, 19) as it is sometimes used in Actor-Network-Theory. However, as cars are at the moment, there is a very clear division of labour between the car and the driver such that the car provides motive power and the driver manages the place of the vehicle in traffic.

8 See also McLuhan, 1964, 217.

9 In the UK in 1981 there were 6 000 road accident deaths but in 1997 only 3 800. There has been an reduction from 67 fatalities/serious injuries per billion passenger km in 1986 to 42 per billion in 1996 (*Social Trends*, 29, 203).

Chapter 10

ORDINARY AND DISTINCTIVE CONSUMPTION; OR A KITCHEN IS A KITCHEN IS A KITCHEN

Dale Southerton

INTRODUCTION

The symbolic capacity of consumption for mediating social relations is well documented in the sociological literature. For some theorists, consumption patterns are symbolic of the resources available to individuals and act to re-produce the existing social order (Bourdieu, 1984). In contrast, theories collapsed under the umbrella of 'post-modernity' suggest that symbolic consumption has become the 'play-thing' employed in individual life-style projects that are free from the normative constraints associated with class, gender and age (Bauman, 1988; Giddens, 1991; Beck, 1992). The difficulty in assessing these two theoretical positions is that both lack systematic empirical evaluation of ordinary consumption. In the former, evidence tends to be drawn from survey approaches that are 'variable centred', Bourdieu's analysis focusing upon questions concerning preferences for particular types of consumption, which are then taken as symbolic of social group distinctions. Postmodern arguments tend to draw upon the extra-ordinary consumption of 'spectacular groups', such as the gentrified new middle classes (Featherstone, 1991), to support their theoretical claims.

In addressing ordinary consumption this paper draws upon thirty-five in-depth interviews with couples who live in a Southern English New Town called Yate. Three groups are identified within this 'unspectacular' sample comprising white, working and middle class people who are all homeowners, living as married and mostly aged between 35–54. The first group was Bowland Road residents, charac-terised by low economic, cultural and social capital, short-range geo-graphical mobility and who have lived in their present home for over 15 years. The second group, who lived in Cartmel Street also had low cultural and social capital but comparatively higher economic capital, longer range and recent geographical mobility. Finally, Lonsdale Avenue residents held high levels of economic, cultural and social capital and can be divided between 'established' and 'newcomers', according to length of residence within the street (above or below 10 years). All Lonsdale residents have experienced long range geographical mobility. Previous research has demonstrated a strong north-south housing status division within the Town (Southerton, 1999), the latter two groups residing in the northern area.

Interviews enquired into kitchens as an 'ordinary' form of consumption. Being located within the routine everyday practices of domestic life, kitchens are instructive because they are not highly visible unless guests are invited into its space; might hold emotional meanings attached to the family (Corrigan, 1997); are standardised in design and yet hold the possibility for stylisation (Miller 1988). The collection of these features affords kitchen consumption with the potential to be symbolic of social distinctions and identity. However, given the range of practices and meanings that relate to the kitchen, contextual interpretations of this symbolic potential of kitchen consumption may be important in narratives of distinction.

This chapter adapts the analytical approaches of Holt (1997a) and Lamont (1992). Holt argues that when considering the significance of consumption, it is necessary to appreciate the relationship between *what* and *how* collections of objects are consumed. Lamont's approach advances a conceptual framework focusing upon symbolic boundaries to decipher the differential values attached to consumption in the interpretation of social status. By adapting these approaches, this chapter demonstrates that levels of economic and cultural capital may socially organise consumption orientations but the significance of consumption in mediating interpretations of social status depended upon the degree of embeddedness within local contexts. This is important because it indicates how consumption conveys messages and establishes social boundaries in a variety of ways which cannot be entirely reduced to levels of capital nor described as individual life-styles that are free from normative constraints.

CONSUMPTION AND CLASS-BASED SOCIAL DISTINCTION

Social class is widely accepted as the fundamental structure organising social relations within modernity. Contemporary accounts within this tradition relate consumption to the parameters of distribution, display and normative group expression. Bourdieu (1984), the most sophisticated exponent of such accounts, employs concepts of capital to explain the mechanisms through which class cultures and norms of consumption are produced (Warde 1997). Volumes of economic, cultural and social capital are advanced as the resources that constrain and organise the consumption dispositions of agents. Economic capital refers to material wealth. Cultural capital is operationalised as levels of education but in definition also includes occupation and lived experiences (such as travel or living in cosmopolitan centres). Social capital, the most conceptually diffuse of the three resources, refers to 'various kinds of valued relations with significant others' (Jenkins, 1992, 85) or, at its most basic level, extent of social networks. How social capital operates is unclear. For example, Bourdieu discusses neither the type of resource that it offers nor the types of social networks (friends, family, work colleagues) that are important. Lamont (1992) however, does indicate that social capital might provide important sources of information for legitimating cultural tastes.

Levels of capital are important because they effect judgments of taste and, for Bourdieu, tastes are symbolic of class position. Tastes can be classified (as 'highbrow', 'middlebrow', 'lowbrow', 'refined' as opposed to 'vulgar') and indicate agents' expectations concerning the preferences, practices and social values of different groups. For example, Bourdieu argues that the working classes, constrained by their low economic and cultural resources, develop a 'taste for necessity' that validates their consumption dispositions by rejecting the tastes of those with high economic and cultural capital as wasteful and extravagant. It is this process of differentiation that organises consumption dispositions according to class and makes consumption indicative of social relations.

Bourdieu's strength is his concept of cultural capital because, while levels of economic capital have obvious constraints on consumption, increased affluence (Corrigan, 1997) and the growing range of similarly priced goods in the market place (Miller, 1987) makes the capacity of economic capital for indicating clearly defined social positions problematic. Applications of cultural capital as a concept for analysing tastes, however, vary dramatically. Halle (1993) and Hall (1992) argue that the only significant difference in orientations toward the consumption of art in the United States is that the cultural elite value high culture and the majority of people favour popular culture. Since the cultural elite represents a marginal group, cultural capital is argued to hold little explanatory power for understanding the social organisation of consumption. In a rather different analysis, Erickson (1996) claims that contemporary judgments of taste relate less to a command of knowledge within a particular field of consumption, and more towards limited but broad knowledge of many genres and fields (cultural omnivorousness).

Part of the problem is the basis upon which tastes are analysed as symbolically meaningful. Gronow (1997) demonstrates that 'taste' can be interpreted through two categories of meaning. First, it is associated with interpretations of aesthetics and style in the consumption of objects. Second, it relates to evaluations of social practices that revolve around moral categories such as decency and judgments of right and wrong. It is this distinction between the association of taste with objects and practices that forms the basis for Holt's (1997a) criticism of accounts which analyse cultural capital solely in terms of material tastes or 'preferences for particular categories, genres or types of cultural objects' (ibid. 102). Holt suggests that cultural capital is best operationalised through interpretations of taste that account for practices of consumption. To illustrate, Holt contrasts Bourdieu's concept of cultural capital (1984) with Erickson's (1996) cultural omnivorousness. Erickson's evidence suggests that knowing the name of various sports stars, specific restaurants and clothes designers, act to symbolise that an individual is culturally well endowed. Bourdieu's point is that such 'book learned' knowledge and the apeing of fashion are precisely the types of *practice* that cultural elite's judge to be bad taste. In this way, judgment of taste is less concerned with '*what*' is consumed and more with '*how*' it is consumed.

Holt argues that, for comparative reasons, cultural capital should be systematically measured within given fields of consumption by accounting for the relationship between judgments of what people consume (material tastes) and how they consume it (practical tastes). However, he does not address how the symbolic meanings that practices of consumption may hold are translated into narratives of distinction. This is precisely what Lamont's (1992) research does by employing the analytical tool of 'symbolic boundaries'. Symbolic boundaries are the 'mental maps which they [people] draw upon to organize the raw 'data' they receive of others' (Lamont, 1992, 2). In the process, boundaries explicate the 'conceptual distinctions that we make to categorise objects, people, practices and even time and space' (*ibid.*, 9). Taking this premise, Lamont investigated the symbolic boundaries drawn by American and French upper middle class men and extrapolated three fundamental frameworks employed to judge social status.

First, *socio-economic* frameworks encompass boundaries that judge social position according to wealth, power and professional success. Alternatively, they can include perceptions of money as 'impure'. Second, boundaries drawn within *cultural* frameworks include emphasis upon education, intelligence, manners, taste and command of high culture or, alternatively, embrace senses of cultural snobbery. Finally, boundaries drawn within *moral* frameworks revolve around judgments based upon personal characteristics such as honesty, work ethic, personal integrity and consideration of others. Boundaries within this framework include classifications of 'the phoney' (lack of sincerity), the social climber and self-association with 'volunteerism'.

Lamont demonstrates that despite holding the same levels of economic and cultural capital, respondents varied significantly in the frameworks they employed to judge social status. For example, American men extensively employed socio-economic frameworks, while French men emphasised cultural frameworks. However, variations were not only found between national contexts. American men varied systematically according to place of residence, those living in cosmopolitan cities drawing more extensively upon cultural frameworks than those who living in suburban towns. The implication is that classification is not a 'zero-sum' game because narratives of social differentiation did not only vary according to levels of capital. The impact of contexts, such as residential locality, upon the frameworks employed to interpret social status means that people with similar levels of capital can draw different conclusions with regards to social differentiation. For example, returning to Bourdieu's (1984) concept of a 'taste for necessity', it would be expected that those with low economic and cultural capital would value non-extravagant consumption orientations. Yet, as Slater (1997) points out, what constitutes a 'necessity' is open to various cultural and moral evaluations and, therefore, not all people with low levels of capital may agree upon, or even recognise, the same consumption orientations as 'necessary'. By focusing upon symbolic boundaries, it is possible to uncover the symbolic meanings that different social groups apply to a particular form of consumption.

MATERIAL TASTES

Adapting Holt and Lamont's approaches, this section examines narratives through which interviewees described the symbolic significance of the material form of their kitchens, including objects and style. The three groups are shown to have variable orientations toward four key principles of kitchen consumption, order, unity, originality, and quality.

ORDER

For Holt (1997a), a principal orientation of taste relates to how material constraints are managed. For those with low cultural capital, taste is primarily ordered according to function and practical evaluations. In contrast, those with high cultural capital do not encounter the same degree of material constraints so that the economic value of goods becomes of less importance than taste as a means of self-expression. Tastes in the material form of kitchens can, therefore, either be ordered to maximise utility and function or be stylistically ordered, with the collection of objects viewed as an expression of personal taste.

Bowland Road and Cartmel Street

For these low cultural capital respondents, the kitchen was ordered according to principles of utility and household efficiency as reflected in descriptions of 'modern' actual and ideal kitchen styles. Simon described his kitchen as, 'a modern one… it's white, the plastic Formica cupboards, you know it's easy to clean. All the appliances are white and modern. That's it really, what more can I say'. Other examples referred to daily practices: 'it's a kitchen, what else can I say. I cook and clean in it, so yeah, it obviously has to be easy to use' (Claire). The more affluent Cartmel respondents elaborated most upon the style of their functional kitchens: 'It's white, you know wood effect Formica units, it's got a grey speckley surface. So it's a light modern kitchen but with a traditional layout, nothing fancy' (Patricia). Higher economic capital allowed Cartmel respondents to consider style and the material form of kitchens, although their narratives always returned to function: 'I do like those pine kitchens, they look great… but well, they're not always that practical. Like you have to go the whole hog and that involves hanging pans and that and cluttered surfaces, and it's just not practical really, not in a working kitchen' (Sarah).

When describing their ideal kitchens, both groups answered in relation to 'material abundance' (Holt 1997a), although Bowland residents were uneasy about the question: 'I don't know, we're happy with what we've got' (Wendy); 'Something bigger I suppose' (Claire); 'umh, well, I suppose something bigger and a dishwasher maybe' (Bob). Cartmel narratives were similar in content but less hesitant in reply: 'Ohh, something bigger. We're alright for space but it would be nice to have a utility room and a new washing machine… ideally I'd get all the mod-cons' (Nicola). In Christine's case: 'Ideally, a big country kitchen with an island and flowers and veg and utensils and a big table and an Aga, all that. In reality, I'd go for something more practical, imagine trying to clean that!' Overall, Bowland and Cartmel residents shared an orientation toward a functionally ordered kitchen, but Cartmel residents demonstrated greater awareness of consumption styles.

Lonsdale Avenue

While the kitchen was viewed as a space of household organisation that must be practical, this was largely 'taken-for-granted' as 'obvious'. Emphasis was instead upon stylistic order as a form of self-expression. A prominent example was the 'working kitchen' aesthetic, a style which expressed cooking as a personal enthusiasm:

> 'We both love cooking so it's arranged around that and I think it looks really good to be honest. So we have pots and pans on the wall, the knives are placed in a handy position, we've jars with herbs and spices on display and all that... it looks good, first because the kitchen looks real and used and second... it shows we love food and cooking.' (Colin, established resident)

For this group, the material ordering of the kitchen needed to achieve a balance between practicality and personal expression:

> 'I've got a framed photo on the wall of a holiday cottage which we stayed in with friends... The boys brought us... a tiny mouse which has got scissors, glasses and string for a tongue... it's our own personal style. I've also got shelves with glasses, but if you have too many it becomes a nightmare to clean. For me it's like functionally aesthetic.' (Judith, established)

In terms of ideals, *all* high cultural capital respondents preferred a farmhouse kitchen style which, while being practical, would provide scope for greater stylistic and personal improvisation including having vegetables, herbs and pans on display and various personal ornaments strategically located, as detailed by both Colin and Judith.

UNITY: 'OBJECT VERSUS SUBJECT UNITY'

Building upon the ordering of taste, notions of what constitutes 'unity' in style was a second prominent principle of consumption. Corrigan (1997) argues that stylistic unity is presented in two forms, object and subject unity. The former refers to the matching of objects according to brand or range; the latter is achieved through the imposition of personal biography onto stylistic order. Corrigan's example is the distinction between matching teacups and a mug collection, the latter being inscribed with the owner's biography.

Bowland Road and Cartmel Street

Low cultural capital respondents described object unity. This amounted almost exclusively to the colour co-ordination of utensils and appliances. Kitchen décor unified in this form resulted in little stylistic interpretation beyond the combination of formally complementary objects: 'We've got like the same colour bin and washing-up bowl, drying rack and that, all beige plastic. You know we don't want it to look like mix and match' (Robert). Object unity also provided important criteria for evaluating bad taste. Joan explained: 'I don't know, I suppose like if things didn't match, like white cupboards, green kettle and red floor, or something like that'. Orientation towards style amounted to little more than avoiding colour clashes. Cartmel respondents elaborated most upon object unity, all discussing how they planned 'colour themes' that embraced major kitchen appliances and not merely utensils, as was the case for Bowland respondents.

Lonsdale Avenue

High cultural capital respondents favoured subject unity. Matching colours were important, although less so than the imposition of biography upon the unity of goods. One woman had no qualms about placing a pine table in her oak unit kitchen, pine tables being significant from her childhood, even though: 'It's a bit of a botched farmhouse, because we've kept the original units...Of course this [the pine table] doesn't really go with the units [oak], especially if you go by the magazines' (Anne, established). The 'working kitchen aesthetic' described by Colin was another example. In his case, objects were unified according to the user's creative cooking capacities and the context of the kitchen design itself, pans being placed in strategic locations to maximise efficiency when cooking but also serving to create a stylistic impression of 'serious' cooking practices. The principle of object unity was a prominent basis for judging bad taste for Lonsdale newcomers; as Tracey explained, 'I think white, sterile kitchens are naff... [they] have no imagination, no life to them... they are cold... too manufactured and show no individual touch'. Established residents had a tendency to identify their own good taste through subject unity, whereas newcomers would contrast subject with object unity and discuss the bad taste of others.

The uniformity associated with mass production and consumption has been met with great 'fear' by the middle classes who associated it with the passive and uncritical acceptance of standardised goods which blunt the imagination and reduce consumption to a practice of uniformity and apathy (Slater, 1997; Warde, 1997). Yet, many theorists claim that consumption is a site for the pursuit of individuality, because agents can re-appropriate cultural meanings from the most commodified of objects. In Holt's analysis of cultural capital, he argues that those with high cultural capital express greater concern with the homogenising effects of mass consumption and in response, 'are more energetic in their attempts to individuate their consumption... through authenticity and connoisseurship' (1997a, 113). By contrast, Holt argues, those with low cultural capital perceive individuality through 'community acknowledgement of particular tastes and practices' (*ibid.*, 114). In essence, low cultural capital reduces horizons of perception, and individuality is perceived not in relation to mass culture but within local and collective frameworks.

Bowland Road and Cartmel Street

Consistent with Holt, Bowland residents did not express great concern over mass consumption, after all 'a kitchen's a kitchen' (Yvonne). They did not perceive mass manufactured products as infringing upon individual expression, precisely because they did not view consumption of the kitchen as personally expressive. In addition, comparative, collective and local frames of reference were prominent. Mavis described how, 'Over here [south Yate] everyone would see it as a working room, I mean, I've not seen a kitchen over this side which isn't primarily geared towards household chores'. In Claire's opinion:

> 'It depends on the sort of person. I mean, 'round here, we're all, well they're not big kitchens are they and we're all like practical people who use them... then there's like, your sort of manager type person and well they probably get take-aways more and that, so they use it less and perhaps that's why they'd have, like, shop-floors ones.'

Cartmel respondents were more aware of mass consumption and while their narratives inferred distance, they utilised mass culture as a means of information: 'in the brochures, it said something like 'close equivalent to farmhouse pine'... and that is the sort of style we wanted... Of course it's not real pine that would be too expensive but it's modern' (Sarah). Given perceptions of the kitchen as having limited potential for personal expression by all low cultural capital respondents, it was not surprising that massification did not form a major concern.

Lonsdale Avenue

As indicated through narratives of subject unity, Lonsdale respondents took a different stance. Aversion to mass consumption was most prominent in the celebration of 'original kitchens', described by Tracey as, 'dark oak cupboards and the wooden beams in the ceiling, with a white plastic work surface and heavy large, grey splash tiles, oh and the heavy red quarry tile flooring'. These kitchens were fitted as standard in the 'top of the range' (Peter, newcomer) and 'de-luxe' (Beatrice, established) Lonsdale houses, and were seen as distinctive because no other local houses had these kitchens and nor were they available in the open market (according to most Lonsdale respondents).

Established residents celebrated 'original kitchens' for their perceived cultural authenticity. Colin explained: 'the oak is really special, it's French oak and you just can't get hold of it any more, it's so expensive.' Tom and Sylvia placed the symbolic significance of 'original kitchens' directly within local context:

> Tom: 'They're unique right, you won't find them in any other house'; Sylvia: 'In Yate, most houses have those horrible turquoise kitchens, so these are special. But they also did a good job and I must admit, this type of kitchen is back in fashion but they're not the same. Oak needs to age'.

By contrast, newcomers emphasised the economic value of 'original kitchens'. For example, Charlotte appeared unable to decide if she liked her recently acquired kitchen: 'I don't like it, it's so dark, it's like being in a coffin... no I'd go for a stainless steel one... but it's different... There's something about them, it would cost an absolute fortune to buy one like it because it's so rare... and I do like the oak, it's got character'.

In terms of Holt's analysis, while high cultural capital respondents did demonstrate an aversion to mass consumption (as highlighted by their objections to object unity), they also discussed this through comparative and collective local contexts. They may have presented more considered views of massification but, as with low cultural capital respondents, individuation did not necessarily arise through senses of individuality in kitchen consumption. Furthermore, the symbolic significance of particular material tastes depended as much upon embeddedness within local contexts (as determined by levels of geo-graphical mobility) as on levels of capital.

Aversion toward mass culture relates to the final principle of kitchen consumption, which refers to quality. Holt's (1997a) distinction between 'critical versus referential appreciation' is instructive. Holt employs this dimension to analyse taste in media genres, concluding that those with high cultural capital favour critical interpretations of cultural texts, rather than evaluations in terms of their applicability to the 'real' world and lived experiences. In essence, this distinction amounts to the degree of abstraction employed when evaluating good taste.

Bowland Road and Cartmel Street

For Bowland residents, the quality of materials used to produce kitchen units and various utensils was only mentioned through passing reference to utility. As a form of 'referential appreciation', quality was only discussed in terms of proven durability as with, for example, old and trustworthy pans: 'they're good quality, I think we've had 'em, what, twenty years. And they're as good as new' (Wendy). For Simon: 'We've got my Mum's old set of knives, they've lasted ages and are in great condition'. In the case of Cartmel respondents, quality was additionally judged through rational exchange value: 'I'd rather pay a bit more for good quality, otherwise it's false economy as they'd not last so long' (John). For Stephanie: 'I'd not buy cheap. I once got a cheap wok and all the non-stick coating flaked off in a stir-fry.'

Lonsdale Avenue

In sharp contrast, Lonsdale respondents discussed quality in terms of rarity and distinction. The retention of the 'original kitchen units' by all members of this group served as a good example. The rarity of the oak, its French origins and symbolism of housing superiority within the local context, allowed for the quality of the kitchen to be abstracted. In another instance, 'craftsmanship' was emphasised. Barbara (newcomer) explained how it was:

'really important that we have the right lighting... The lighting was dreadful... so we got someone in who did a wonderful job, he put in some under wall unit lighting and some spots... The quality of his work was fantastic... I'd say we have high quality lights!'

SYMBOLIC BOUNDARIES AND THE VALUE OF KITCHEN CONSUMPTION

Levels of cultural capital had particular effects upon orientations toward kitchen consumption. High cultural capital respondents actively engaged with and reflected more upon the symbolic potential of their kitchens. Among low cultural capital respondents there were variations, Cartmel residents' higher economic capital appeared to allow greater consideration of issues concerning style. Importantly, these small differences had significant implications for the symbolic boundaries advanced by these two groups. For Bowland residents, the kitchen, being a room primarily of functional value, had limited symbolic potential for distinction. However, boundaries were still apparent, most clearly in perceptions of the extravagance of others. Advanced through collective orientations ('Us'), Bowland residents assessed style as, firstly, an excessive concern with consumption and, secondly, false senses of social status:

'It's a middle class thing. There's no point in getting too carried away like some people do. You hear of all the pretty kitchens in north Yate… but you know, a kitchen has to be easy to use and clean, I mean what's the point, it's a functional thing. Well it is for most of the people around here' (Martin).

'I mean it's not a showhouse, it's a home. It's a working thing, I don't believe in a showhouse, it's too perfect, after all, when all's said and done, you have to cook in there, you don't want to be scared to dirty a pan… there are people like that, you know the sort, professional people' (Mavis).

'people who pay an extra £20 for pans from Marks and Spencer's or whatever, I don't see the point… you can't leave the label on!' (Yvonne)

In addition, while these boundaries were anchored within frameworks of socio-economic evaluation they also encompassed moral judgments. In discussing being 'happy with what we've got' (Wendy) and aversions to the 'showhouse' kitchen (Mavis), the rules of function and practicality are suggested to be broken by others and 'phonyism' implied. Phoneys are those who judge themselves as culturally superior on the basis of wealth and superficial measurements of status, as opposed to personal characteristics such as integrity and being 'down-to-earth' (Patrick). In this form, being concerned with style in an ordinary and everyday form of consumption such as the kitchen is rejected as extravagant and misplaced, evidence of evaluations of social status according to material, rather than intrinsic criteria.

Levels of economic capital were important because Cartmel residents, while also advancing socio-economic boundaries as salient frameworks, were more aware of the symbolism of kitchen consumption. Rather than classify by discrediting style, they anchored taste in narratives of function and practicality but described their kitchen style as symbolic of their comparative affluence with respect to south Yate residents:

> 'I don't like the modern ones, they date too easily... but it should fit in with the style of the house, like in my opinion, the dark oak in a modern house is okay, but if you go for the like, cottage kitchen you see in the magazines, well in a new house that looks dreadful. Saying that, the sort of cheaper standard white kitchens are naff, they're like, you know, exactly the same as what's in B&Q.' (Stephanie)

Yet, greater economic capital alone does not adequately explain why Cartmel residents were more concerned than Bowland respondents with the symbolic value of consumption. Geographical mobility provides another route of analysis. Long range and recent mobility affords these respondents little knowledge of their neighbours. As such, they lacked the certainty of knowing shared intrinsic qualities required to advance moral boundaries in the form presented by Bowland respondents. Consequently, highly visible forms of consumption provided the basis for legitimating distinctions. For example, when discussing home consumption more generally, Cartmel residents employed cultural boundaries relating to competence, again drawn in comparison with south Yate residents:

> 'if you look at people's gardens, they might tell you what the person is likely to have their house like inside, you know if it's really flashy... a real mess or just well looked after. And I think 'round here everybody looks after their garden, there are very few who have really spectacular gardens, in fact I can't think of any in this part of the Yate but very few which are untidy.' (Angela)
>
> 'Generally, 'round here everyone keeps to the white Georgian windows, whereas Fylde Road [south Yate] is a hotchpotch of windows, shutters, brown windows, white windows, yellow windows... people don't want to stick out... someone has tarmaced over the whole of their front garden so they can park their cars. Now in south Yate, without being snobby, you'd probably expect it, but you definitely wouldn't expect it in Cartmel Street.' (Andrew)

In sum, while respondents with low cultural capital employed collectively derived socio-economic frameworks as the most salient boundaries of differentiation, the significance of symbolic consumption varied among them. In the case of Bowland residents, functional imperatives, coupled with moral aversions to material-based judgments of status, resulted in low recognition of ordinary consumption as a marker of distinction. For Cartmel respondents, symbolic capacities received greater consideration, first, because they have the economic resources to indulge in such considerations and, second, because generic assumptions of what constitutes collective cultural competence injected ordinary consumption with symbolic meanings that legitimated perceptions of social status.

In the case of Lonsdale residents, issues of style and taste received the most attention through expressions of personal investment in kitchen consumption. For Holt (1997a, 114) 'personal style is expressed through consumption practice even if the object itself is widely consumed'. Senses of individuality can, therefore, be maintained (at least in an illusory fashion) despite processes of massification through the investment of cultural and personal meanings in the material form of the kitchen. The principle of subject unity, for example, allowed high cultural capital respondents to take mass produced items and order them in a way that de-commodified and re-appropriated them (Miller, 1987). It is in this way that Lonsdale residents demonstrated greater faculty in symbolic consumption, drawing upon cultural boundaries to emphasise senses of refinement, distance from mass culture and knowledge of 'good taste'. Yet, socio-economic boundaries were not redundant and narratives that focused upon their 'original kitchens' linked cultural boundaries to social status.

Geographical mobility is again important for explaining the emphasis placed upon socio-economic boundaries, Lonsdale new-comers tending to consider their kitchens as symbolic of their achieved social status (as hinted by Charlotte's change of mind regarding the symbolic properties of her 'original kitchen'). As for low cultural capital groups, length of residence within a given street affected whether ordinary consumption was thought to symbolise social distinction. Knowing little about the shared orientations of their neighbours, Lonsdale newcomers described shared senses of cultural refinement through evaluations of the exclusivity of their material tastes. By contrast, Lonsdale established residents, who were firmly embedded within local contexts and most secure with regard to their local social status, went beyond narratives concerning the symbolic value of objects to emphasise kitchen practices as the most meaningful markers of distinction.

KITCHEN PRACTICES AND SOCIAL DISTINCTION

Because the kitchen is a room of everyday use, its symbolic meaning cannot only be reduced to material tastes. As stated earlier, taste also embraces moral categories and judgments of consumption practices.

How kitchens are used should, therefore, offer insights into the social and symbolic role of its consumption. During the course of interviews, kitchen usage illustrated a number of important associated 'meanings' concerned with (re) producing the family, marital relationships and sociability.

(RE)PRODUCING FAMILY: THE ROLE OF THE KITCHEN TABLE

DeVault's (1991) research on the social construction of family argues that different social groups engage and understand discursive forma-tions of family ideology in different ways. Her working class female respondents 'absorbed discourses from the margins' and family life was thought about in relation to familiar practices revolving around 'patterned customs'. A similar case can be made for respondents in Yate with low cultural capital, who discussed the relationship between family life and the kitchen through discourses associated with hygiene (narrated mostly by women): 'It must be easy to clean, I couldn't bare the thought of germs and that when I'm making the tea' (Sally). For Yvonne, 'you have to keep it clean. It's no good if we all catch a bug because it's not been disinfected properly'. In line with their utilitarian orientations toward taste, they did not engage with discourses concerning the role of kitchens in family relationships.

In addition to hygiene, vigorous narratives of the kitchen as a family room were dominant for established Lonsdale residents, particularly the kitchen table as symbolic of meaningful family interaction. Tom explained that kitchens 'should have a table… you can sit as a family and eat as a family, very, very important. A kitchen should be seen as a central room to the house and the family, a place for all the family to sit and talk'. Anne agreed: 'all the family can sit around this table… I think that's very important because I'm used to having, always having the kitchen as the focal family room, and we try and sit down as a family and eat and I know a lot of families don't do that'. Narratives of the table and family co-participation indicate this groups concern with contemporary discourses that emphasise a sense of 'loss' or decline in the 'well-being' of the family (Morgan 1991). This decline was associated with a perceived lack of time in daily life, in which the family can spend 'quality time' (Southerton 1999). These narratives of family relationships are important in relation to the taste orientations of respondents, established Lonsdale residents emotionally investing in the kitchen as a space symbolic of family values. The only low cultural capital respondent to discuss issues surrounding a table was

Christine (Cartmel), and for her this was simply a stylistic prop following the principle of object unity: 'I'd have liked a matching table, like in the brochure. It just sets the room off.'

MARITAL RELATIONSHIPS AND SOCIABILITY

Similarly, kitchen tables were also symbolic of marital relationships. Low cultural capital respondents did not discuss marital relationships. However, Lonsdale respondents perceived the kitchen as a space of intimacy:

> 'We [herself and husband] also like to sit in here when we have time to ourselves, it's nice to have a meal alone in here, just the two of us, it gives us the chance to have a nice meal and to talk, that's important to us.' (Anne)
>
> 'Actually, we'll sit in the kitchen when we're sorting out bills and that. I don't know, you have proper conversations, less distractions.' (Michelle, established)
>
> 'We both like to cook, so we do it together which is great. Get the kids off and then we can sit and cook for ourselves, and we have a chat and a laugh and some proper time to ourselves.' (Alex, newcomer)

For Bowland and Cartmel respondents, the kitchen is not a space of sociability for the family, partners or friends. Bowland residents did not socialise within their homes. Cartmel respondents did invite other couples (but not groups of couples) into their home for meals, but the kitchen was off-bounds to these visitors. Andrew and Patricia explain the dominant format:

> Andrew: 'we'll sit in here [lounge], have a drink then move to the dining table'; Patricia: 'I don't like guests seeing what I'm cooking [laughs].'

When I asked Angela if her dinner guests visited the kitchen, her confused response was: 'we've got a hatch so they don't need to... anyway, it's a bit rude to expect guests to collect dishes for the table.'

Lonsdale respondents, however, used the kitchen as a social space with the table again playing an important symbolic role: 'when people come around we often or usually sit in the kitchen. We tend to socialise around the table rather than in the lounge' (James, established). When friends visit Tracey, 'they tend to come and have a drink with me in the kitchen... there's no sort of ceremony, they like to be in the thick of it and helping'. In Judith's case: 'we always start off in the kitchen, like if we have people around for a meal we don't usher them straight in here (lounge) they go straight to the kitchen and start opening wine and things' (Judith). The kitchen as a space of sociability and its visibility to others indicates that, for this group, the kitchen has meaning at various levels: it is a room of intimacy for couples; a room in which ideal family relationships can be achieved and performed; and a visible space open to symbolic consumption by friends, acquaintances and neighbours.

KITCHEN PRACTICES AND SYMBOLIC BOUNDARIES

For Bowland and Cartmel residents, kitchen practices provided few additional interpretations of the symbolic meanings associated with kitchen consumption. Indeed, the only further consideration came in relation to hygiene, which was interpreted within the principle of the kitchen as a functional space. Lonsdale residents, however, employed kitchen practices to advance nuanced articulations of the symbolic meanings associated with particular aspects of kitchen consumption. Narratives of kitchen usage, which embraced family interaction, marital relationships and sociability, provided additional symbolic meanings of ordinary consumption. For example, established Lonsdale residents placed great emphasis upon kitchen tables when drawing moral boundaries that referred to the shared family values of their neighbours. Furthermore, their confidence in discussing the personal orientations of other social groups was underlined by comparing their own moral values within the local context:

> 'I suppose the people in south Yate... don't spend lots of time in the kitchen, cooking and things... they are likely to eat off trays, you know, all in front of the telly and not talking... I would say that people in this street... use and see the kitchen in a very similar way to us. It's funny really but we are very similar in that sense.' (Judith)

While such narratives were not redundant for Lonsdale newcomers, these geographically mobile residents continued to extensively employ descriptions of style, particularly images of hearth. Barbara provided an example:

> 'we need a new one and we know which it is... rectangular, dark stain... it's just important because like, when Amelia's older, she can do her homework or now, she could do some painting and playing, you know, while I get on with dinner... and dark stain complements the oak cupboards and it would be lovely.'

Such images are evoked by the farmhouse style kitchens and the material tastes of these respondents, discussed in an earlier section. In this form, the kitchen table is as much part of the symbolic repertoire of a particular kitchen style as it is an exclamation of a boundary that draws upon moral values to legitimate claims of social distinctions.

Overall, the lack of symbolic significance attached to consumption of the kitchen by low cultural capital respondents was confirmed by their one-dimensional view of the kitchen as a functional space. For high cultural capital respondents of Lonsdale Avenue, ordinary consumption received symbolic meaning in developing boundaries of distinction. In the case of established residents, the kitchen was afforded symbolic meaning through understandings of shared practices that facilitated narratives of moral values as well as cultural differences. For newcomers, knowing little about the kitchen practices of their neighbours reduced the possibility for advancing moral boundaries, and the kitchen became most significant through reflection upon material tastes. In sum, established residents focused symbolic meaning upon kitchen practices and how kitchen objects are consumed, while newcomers placed greater emphasis on what people consumed as symbolic of social status.

THE VARYING SYMBOLIC VALUE OF KITCHEN CONSUMPTION

The symbolic significance of the kitchen in the process of social distinction varied according to levels of economic, cultural and social capital, and patterns of geographical mobility. These variations are highlighted by the relationship between material tastes and kitchen practices, which together disclose the salient frameworks employed to narrate symbolic boundaries. Importantly, for all groups, boundaries were collectively derived, as illustrated by the constant references to locally derived senses of 'Us', 'We' and 'Them'. Moreover, boundary narratives were always advanced in relation to contexts, particularly the Town and the kitchen as spaces of interaction. Whether contextual narratives embraced domestic organisation (as in the Bowland case), local comparisons of affluence (Cartmel and Lonsdale newcomers) or a variety of morally derived values regarding practices (established Lonsdale residents), is of less importance than the demonstration that the symbolic meaning of ordinary consumption is context dependant. For all respondents, local contexts were important and the degree of embeddedness within these contexts affected the frameworks employed to identify the significance of consumption for interpreting social relations.

This empirical research indicates that the meanings applied to the symbolic value of consumption vary systematically according to levels of capital and patterns of geographical mobility. This demonstrates that ordinary consumption is not a 'realm' of individual 'free' choice, but nor is it determined by levels of capital alone. The meaning of forms of consumption is interpreted in context-dependant ways (whether 'Others' will view the kitchen, levels of embeddedness in local contexts, the ways in which kitchens are used and organised) and according to the constraints of experiences such as geographical mobility. Furthermore, the impact of geographical mobility indicates how the symbolic dimension of consumption is only one of several criteria that can be employed in the articulation of social distinction, moral evaluations being more important for many respondents in this research.

Chapter 11

THE ROLE OF STATES IN THE CREATION OF CONSUMPTION NORMS

Terhi-Anna Wilska

INTRODUCTION: CONSUMPTION AND THE WELFARE STATE

In sociological studies the connection between welfare state, social citizenship and consumption is almost totally neglected, although it is widely accepted that a person's social identity in post-industrial societies is determined less by employment position and more by consumption and lifestyles (e.g. Bauman, 1988; Lunt and Livingstone, 1992; Bocock, 1993; Gabriel and Lang, 1995). However, the connection between the welfare state and the consumption of public services has attracted more attention than the connection between welfare state and private consumption (e.g. Gabriel and Lang, 1995; Hugman, 1994; Walsh, 1994; Lury, 1994). The reason for this is probably that the consumption of collective social services has traditionally not been seen as 'real consumption' of the sort which creates consumer identities, since a consumer's right to choose between public services provided directly by the state, is often limited.

An interesting question is whether the definition of 'proper' consumption really requires consuming *individually chosen* goods and services. In Finland, for instance, the share of public spending of the GDP grew notably in the late 1980s and 1990s, and the number of people, whose total consumption consisted largely of public services provided by the state, such as education and health services, who benefited was considerable in the 1990s (Honkanen, 1995, 27; Parkkinen, 1996, 55–60). In Britain, by contrast, the relative share of public spending of the GDP was significantly lower in the 1990s than in the early 1980s, and the share of private consumption was clearly higher than in Finland (CSO, 1996, 126, SYF, 1996). Some reasons for this were the Government's privatisation and the 'empowerment' schemes in the late 1980s and early 1990s. The empowerment of citizens means that the state no longer provides welfare services, but only controls the *market* of a wide range of public and private organisations, thereby turning the citizen of the welfare state into *a consumer in the market society* (Walsh, 1994, 191–194). Thereby, the using of public services and the claiming of different social benefits can be seen as *the consumerism of the dependent.*

The main problem of this chapter is how the modes of welfare provision affect welfare recipients as consumers and citizens. Another problem is how different macro-economic circumstances, such as economic recession, affect the market of welfare services in a consumer society. This study examines particularly how young adult consumers aged 25–34, who are dependent on social benefits, survive as consumers in two very different welfare states, Finland and Britain. The period under examination is 1990–1994, which was a period of slow-growth in the British economy and a deep economic depression in Finland.[1]

WELFARE STATE AND WELFARE DEPENDENCE

The traditional definition of the aim of the welfare state is to secure basic welfare for its citizens through a public-financed safety-net. However, a question arises from this kind of definition: what is meant by 'basic'? Does the word 'welfare' imply more than just minimal needs (Esping-Andersen, 1990, 19, see also Marris, 1996, 9)? According to Bauman, welfare is survival with *dignity*, which it is the difficult duty of the welfare state to guarantee (Bauman, 1998, 45, original emphasis). Particularly from the consumer's viewpoint, this implies that a person should also be able to lead a 'normal', socially acceptable lifestyle (Townsend, 1979, 250–262). Inclusion for everybody is one of the main duties of the (post)modern welfare state.

Different welfare states, such as Finland and Britain, have different success rates in meeting their duties and obligations. According to Esping-Andersen's classification of three types of welfare regime (Scandinavian, Liberal, and Corporatist) (1990, 19–33), the Finnish welfare system is usually seen as a typical Scandinavian model; where the public sector is large, there is a universal state social security and social service system as well as an income-related one. The Finnish welfare state developed late, only from the 1960s onwards, but it did so very rapidly, and in the 1980s the level of social security was one of the highest in the world. Characteristic of the Finnish welfare state in the 1980s was a very important role for public income transfers that succeeded particularly in alleviating poverty (Ritakallio, 1994).

The traditions of a welfare state are longer in Britain than in Finland. Since World War II and the reforms advocated in the Beveridge Report (1942), income transfers and public services have served large groups of the population. The British welfare state, however, never became as comprehensive as in Finland and other Scandinavian countries. The ideal in British social policy in the post-war era was universal welfare provision, but Margaret Thatcher's neo-liberal policy in the beginning of the 1980s shifted it very close to the Liberal model (Twine, 1994, 108). In the Liberal model the role of the market is central in social services provision, social support is targeted rather than universal, and the level of the means-tested benefits is low (Esping-Andersen, 1990, 33).

In the Liberal welfare state model the, often means-tested, modest social benefits are targeted particularly at those on low income, and thus stigmatise the recipients. This is likely to cause 'relative equality of poverty among state-welfare recipients, market-differentiated welfare among the majorities, and a class-political dualism between the two'. In the Scandinavian model, the majority of social benefits are aimed at the large middle classes, ideally upgraded to levels that would satisfy 'the most discriminating tastes of the new middle classes'. All benefit and all are dependent (Esping-Andersen, 1990, 27–28), hence state dependency will not stigmatise. This sounds very idealistic, and in reality it is difficult to imagine living on social benefits satisfying discriminating tastes. Moreover, the universal welfare state model is crucially resource-dependent, requiring heavy taxes and a steadily growing national economy. Therefore, another interesting problem is how changes in national economies affect the provision of the welfare states. Esping-Andersen argues that in the Liberal welfare state model, social inequality between citizens is likely to increase during economic recession. Conversely, the Scandinavian model is supposed to maintain equality even in the non-growth periods in the economy. However, there is contrasting evidence about this (*ibid.*, 1990, 57).

The decade of the 1980s was a prosperous period for most people in Finland. At the beginning of the 1990s, the deepest and most rapid recession since World War II ensued. It began in 1990 as a decrease in private expenditure, due to severe private indebtedness. Indebtedness in the public sector, too, was characteristic of the beginning of the decade, as well as bank and financial crises (Honkanen, 1995, 53–56.). The unemployment rate rose from three per cent to nearly 20 per cent of the population and reached 40 per cent among young people aged under 25 in 1994 (Kosunen, 1997, 38).

As a result of the depression, and particularly unemployment, the number of households receiving income support rose from 180,000 to 330 000 between 1990 and 1994 in Finland. The increase in the number of households containing long-term unemployed during the same period was even more dramatic: from 18,000 to 210,000 (Ruotsalainen, 1996, 14). However, the general poverty rate increased only a little in Finland during the 1990s, from 2–3 per cent to 4–6 per cent, depending on the source, although the number of social aid recipients increased, and there were also cuts in social services (e.g. Ruotsalainen, 1996; Kangas and Ritakallio, 1996). The incomes of *most* households decreased evenly during the 1990s, and the general disparity in income remained rather steady (Jäntti, 1994, 64–72). The distribution in wealth did not change notably, either; in 1994 the wealthiest 20 per cent of population owned 51 per cent of the total wealth, which was about the same as four years earlier (Säylä, 1996, 5).

In Britain, economic growth was slower than in most European countries during the 1980s, and unemployment reached high figures. In most areas of welfare, the restructuring of the 1980s led to major cuts in social benefits and services, and thus increased poverty and inequality. The most apparent reason for this was the relative decline in the basic state pension, but the level of income support and unemployment benefit fell too. In general, the number of people not in work increased during the 1980s, as did the number of people working part-time. Families with a person in work enjoyed a rise in prosperity in the 1980s, but inequality increased even among them (Atkinson, 1995, 32–36).

The British economy improved slowly in the late 1980s and early 1990s, and unemployment started to fall in the late 1980s. The decrease in the unemployment figures, however, was at least partly due to the constant altering of the definition of unemployment. Inflation, too, was a problem in the late 1980s and early 1990s (Johnson, 1991, 206; 220–222). The disparity of income increased steadily, however. The real rise in disposable income after housing costs was just 1 per cent in the lowest income quintile, 13 per cent in the second, 28 per cent in the third, 38 per cent in the fourth, and 46 per cent in the highest between 1981 and 1993 (CSO, 1996). In Britain, the wealthiest 10 per cent owned almost 50 per cent of the total wealth in both 1990 and 1994. Inequality and increased poverty are the reason for more people living on income support and receiving housing benefit in the 1990s than in the 1980s, despite cuts in public spending. In 1993, 5.6 million households received income support, whereas the number was 4.2 million in 1989 (CSO, 1992 and 1996).

According to the Family Expenditure Surveys, among the age group 25–34, living mainly on social benefits (such as income support and/or unemployment benefit, or annuities and pensions) became more common in both countries in the early 1990s. The share of the dependent increased particularly in Finland. In the period of a strong economy in Finland, there were remarkably few young adult households whose main source of household income were social benefits, but the proportion tripled between 1990 and 1994. The share of dependent young families grew in Britain, too, and was more than a quarter of all households in 1994, as can be seen in Tables 1 and 2.

Tables 1 and 2 also show the average values of the income and consumption of the independent and dependent in 1990 and 1994. The difference in income and expenditure between the independent and the dependent are shown in percentages as parentheses, so that the independent households have the value 100. Table 1 shows that the difference in the weekly disposable income per consumption unit between the independent and dependent households was approximately the same in Britain in both years, such that the dependent young families earned *less than one third* of the earnings of the independent. The value of dependent households' expenditure was a little under 40 per cent of the spending of independent ones, which means that dependent households

Table 1: Weekly disposable income and total expenditure (£) per consumption unit among the independent and dependent young households in Britain 1990 and 1994/5 in 1994 prices.

Year	1990		1994	
Position	Independent	Dependent	Independent	Dependent
%	85	15	74	26
Income	182 (100)	54 (29)	204 (100)	60 (29)
Expenditure	164 (100)	63 (38)	184 (100)	72 (39)
Difference (%)	18 (9)	−9 (−17)	20 (10)	−12 (−20)

Table 2: Annual disposable income and total expenditure (FIM) per consumption unit among the independent and dependent young households in Finland 1990 and 1994 in 1994 prices.

Year	1990		1994	
Position	Independent	Dependent	Independent	Dependent
%	92	8	77	23
Income	80 045 (100)	57 875 (72)	70 911 (100)	45 557 (64)
Expenditure	75 641 (100)	59 617 (78)	69 428 (100)	50 952 (73)
Difference (%)	4404 (6)	−1742 (−3)	1493 (3)	−5392 (−12)

either constantly made credit purchases, or, more probably, received money for consumption from private sources.

In Finland the dependent households earned relatively more than in Britain; the disposable income of households on benefits were almost three quarters of the income of the independent households in 1990. However, the percentage went down between 1990 and 1994, and the income of the dependent was only two thirds of the income of the others in 1994, as Table 2 shows. Similarly to Britain, the expenditure of the Finnish dependent households was bigger than their income, but the difference between the income and the expenditure was only 3 per cent in 1990. In 1994, however, it was clearly higher, which suggests that informal sources of income or credit purchases became more important. The value of the expenditure, however, was not much lower than that of the independent, particularly in 1990, when the dependent households spent only 20 per cent less than the others.

The relative differences in the income and expenditure of the dependent households between Finland and Britain clearly indicate the difference in the level of welfare on the one hand, and the difference in the 'degree' of dependence on the other. The total value of different social benefits in Finland could exceed the value of wages, leaving some dependent households with substantial total incomes, even to the extent of rendering the concept of dependence questionable. On the other hand, in Britain dependent households earned less than a third of the income of the independent; they are poor regardless of the methods by which poverty is measured.[2]

Although the poverty rate had been steadily rising in Britain during the 1980s, the concept of poverty seems to be difficult to deal with. The Conservative government of Thatcher even refused to acknowledge the existence of poverty and rather talked about 'vulnerable' people (Johnson, 1991, 239). The problem of poverty was also belittled in popular talk and media in the 1990s. *The Economist,* for instance, argued that poor people were 'consumers like the rest of us', whose households were better equipped than ever (The Economist, 24 February 1996).

Interestingly, it is the *private consumption* of the poor rather than their income that makes the media question the 'real' poverty of the poor, as if there *were* norms according to which poor people should consume. Indeed, for those who are dependent on income support there are definitions of 'reasonable' consumption in Finland. The Social Office calculates acceptable expenditures, such as subscription for *one* newspaper, television with licence, a certain sum for buying clothes, acceptable travel and fares costs, etc (Aatola and Viinisalo, 1995; Ritakallio, 1994). In Britain there are estimated budgets for different types of household that follow 'subsistence minimum' or 'low cost level' (JRF, 1992, 3)[3]. Thereby, the welfare state gets an important role, not only in helping to survive, but also, to some extent, in controlling the use of money of its dependent populations.

The control of the state is, of course, more obvious in public service provision than in private consumption. As mentioned above, in the late 1980s and early 1990s in Britain, the Government's privatisation and decentralisation schemes turned collective services over to public and private organisations operating through market mechanisms. Citizens that used the services, in turn, became consumers in the market (Walsh, 1994, 191–194). In Finland, the role of the welfare state as the service provider had been taken for granted. However, during the depression, neo-liberalist values and attitudes began to spread, and they were implicitly included, not only in the Government's savings schemes in the early 1990s but also in the debates over the role, need, and aims of the expanded public sector. This is easy to understand in the light of the state's increased inability to sustain the growth of public welfare during the depression. What followed was that cutbacks in social security gave space to an expanding market of private social and health service organisations (see Kovalainen and Simonen, 1996).

THE 'UNDERCLASS' AND THE 'EXCLUDED'

Gabriel and Lang argue that by turning citizens into consumers the state justifies the dismantling of the welfare philosophy and the disowning of responsibilities. As it is up to the citizens as consumers to decide whether they want a service from the state, and what quality they are prepared to pay for, the result is that, for both citizens and consumers, rights have become dependent on income and wealth. Consumers do not face discrimination, as long as they can pay. Through money, consumers may acquire a number of things, including 'citizenship', the right to participate in a certain way of life (Gabriel and Lang, 1995, 174–177). According to Bauman, people living in poverty, due to either unemployment or a large number of dependants, for instance, do not have the free choice over marketed services, and therefore have neither the option to 'exit' from the supervision of state bureaucracy nor a loud enough 'voice' to exercise control over the powers that dominate them. In a consumer society these people are regarded as failed consumers, unable to choose and make decisions of their own, and that is the main justification for decisions being made for them by the state (Bauman, 1988, 83–84).

According to Bauman, the poor of a consumer society have no access to a happy life (or even to normal life), and are thus banished to 'internal exile'. The poor are defined (even by themselves) as 'blemished, defective, faulty and deficient—in other words, inadequate—consumers'. Inaccessibility to consumer lifestyles is 'the most painful of deprivations' (Bauman, 1998, 38). Bauman argues further that as the (Liberal) welfare state is the last resort of the traditional work ethic, those who are not working, have not *earned* their inclusion in the consumer society, and should be punished (*ibid.*, 66–69). Indeed, the Liberal welfare state punishes and excludes, mainly by keeping the dependent population poor by providing inadequate benefits, but also by stigmatising the welfare recipients.

In the Anglo-Saxon discourse, problems of poverty, dependence and social exclusion have led to widespread debate about the concept of the 'underclass'. Typical of the underclass is dependence on the state. According to Morris, being dependent on the welfare state is often seen as a badge of inadequacy, and not as a means of guaranteeing social inclusion (Morris, 1994, 134; see also Roche, 1992, 57 and Marris, 1996), which is quite opposite to the ideals of the welfare state. Most authors agree that the underclass today is not a homogeneous and marginal group, but rather a mixture of excluded people in very different situations. According to Leonard (1997) and Bauman (1998), post-industrial consumer society is likely to exclude totally new segments of population, mainly due to long-term unemployment or under-employment, making them 'useless' (Leonard, 1997, 131; Bauman, 1998, 66–69). In Britain, unemployment was not as major a problem in the early 1990s as it had been in the early 1980s. Instead, the problem in Britain was secondary employment; secondary jobs on low wages, and underemployment; insecure, part-time and seasonal jobs. Morris argues that the central group of people in this kind of employment were women: the structure of the whole British labour market was based on women working for secondary wages, and the males being the main breadwinners (1994, 122–123). This puts single mothers, for instance, into a vulnerable position, and they are much more likely to become welfare dependants than women in conventional families.

Between 1981 and 1994, the total number of single parent families in Britain grew from 900 000 to 1.5 million. Simultaneously, the average number of children living in single parent families increased from 1.5 to 2.8 (Haskey, 1998, 7). The percentage share of all children living in dependent or low-income families increased steadily during 1980s and 1990s in Britain. In some industrial areas up to 20 per cent of all children come from lone-parent families and in those areas child poverty is also the most widespread (Wong and Coombes 1996, 72).

According to the Family Expenditure Surveys, the main reason for living on benefits in Britain in the age group 25–34 was being unoccupied, as can be seen from Table 3. Not surprisingly, the type of household most prone to dependence was 'single parent' (over 90 per cent of whom were women), while two parents with children were usually independent. The dependent also had more children in their households than the independent. The profile of British dependent households changed slightly over the period 1990–1994, though, including more single persons and fewer families with many children. There were also more heads of households in part-time work on apparently low wages, and slightly fewer unemployed and unoccupied in 1994 than in 1990.

The main reason for the high dependence rate for single mothers is that British welfare policy has traditionally served to reproduce the patriarchal structures of family life. Morris argues, as does Crompton, that women have been incorporated into the welfare state not as full 'public' citizens, but as 'private' citizens in the role of dependants and welfare providers—wives and mothers. Housewives, for instance, are exempted from unemployment and work pension schemes (Crompton, 1993, 148–149). According to Morris, single mothers living on income support, as stigmatised members of the 'underclass', lack both the public and private forms of social citizenship. They are seen as failing, not only in their roles of workers and consumers but also in their 'female' role of socialising the next generation (Morris, 1994, 122–135).

In the social and political discourse in Scandinavian countries, the concept of 'underclass' is usually replaced with the term 'excluded'. Particularly during the depression in Finland in the 1990s, talking about the problems of the 'excluded' dominated the debates between politicians, social workers and researchers. It got a specific meaning of being permanently excluded from the labour market, which eventually results in passivity and lack of social contacts. According to Kortteinen and Tuomikoski, even *after* the economic depression, there were still about 100 000 long-term unemployed (about 5 per cent of the total

Table 3: Household characteristics in percentages among independent and dependent households in the age group 25–34 in Britain 1990 and 1994.

Econ. position of household of the head %	Year Dependence	1990 Independent	Dependent	1994 Independent	Dependent
Self-employed		14	2	12	2
Ft. employee		81	2	80	0
Pt.employee		3	7	4	14
Unemployed		1	28	3	27
Unoccupied		1	61	1	57
Total		100	100	100	100

Household type %		Independent	Dependent	Independent	Dependent
Single person		21	13	27	24
Single parent + children		3	60	5	51
Couple		26	1	25	3
2 parents + children		49	26	43	22
Other		1	0	0	0
Total		100	100	100	100

Table 3: Household characteristics in percentages among independent and dependent households in the age group 25–34 in Britain 1990 and 1994. – *continued*

Number of children under 18 %	Year Dependence	1990		1994	
		Independent	Dependent	Independent	Dependent
0		47	12	51	24
1		19	31	21	22
2		25	27	20	34
3		8	21	7	13
4<		1	9	1	7
Total		100	100	100	100
			(N=1345)		(N=1344)

workforce, which is ten times more than before the depression). About 20 000–30 000 of them are poor and likely to remain permanently unemployed (Kortteinen and Tuomikoski, 1998, 11, 179).

Table 4 shows that unemployment was a more common reason for dependence in Finland than in Britain, particularly in 1994. In 1990 the most typical dependent households were either families with children and the head of household working or unoccupied, or unoccupied persons in unconventional types of household. By 1994, the profile of dependent household types resembled that of the independent, except that unemployment was a more common reason for dependence. Single parenthood was not as apparent a reason for dependence as it was in Britain, since in Finland child care was not as big a problem as in Britain. The Finnish local authorities are obliged to provide childcare at means-tested prices for every child under the age of three. Largely for the same reason, part-time working was much less common in Finland than in Britain.

The typical household composition of the dependent in Finland was not exceptional. The proportion of single parents was somewhat higher among the dependent than among the independent, but still single parents represented only 12 per cent of all dependent households. Considering also the small differences in the amounts of incomes and expenditures between the independent and the dependent, it is very difficult to regard the dependent in this age group as a marginal group in a consumer society, as was clearly the case in Britain in both years.

THE DEPENDENT AND PRIVATE CONSUMPTION

It is not only the volume but also the structure of consumption that gives information about the social and economic position of the dependent in a welfare state. When comparing the structures of private consumption of the independent and dependent households, there are greater differences in Britain than in Finland, as can be seen from Table 5. In Finland the depression changed the general consumption patterns only a little, and only in some particular expenditure categories, such as housing and travelling. The differences between the independent and dependent in 1994 were very small: there were notable differences only in motoring expenditure. In 1990 there were more differences between the independent and the dependent, particularly in terms of items such as travelling and housing. This suggests that although the recession increased the number of dependent young

Table 4: Household characteristics in percentages among independent and dependent households in the age group 25–34 in Finland 1990 and 1994.

Econ. position of the head of household %	Year Dependence	1990 Independent	Dependent	1994 Independent	Dependent
Self-employed		11	19	9	7
Ft. employee + =		87	40	79	19
Pt.employee		1	15	5	4
Unemployed		1	15	3	35
Unoccupied		1	26	4	35
Total		100	100	100	100
Household type %					
Single person		15	17	21	24
Single parent+children		3	14	2	12
Couple		26	11	28	12
2 parents +children		45	32	45	45
Other		11	26	4	7
Total		100	100	100	100

Table 4: Household characteristics in percentages among independent and dependent households in the age group 25–34 in Finland 1990 and 1994 – *continued*

Number of children under 18 %	Year Dependence	1990		1994	
		Independent	Dependent	Independent	Dependent
0		50	50	53	43
1		19	22	19	25
2		23	19	23	22
3		6	7	5	6
4<		2	2	1	3
Total		100	100	100	100
		(N=1486)		(N=404)	

Table 5: Composition of household expenditure in the main expenditure categories by position of the household in Britain and Finland 1990 and 1994.

Country, Age	Britain, 25-34				Finland, 25-34			
Year	1990		1994		1990		1994	
Position	Ind.	Dep.	Ind.	Dep.	Ind.	Dep.	Ind.	Dep.
Food, drink	22	29	18	28	20	21	19	21
Clothing	8	11	6	6	6	7	5	5
Housing	20	20	24	21	20	24	26	28
Household equipment and services	11	11	13	14	10	10	10	9
Motoring	13	5	13	5	14	13	13	9
Travel & fares	3	3	2	3	9	5	3	4
Alcohol	5	3	4	3	3	2	3	3
Tobacco	3	7	2	6	1	2	1	2
Leisure Goods	5	3	5	4	4	4	6	5
Leisure services	5	4	8	5	4	2	3	3
Personal goods & services	4	4	4	4	8	8	11	11
Miscellaneous	1	0	1	1	1	1	0	0
Total	100	100	100	100	100	100	100	100

households, in the field of consumption the gap between them and the others narrowed.

In Britain there were more differences. In 1990, 71 per cent of the total expenditure of dependent households was spent on food, clothes, housing (net), and household goods and services. As housing benefits covered most of the direct housing costs (rents etc.) of the dependent households, their housing expenditure consisted mainly of fuel, light and energy. In food expenditure, the difference between the shares of the independent and the dependent increased between 1990 and 1994, and it was very marked by 1994. In both years, the share of total expenditure on motoring was almost three times greater for the independent than for the dependent. However, the dependent spent double the share of the independent in 1990 on tobacco products , and almost three times more in 1994.

The above results may not seem very striking, but what is interesting is the different development of the countries between 1990 and 1994. The most distinctive feature in the structure of consumption for the independent and the dependent in Britain during that period was the big (and growing) difference between them when it came to spending on necessities, particularly on food. In Finland, by contrast, the differences between households on benefits and the others were surprisingly small, at least when only looking at the main expenditure categories. Moreover, the main expenditure categories do not tell the whole truth, as the imputed values of the benefits-in-kind in Britain are included in the expenditures, such as living in a council house, having free milk and nappies etc.

Being a recipient of benefits-in-kind in Britain is precisely the kind of 'consumption' by which the state restricts the consumer's right to choose. In Finland, only those on income support face direct control by the state. More indirect forms of control, like higher prices of private social and health services, force people to rely on the free, lower-standard public provision. For the unemployed, travelling as leisure time consumption used to be controlled, since the jobseekers had to be in the reach of the employment office, which excluded, for instance, holidays abroad. The system was changed in most employment offices along with the increasing unemployment rates, and now most unemployed may travel wherever they want, because they can easily be reached on their mobile phones (!) (HS, 12th August 1998).

The ownership of durable goods and 'unnecessary' items such as mobile phones is usually the kind of consumption that leads the media to question the 'real' poverty of the dependent households. Indeed, possessing durable consumer goods was fairly similar between the independent and dependent young adult consumers in either countries. There were notable differences only in the ownership of cars and some hi-tech products, such as CD-players. In Britain the differences were slightly larger than in Finland. However, we cannot see from statistics how well-functioning the owned appliances were. There may be tremendous differences, particularly between more expensive items such as cars that can be new and shiny or old and banged-up. What also makes the comparison between two countries difficult in this respect is sometimes the different 'status' of the item in question. A good example is the mobile phone, which may still have some prestige in Britain (where the calls are quite expensive), but which in Finland is owned by almost every teenager!

CONCLUSIONS AND DISCUSSION

The main problem of this chapter was to analyse how welfare states with different histories and social structures affect dependent young adult consumers; how likely they are to become excluded from the consumer society. Statistical analyses give important information particularly about the characteristics of the dependent households, as well as about the gap between the resources of the dependent and the independent. According to the Family Expenditure Surveys, the structure of the welfare state undoubtedly affects the distribution of economic resources and the nature of economic dependence, as well as the position, attitudes, and self-esteem of people at different life course stages.

The analyses show that the dependent are in a clearly worse position as consumers in Britain than in Finland, despite the depression in Finland in the early 1990s. The important difference between the Finnish and the British 'excluded' manifests itself in the problem of whether the subjective feeling of exclusion primarily arises from a low ability to participate in the consumer culture or from being out of a working community. In Finland, being out of employment was probably more frustrating than being unable to buy certain things. Moreover, even among the dependent, few young adult households were so poor or so profoundly under the control of the social services that they were totally excluded from the consumer culture. More than anything else, the exclusion of the long-term unemployed seemed to be related to the social and status aspects of work, although in Finland, too, the dependent had to struggle to make ends meet. Dependence inevitably makes it more difficult to participate in a modern consumer culture which implies choosing, pleasure-seeking, and self-fulfilment. As Gabriel and Lang put it: 'It would be bizarre to envisage a single mother shopping for her weekly groceries as being lost in the reveries of pleasure' (1995, 109).

In Britain the dependent were not only relatively poorer than in Finland, but also more likely to remain poor and dependent, since in Britain poverty and exclusion of some groups of population was not primarily caused by macro-economic changes. The most important reasons for dependence were single parenthood and secondary employment rather than unemployment. The Liberal welfare state structure in itself, the long tradition of inequality between classes and genders, and the continuously growing disparity of income are the main reasons for the more or less permanent 'underclass' in Britain. In addition to the disparity of economic resources, the stigmatising and patronising social benefit system also exclude the 'underclass' from the 'legitimate' consumer culture.

However, social exclusion, especially in terms of consumption, is relative, and has to be looked at in the particular social context. In the densely populated, culturally heterogeneous British society in particular, there are plenty of opportunities for creating new consumer sub-cultures. In a country bristling with informal social groups for all unoccupied groups on the one hand, as well as all sorts of second-hand sales such as car boot sales, low-price shops and Sunday markets on the other, there are chances for a special kind of social belonging to the consumer groups who are used to bargain-hunting. Moreover, even with scarce economic resources, one can derive satisfaction from everyday 'routine' consumption, which is not clearly distinctive or hedonistic, such as shopping in the superstores. Trying new washing powder tablets or buying ice-lollies with a new flavour for the children may be enough to support a feeling of social inclusion in the consumer society for the single mother with her weekly groceries.

Notes

1   The data material used consists mainly of datasets derived from the Finnish Household Expenditure Surveys, and the British Family Expenditure Surveys 1990 and 1994. The British samples contain about 8 000 households each year, consisting of about 13 000–17 000 individuals. The Finnish samples contain about 8 000 households as well, except the dataset of the year 1994 which contains about 2 500 households. The samples of the age group 25–34 contain about 1 500 households, except the Finnish 1994 sample, which contains about 400 households. Both datatsets are based on household expenditure diary records and interviews.

2   There are innumerable ways of measuring poverty, direct and indirect, based on both income and consumption, defined by experts, political decisions, public opinion and persons individually (see Kangas and Ritakallio, 1996). The most commonly used official method is the relative income method, which means that the poverty line is 50 per cent of the median disposable equivalent income.

3   The subsistence minimum is estimated to be only half of the adequate level of consumption. Moreover, the social support in reality was even worse. In 1992, the Government's Income Support Scale was only 74 per cent of the low cost level for two-parent families, 77 per cent for single parents, and 108 per cent for single persons (JRF, 1992, 3).

Chapter 12

SMART LIFE, VERSION 3.0
REPRESENTATIONS OF EVERYDAY LIFE IN FUTURE STUDIES

Katja Oksanen-Särelä and Mika Pantzar

'Technological forecasts tell more about the times in which they were made than they do about the times they seek to predict.' (Schnaars, 1989, 61)

INTRODUCTION

This chapter focuses on the ways futurologists describe everyday life in the future. It is based on an analysis of a sample of futurological texts, which seek among other things to anticipate the demand for new goods and technologies (see Appendix). We suggest that current, mainly American, visions about the future overemphasize rational aspects of daily life, e.g. self-management and purposeful decisions, while the less overt and meaningful aspects are ignored. Most importantly, there is no reference to the ways in which technology is transformed from freely chosen objects to habitual routines.

The way we approach future visions could be called a variant of constructivism. Inventions are created in a certain social and political context. Technological artefacts are culturally constructed, their development is guided by different interpretations and predictions (Bardini, 1995; Bijker et al., 1987). Therefore representations of the future matter. The scenarios are typically written by business consultants whose task is selling different futures to business-oriented people. Often, the authors are consultants with a university background. The introduction and legitimisation of the authors is based on three factors: he/she is acting as consultant to Fortune 500 companies, he/she is or has been a professor, and the list of earlier publications.

We are not interested in single predictions but in the general message carried by all the books, a specific kind of the 'dominance of the technology'. Subtitles like 'effects of science and technology' imply linear causality and technological determinism. We argue that this reasoning may influence the ways in which many innovative companies orient to the future and also create consumer representations.

Technology does not develop as a one-way process from the designer's desk to the hands of the consumer. Creating the consumer and the use or uses for the product are a central element in the invention process. Steve Woolgar (1994,1996) calls this process 'user configuration'. User configuration leads to the formation of a 'script' (Ackrich, 1992, 1995; Ackrich and Latour, 1992) which the consumer follows when faced with a novel product.[1] From the manufacturer's point of view, creating a need and a market for the product is as important in the domestication of technology as is technical inventiveness.[2]

The extent to which various kinds of scenarios or market visions shape reality is an interesting question in itself. For instance, the creation of images of the modern consumer has been essential for the success of the television and car (Pantzar, 1999, 2000). It may be, paradoxically, that the imaginary consumer segments of marketing in fact produce real consumer segments (Miller and Rose, 1997), because reality is partly created through different representations. The question whether users or consumers can be divided into different segments by their relationship to technology is inverted: new 'versions of human beings' emerge as a result of both segmentation activity and emerging technology.

It has been stated that every era calls for a certain kind of person. Just as the industrial era produced a 'civilised', disciplined man, the digital era, or rather representations of the digital era, may produce a certain kind of person. This is the imaginary person, whose qualities we are trying to explore in this chapter. When technology around us is shaped in a certain way, it also shapes our experience and actions. This does not mean that technology is autonomous and has some kind of effects on its own. Technological choices are shaped by certain interests–and the scenarios are no exception to this.

Let us start by looking at the future scenarios from the viewpoint of everyday life. What kind of assumptions about the potential user can we find in these visions? What kinds of motivations to choose new technology are suggested? How is the relationship between individuals and technology constructed?

'RATIONAL WORKERS' OF EVERYDAY LIFE

The newest information technology reinforces the traditional picture of the 'rational consumer'. We might say that *homo oeconomicus* is inscribed in the manual of the information society. Earlier, when new technologies were introduced, their uses were envisioned as useful and rational from the producer's side. The ideal user was educated and rational. This was the case with telephones and personal computers when they were commercialized (Pantzar, 1999; Oksanen-Särelä, 1999). In official Finnish information society documents there has been a recent shift. The idea of correct use of technology has changed since Nokia, the world's leading mobile phone company, has increased its dominance in the national economy. Also, in current official documents social communication is associated with the correct use of IT technology (Pantzar, 2000).

The utilization may prove to turn out a winner of information technology, because it is so easy to talk about it in line with our cultural norms: technology is a servant and consumers are the users of instruments (Eriksson, Oksanen-Särelä and Pantzar, 1998). In future scenarios rational use of technology is described in different situations, which may be called different subcategories of the rational discourse.[3] Let us look at three subcategories, which represent special cases of the information technology user within the rationality discourse: dealers, homesters and self-observers.

a) Dealers (and e-commerce)
It has been predicted that electronic shopping will profit most from home networking. Judging by the precursors of teleshopping (e.g. Amazon.com, CdNow.com, Peapod.com), the only conclusion to be drawn is that the formerly unrealistic ideal of *homo oeconomicus*, cherished by economics, is finally being realised in network shopping. (Through the internet we are selling, buying and auctioning everything: e.g. goods, intellectual capital, attention, work effort and bank savings.)

It is assumed that microprocessors, the internet and information services will empower consumers. They will become expert buyers. Armed with pocket PCs, wireless modems and access to comparative shopping information services on the internet, they will be able to make buying decisions without leaving home. They will be able to compare prices by brand and by store: 'Consumers will become more sophisticated technophiles, spurred on by their passion for information, entertainment and faster, better, more personalised solutions' (Roberts 1998, 90–91).

> Her online gift shopping on the living room computer is almost done when she decides to take one last look at the Deere Tractor sale and, bang, a great need is unearthed: a small lawn tractor with an attractive price. She quickly skims through a short video of the machine at work, and, despite the exaggerated advertising, is still surprised to see the heavy landscaping the compact machine

can handle. She asks for a drawing of the tractor, which discloses the extensive use of carbon composite materials in its construction. With mounting interest, she fires off two requests—one for consumer reports on the product, the other a call for anyone who might be interested in selling her a used model.—Just to be safe, because the amount of money is considerable, she decides to go for a list of actual user complaints. That costs her a few extra dollars, paid to one of the many services that specialize in compiling consumer reports on outdoor equipment, but it is money wisely spent. She is happy to find out that the complaints are few and minor. Back at the Deere Tractor site, she asks a few questions about maintenance costs and ease of changing attachments and finds herself controlling an interactive video that deals with these topics. All right. She takes a deep breath and says the magic words: 'I'll buy it.' (Dertouzos, 1997, 124–125)

Electronic shopping makes it easy for the user to make price comparisons, and the different alternatives are offered in a very concrete form with unit sizes and prices. The user will be able to read the book reviews in an electronic bookshop before deciding to buy. He/she will get an itemised bill from each purchase indicating, for example, the price of transport. Moreover, since the time savings are considerable, electronic purchasing responds to social pressures and offers a real opportunity to the user who wishes to optimise his leisure time, effort and budget. This is what numerous visions of electronic shopping lead us to understand. In any case, a shopping revolution has been waiting just around the corner for a number of years already. The visions of electronic shopping are closely connected to a vision of safety at home.

b) The homester in his/her smart home
In the visions we have explored there are all kinds of new devices, which make the home smart. In the home there will be different control mechanisms, which should make the home safer from outside intruders. What is essential is that all technical functions are integrated. The remote controller enables the residents to affect the energy consumption and air conditioning in the building as well as the influx of information and entertainment. Smart cards, entrance surveillance systems and television cameras create a feeling of security.

There appears to be a typical American vision of an 'intelligent' and, in particular, a safe home (Dertouzos, 1997; Popcorn, 1991). The homester is a teleworker and a teleshopper. His/her children are tele-learners, utilising the most advanced technology. The intelligent system allows access through only one entrance and permits moving about only in daylight. Public space is visited only by abnormal actors for whom home is not paradise: predators and weak individuals—the homeless, in a broad sense. The image of the homester is one of a tiny mouse in its hole, safe from the cat and the dangers of the surrounding world.

'Besides the auto-cook and automated cleaning gadgets, home will offer a host of sensors and controls for lights, temperature, door latches, burglar and fire and gas alarms. It will also provide entertainment, health monitoring, babysitting, and package reception systems, live or changeable visual displays; multiple communications pipes to cable, telephone, wireless and satellite links; and outdoor amenities like pool water purification and garden irrigation. Once the electronics are integrated into the house and with one another, you will not notice them any more or less than you notice your present hot water heater, furnace, refrigerator, washer and dryer and other electromechanical gadgets. The difference, of course, is that the new devices will communicate with one another about their goals and their problems' (Dertouzos, 1997, 130).

In these scenarios technology takes care of everyday household chores. This reminds us of the early days of automation when it was believed that kitchen apparatus would diminish household work. But automation of household work has not gone far—and even if it had gone further, the workload would not necessarily decrease. Washing machines and other devices did not actually diminish the time consumed because they raised the standards of cleanliness (Schwartz Cowan, 1983; Markussen, 1995).

In any case, what should be done with the time or effort saved? The Taylorisation of household work did not give free time to the user because the time saved was filled with other household work. Moreover, many of the applications of intelligent buildings have focused on trivialities and not on real problems. Consider two experiments from America: a vacuum cleaner which switches off when the phone rings, and a robot, 'robutler', which serves refreshments but needs the help of a human to pour the drinks into the glasses (Berg, 1996).

The visions of the intelligent home seem to represent the early 20th century ideal of centrally controlled technological systems. Are we thereby planning the technology of the 21st century on the Tayloristic values of the early 1900s, where the ultimate goal was to minimise the diversity of human life? The terms used for the intelligent building are illuminating: 'total house, automatic house, global house, smart house, intelligent house' (Lorente, 1996). But what happens when there are technical problems, total disorder? Are we to expect that the smart system could be switched off if we so wished?

As highlighted earlier, products set some limits for their users. This is particularly clear with visions of the smart home. It is not just that people construct their homes according to their likes and dislikes; the home also requires adaptation and adjustments from its residents. Unsurprisingly, children and the elderly are objects of control in many visions.

> Robositter: the babysitter's best friend... The robositter is a simple robotic device that makes it possible for daycare workers or parents to more easily and with greater security watch children... The device relies on an electronic badge worn by the child... is programmed to follow the child and monitor his or her activities... Upgraded version can monitor the child's breathing, and observe what it puts in its mouth... Infant care has never been easier, the institutions and technologies at play today give parents an unprecedented sense of security. (Coates et al., 1997, 441)

The ideals of intelligent home are intensified in these visions where the home has turned into a kind of laboratory. This kind of system requires an active user who is constantly interested in his condition.

c) Observing the self

In the scenarios there is a recurrent image of preventing illness and other harms to the body through self-monitoring devices. Devices make it possible for us to check our blood pressure, pulse, blood sugar, etc. If necessary, the machine can also serve as a home kidney unit, insulin syringe, etc. In the morning we will ask the machine to tell us whether or not we are fit for work. The machine replaces the family doctor, dietitian and personal fitness coach. If we are in danger of putting on weight, the machine will give us dieting instructions and advise us to go jogging. The 'help desks' of the future will no longer deal only with computer problems but with human problems as well. A cardiac monitor or an intelligent WC, which performs analyses, will send our data directly to the nearest health care center. In case of alarming results the message will be passed to the doctor in charge at the interactive call center, who will then contact the patient.

> Fully awake, you head to the bathroom. You brush your teeth, and some of your mellow disposition starts to disappear. That terrible sink is at it again. It has detected minor traces of blood from your gums and is now scolding you in a deep parental voice: 'At the rate you are going there is a fifty-fifty chance that you will have a periodontal incident in twelve to fifteen months

and a loss of half your teeth by the time you are fifty-five years old'. Mumbling to yourself, you reach for the rubber tip and hope for the best. (Dertouzos, 1997, 117)

Robert wandered into the bathroom, which turned on its lights when it detected his arrival. 'Your sugar level appears to be satisfactory', announced the house computer, having received the urinalysis from the instrumented toilet in the bathroom. (Cerf, 1997, 34)

You want to focus on the running, and you need peace to think through choices ahead. When you are finished, the cheery voice of the 'treadmill doctor' congratulates you and tells you that you are on target with your chosen weight maintenance program. (Dertouzos, 1997, 115)

The idea of controlling others has been central to different technologies. What is interesting and novel is the idea that the person observes him/herself through technological devices. This is something we will discuss further in more detail.

A LIMITED PRESENT AND A RESTRICTED FUTURE

Managing life with technology

We have seen how people are described as actors in various situations and fields of life. What is common to the situations described is that people are actively managing their life through technology. The possibility of managing time and place is important in this aspect.

People have for a long time developed different machines and technologies to help them in various tasks. These technologies have sometimes been classified as either powerful or intelligent. Powerful machines help with simple tasks while intelligent machines have a more profound effect on human experience because as they have often been designed for the management of time and place. Modern devices (modern 'conveniences') like the electric stove have been effective in saving time and labour. There are also other kinds of devices which make possible a further management of time. Machines which work with a timer like a video recorder do not necessarily make things faster but with them it is possible to arrange and plan one's personal use of time. They do not require the user to be present all the time but operate independently (Warde et al., 1998). With the newest technologies the idea has gone further: a personal agent which organizes data is a good example. In such scenarios the user has overcome the limitations of time and place both by being constantly connected to other people and by using different information sources.

Consider some extracts from a daily round of Ashton, an imaginary person, in the year 2025:

> 7.08 AM The shower stall recognizes Ashton as he enters.. The shower video flips to his preferred channel, MTV-5...
>
> 7.45 AM Ashton uses his breakfast room flatscreen to view the news he needs...
>
> 3.42 PM For any electronic message or information source, Ashton can rely on his knowbot assistant to winnow the information down to a manageable level. The knowbot he has named 'CyberJean' is programmed to anticipate Ashton's information needs...
>
> 3.58 PM Later, on his desk video console, Ashton views a ballot issue from the city council and registers his vote...
>
> 7.00ish Ashton's friend Marcus lives too far away to come to dinner, but he visits by VideoWindow on the condominium's large dining room flat screen...' (Coates et al., 1997, 434–439)
>
> But John Steele was not in his office. He was traveling by himself 90 000 feet above the Pacific Ocean, streaking at 1 700 miles per hour—2,4 times the speed of sound—toward Los Angeles. The meeting participants were similarly scattered over five continents, with no more than three or four being even in the same country. Computer imagery merged multiple audio and video tracks from all over the world to create the illusion of a single meeting room, complete with a conference table and potted plants. It even provided for private chitchat during breaks. (Knoke, 1996, 20)
>
> You finish (the telephone call) with Mom and continue walking along the avenue. To call someone, you would whisper the name and the call would be initiated. To see the latest television news you would glance up momentarily to turn the TV on and click your ring to change channels. You review your personal video messages as you stroll. (Dertouzos, 1997, 65)

Technological devices allow flexibility in a matter of when and where to perform certain tasks. This flexibility is also a means of using time effectively as it allows one to do different things simultaneously. In these visions of (mobile) connectivity there is a strong emphasis on knowing and controlling everything that is happening in various fields of life.

> Emily and Carl have decided to have a baby. They want a girl, and they want her to be born in October. They are interested in choosing characteristics such as height and hair and eye color, but those techniques add too much to the cost. They look forward to being surprised. Their genetics counselling assured them there were no diseases or other problems to worry about. (Coates et al., 1997, 418)

Future people manage sleep as never before. Sleep is no longer downtime for people intellectually:

As brain science began to recognize the complexity of brain activity during sleep, and the purpose of dreaming, scientists deviced sleep-time interventions, to adjust mood, ensure the cognitive recharge people need from sleep, and, at least experimentally, to promote subliminal learning during sleep... teach people while they sleep. (Coates et al., 1997, 440)

The assimilation of real-world data of every form, including video, global position, and radar, enables new computers, including home, office and industrial robots. Radio networks and GPS's (Global Positioning Systems) open up more possibilities by having objects that know where they are and can report their state and that are not just adaptations of cellular phones. Nothing—from keys to cars to people—need be lost. (Denning 1997, 29)

These are images of omnipotency and control—even perfect knowledge about the future. However, although the changes in our environment will be very radical, the ideals connected to future technologies are familiar: efficiency and control. In short, these are modern ideals of rationality. One cannot help wondering whether this is a desirable way of looking into future and the future users or consumers needs.

Forecasts today are actually very similar to the ones made in the end of 1960s when it was predicted what today would be like. In a popular book called *The Year 2000*, Herman Kahn, the director of the Hudson Institute, a well-known future-oriented organization, and Anthony Wiener, proposed a list of predictions where there were e.g. 'controlled and/or supereffective relaxations and sleep', 'automated or more mechanised housekeeping and home maintenance', 'new and possibly pervasive techniques for surveillance, monitoring, and control of individuals and organizations', 'genetic control or influence over the basic constitution of the individual', 'chemical methods for improving memory and learning', 'home computers to run household and communicate with outside world' ... (Kahn and Wiener, 1967, in Schnaars, 1989, 17–20). These predictions are among the most accurate ones—most of the predictions were not realised—but what is interesting is that not only are the areas of improvement through technologies the same as today, but the aims have not changed in over thirty years. The idea of control through technology is at least as pervasive as it was before.[4]

But it is not only the 'other nature' we are aiming to control. What seems to be a novel aspect of the contemporary view is the explicit emphasis of self-governance with the aid of technology.[5] In the image of a self-observer the modern ideals of control are taken further as control is internalized. These ideals represent different degrees of modern rationality, the self-observer being more close to a type that may be called late-modern, reflexive type.

HABITS AND SELF-GOVERNANCE

As we have seen, the need of an individual to have control over his surroundings and himself is emphasized in the scenarios. Hence the people described are similar to the actors described in modern action theories, most notably in the theory of rational choice. Any passive behaviour is transformed into an active action and at the same time the rational aspects of action are highlighted. This kind of action is determined by strong self-control. Weber described this attitude towards life as the methodical rationalisation of life (Campbell, 1996, 150–151). In this sense self-control means refraining from impulsive desires and planning ahead. But the idea can be taken further as the aspect of self-control extends to every aspect of human behaviour, in a Foucauldian sense.

The idea of control and monitoring has expanded as it has transformed into self-monitoring. This self is a calculating self, one which works upon itself in order to improve itself (Rose, 1989; du Gay, 1997). This reflexivity fits well with a 'perfected' experience economy. After 'experience goods' it will be personal transformations that most successful companies start to sell:

> ...transformations turn aspirants into 'a new you,' with all the ethical, philosophical, and religious implications that phrase implies. All commerce involves moral choice. (Pine and Gilmore, 1999, 183)

As new technologies become a part of our functioning in everyday life they disappear from active view, the technology moves from conscious memory to bodily memory (Wise, 1997, 188), and we no longer take notice of it. The scenarios claim that the user will be freed from different routines, like household chores, through technological devices. But they do not acknowledge that the technology itself creates new kinds of routines and dependencies. This can be seen most clearly in the visions of smart home (c.f. Dertouzos, 1997, 130).

Here we face an often stated philosophical question: if a device leads us to act in a certain way, are we actually controlling ourselves or has the machine some kind of independent power of its own?

LIMITATIONS OF AGENCY

> The bathtub controller started to fill the tub with the 98 F water that Robert preferred. 'Stop the bath, Jeeves, I don't have time for it today. 'Yes, sir', replied the home computer, and the bathtub drained itself. (Cerf, 1997, 34)
>
> Just tell the stove what you want to prepare—like most computers, it will understand verbal instructions—and it will display a list of ingredients

on its flat-panel screen. It will announce when the skillet is hot enough to sear a steak, prompt you when the pasta is al dente—— With use, it will remember how you like your food. (Cetron and Davies, 1997, 5)

For any electronic message or information source, Ashton can rely on his knowbot assistant to winnow the information down to a manageable level. The knowbot he has named 'CyberJean' is programmed to anticipate Ashton's information needs based on his interests, profession, place of residence, background, and intellectual type. (Coates, 1997, 438)

According to our cultural norms technology is a servant. In the scenarios this can be read in the vocabulary (CyberJean, Jeeves, Robutler) and in the way people are supposed to adopt new technological devices. In the scenarios the user's relationship to technology is envisioned in a simple way: the user has taken over the appliance, controlling it and letting it ease his/her everyday life management. However, a closer look at the descriptions indicates certain difficulties in the relationship between the individual and technology. It might even be difficult to talk about humans and technological artefacts as discrete entities.

The increasing interactiveness of smart machines is one of the core changes in future technology. Note the term 'intelligent agent'. The pessimistic view is that machines, which are capable of learning in interaction, will lead to completely new kinds of human-machine dependencies. Although we speak euphemistically of 'machines that learn and are customised to the user's preferences', we are possibly dealing with a completely new level of dependency. Take, for example, a personal robot connected to digital TV, which seeks the channels for the viewer's favourite programs based on preferences revealed by previous watching choices. At the same time, the program robot of the media operator continuously monitors the changing of TV channels in households. The program robot learns 'from experience' at what dramaturgical points people stop watching a program. Finally the robot learns to select the programs from the producers' list that will attract a maximum audience. The program-compiling robot in the media production unit then receives this information and begins to prepare combinations of different series of programs offering maximal satisfaction—as well as maximum dependency—to the viewer.

The paradox of modern technology is that people create machines to be servants and slaves; however, as the critics of technology fear, humans have been enslaved by machines. People have always been afraid that their creations may gain power over them, that the relationship between humans and machines may be inverted (Joerges, 1989, 31; Mick and Fournieur, 1998). The development of new

technologies, like smart agents, make this question even more important. William J. Michell discusses the often stated paradox in intelligent
technology: 'We want our agents to be as smart as possible in order to
do our bidding most effectively, but the more intelligent they are, the
more we will have to worry about losing control and the agents taking
over' (Wise 1997, 13).

Though not apparent in the visions, there is a latent fear that our
self-determination diminishes with the use of technology. Since new
devices may have effects on our everyday behaviour, e.g. they may
cause addictions and restrictions, we ought to be reflective about the
technology. How the consumer should act, with communications and
entertainment technology in particular, is assessed in terms of activity
and passivity.

Passive use of technologies has been seen as a route to addiction
and a cause for isolation and detachment from 'human' relationships.
One image of the user that has emerged is of a kind of 'media zombie'
who wants to be passively entertained. The media zombie is a
dystopian human being chained to an entertainment machine: com-
puter-dependency marks the end of rational life. The computer society
and the hundreds of digital TV channels would offer unprecedented
opportunities for the passive reception of stimuli. This image has been
introduced by the critics of developments in the media technology but
is also widely shared by those promoting new media technologies
where the interactive properties of the media technology are emphasised. For instance watching TV is often viewed as a problem, but
surfing on the internet is not. 'In the net you have to think and make
decisions, but television you can only watch and that's dangerous'
(Järvinen, *Turun Sanomat* 20.1.1999, translation K. O.-S.).

The picture of the media zombie fits in well with the long tradition of
consumption critique. The elite is worried about the behaviour of the
masses (Cross, 1993; Slater, 1997, 71). It is not hard to predict that the
future flood of visual messages will provoke the rage of the literati as a
form of 'low-brow' culture at the stage when the multimedia and virtual
stations become a reality apart from advertisers' slogans. How will we
react, for instance, to digital TV or third generation mobile video phones
in the first years of the 21st century? Who will be the first to voice
concern over the effects of digital and interactive TV on our genes or on
the quality of human sperm? (c.f. Chesner, 1997).

In many scenarios the user is the opposite of the media zombie
described above. The user is curious, he has an unsatisfied appetite for
information. He is competent in using the media technology to his

own advantage. This is reflected in the shift in vocabulary. It is no coincidence that the term 'user' is underlined in information technology rhetoric. The users of older media such as TV are 'consumers' and passive recipients. In new technology, however, users are actors and active creators of content. In the future we will no longer watch TV, we will use it. We will not enjoy or consume something, but use it. In the interactive visions, viewing and enjoying has been replaced by creating and managing. As a consumer becomes a user, he/she gains more individual agency and autonomy.

> Get connected and establish a network presence... Don't simply subscribe to a service, use it. Explore the information sources, but more importantly, communicate. Find someone to contact. Gain the critical skills and literacies. Yes, using interactive communications will take some work. It's not like television where information or entertainment are delivered with the press of a button. (Doheny-Farina, 1996, 183)

By 2047, people will no longer be just viewers and simple communicators. Instead, we'll be able to create and manage as well as consume intellectual property. (Bell and Grey, 1997, 10)

The visions of the use of technology have much to do with the notion of competence. The user has to be competent enough to use the technology in a reflective and conscious way—otherwise technology might take control over the individual. This dual image of the user resembles an image of a consumer in consumer theories. In modern thought the consumer has been seen in a two-fold-way: on one hand as a slave to trivial, materialistic desires, on the other hand as a calculating individual who seeks to maximize his benefit through reasonable purchases (Slater, 1997, 33).[6]

The strong willpower and capability of knowing 'what's good for me' distinguish the free man (a prudent consumer) from a slave (a shopping addict, a media zombie). The properties associated with the ideal user (in the visions) are in great degree the same properties which are attached to the image of the sovereign consumer.

It is not only that by making purchases or using products in a certain way one can be a certain kind of consumer. The very acts of purchasing or using a product make the person an autonomous agent since they tell that a person is capable of choosing between various commodities (whether they are material or non-material). This competence makes him what he is. But the conscious choosing is not only a right; it is an obligation. If we are not capable of making decisions, we do not have a personality in a full sense. By choosing the proper things we define our personality, who we are. This can be seen in 'small' things like choosing the right kind of wine at a dinner, or in more profound ones, like in building one's life story by choosing from various alternatives. In future visions different mechanically programmed consultants have an important role. People rely more on experts in various fields on life, even in personal matters which they have earlier managed by themselves. The common wisdom is that since people are busier, they need more help in everyday things. This is a complicated situation: people are getting help in everyday management now, but in the long run they may no longer have the expertise to make decisions.[7]

THE MISSING CHARACTERISTICS

Even though the diversity of the users/consumers is praised in future visions, they are surprisingly similar. The users of technology are seen as mobile, competent and constantly looking for new stimulus. They are active, responsible for their own doings in different life areas, like health, passions, reproduction and safety. They are constantly looking for deeper self-knowledge and self-advancement. One may ask whether this is an appropriate way of looking at the user. If the picture is wrong, what is going to happen to huge investments in digital interactive television, for instance?

Although the future visions say that the market will become more and more fragmented, there seems to be only one group of consumers with internally consistent preferences and beliefs. Some qualities are totally lacking from the visions. For instance, there are not any incompetent users or 'lazy people' who are not willing to invest their time on netiquette or teledemocracy in tomorrow's world. What will happen to the people who are not capable or even eager to adapt and use the new technologies? What about people who want to withdraw from the demands of the constant telesociability? What about people for whom home is no paradise? They are not present in the stories of the future. When we study the predictions, it is the normative values and ideals of today which are revealed.

CONCLUDING REMARKS

What is the intellectual source of the consumer image in future scenarios? Some elements are of earlier background: 'in the United States the positive meanings of technology continue to center around liberty, control, and efficiency ... which represent core American values identified by Tocqueville over 150 years ago' (Mick and Fournier, 1998, 124). In the United States the most important reason to believe in the success of smart home is related to a culture of fear. Consumers are scared of out-siders and criminals. Another reason why American visions emphasise security, but also a controlled environment, is related to the military background of vision-making and -makers. It is often overlooked that military organizations during the Second World War started scientific future scanning and modelling. Cyborg science, computer technology and system modelling still haunt the ways future scenarios see human beings.[8] Is it possible that a simple and mechanistic 'ontology of the enemy' could be found even in current future visions?[9]

Perhaps this very specific intellectual background explains why we have today so restricted, and still similar views, of the potential of future technology. Contrary to many other researchers, we would suggest that instead of technological determinism we are witnessing cultural determinism. Furthermore, a mechanistic view of human beings has implications for innovations. As long as user representations are based on a mechanistic view:

1. It is 'natural' to see machines as replacing human beings in everyday life context.

2. It is understandable that human beings are seen either as simple objects of change (Science finds, industry applies, people conform) or autonomous actors strictly separated from machines.

3. It is likely that real human beings, who are corporeal, have identities and are full of internal tensions, will refuse to buy and use the emerging richness of smart artefacts.

Could we find alternative views to consumers as simple rational calcu-lators? Historical data suggests that motivation to adopt and use new technology is versatile. Pantzar (1996a; 1999) elaborates the historic-ally changing relationship between the user and new commodities as a three-stage process. In the earliest stage of a novelty product, the user's relationship is often such that the product is understood as being a 'message' in itself. The most important thing about the first automo-biles and radios was the excitement these products generated. This stage can be viewed metaphorically as 'consumption as play'. In that case using a product is primarily an activity done for its own sake: the process itself is always more important than the outcome.

However, users will begin to raise their expectations of the novelty commodity (e.g. reliable operation of a motor or quality of an image), and the relationship with the product becomes more demanding. The new commodity will begin to make claims on its environment (e.g. radio and TV as co-ordinators of people's daily schedules). Metaphorically this stage can be termed 'consumption as work', with the user, a rational worker. The instrumental side of the using of the product is central. The future texts above seem to fit well to this specific view. Finally, the relationship to the commodity might become increasingly critical. Consumers begin to question the lifestyle inscribed in the product, and start to analyse their own commodity-dependency. This stage may be called 'the art of consumption', or 'age of reflexivity'. From the user's point of view this is a phase where he/she is no longer restricted by the instrumental use of the product, but has embraced it in a way so it can be a part of identity formation and self-expression (see Table 1).

Table 1: Consumption as play, work and art (Pantzar, 1997)

	Self-purposeful consumption (Consumption as play)	Consumption for instrumental value (Consumption as work)	Critical, creative consumption (Consumption as art)
Collective conception of the product's function	Toy, luxury, 'wonder of science'	Tool, necessity, 'serious' commodity	Critique of the material-intensive lifestyle
Production method	Creative induction	Standardization	Reappraisal of the product's function
Function	Collective, shared experience of use, finding the function	Personal use, routines	Deroutinization, from necessity to play
Motive	Sensation, pleasure, status	Satisfaction of needs, routine	Stylization, collecting, self-expression

Different needs and wants may be viewed from historical perspective but another way of interpreting this is to suggest that representatives of the different orientations (play, work and art) are present simultaneously at all points in time.

In the scenarios the instrumental orientation towards commodities is dominant and, for example, (information) technology shouldn't be used just for its own sake. Their viewpoint might be labelled as utilitarian individualism (compare Heelas et al., 1996, 6, notion of expressive individualism). The use of technology should be work-like. The ideal user is active and knowledgeable in using technologies. The relationship with technology is presented as unproblematic; the user has taken over the appliance, controlling it.

This viewpoint might be too simplistic. Recently aspects which could be labeled as 'expressive individualism' have also emerged in future visions (e.g. Jensen, 1999; Pine and Gilmore, 1999). However, as the playfulness of consumption is increasingly emphasized, the routines of everyday life disappear from future visions.

Notes

1 The concept of 'script' has been used in studying the transfer of technology to developing countries, but it is equally useful in examining, say, the domestication of the refrigerator in Finland in the 1950s (Pantzar, 1996).

2 It is not purely by chance that companies such as Intel, Phillips, L. M. Ericsson or Siemens, for example, are actively involved in the debate about our future: 'So to stay in rhythm, Intel must create 'new uses and new users'—which is in fact the company's slogan for keeping the market in sync with its own pace' (Eisenhart and Brown, 1998, 65). Correspondingly, on a film on design futures made by Phillips, someone says: 'We know there is no need for any of this (i.e. new products). Our job is now to create the need, so that we have the reason to make the products—and sell them' (Butenschon, 1998).

3 It is not claimed the discourses about the user would be some kind of total entities. They are more like situational behavioural patterns, the ways the user is supposed to act in different use contexts.

4 Actually these predictions could be found already in futurology texts of the early 20th century (Pantzar, 2000).

5 Promotion of all kinds of scorekeeping, for personal performance, group performance, and team performance might be one outcome of Information society '(e.g. Coates et al., 1997, 52). Accordingly, 'The collection of ground data by video, audio, and other sensors, night and day round the clock, is routine'(Coates et al., 1997, 53).

6 The concept of cyborg is one possibility to overcome the dualistic way of seeing the consumer of new technology. A human being who monitors him- or herself and is connected to a machine can be called a cyborg of the first or second degree. A first-degree cyborg is one with mainly cosmetic transplants: silicon breasts and silicon lips. A cyborg of the second degree has had part of the vital functions replaced with mechanical and more efficient devices: an artificial heart or a home kidney machine. The artificial parts can be exchanged for newer versions as needed. The vital functions of athletes, for example, can be considerably improved from the current level. Cyborgs of the third degree are continuously connected to machines, so that signals from the brain pass directly to the machines. Fourth-degree cyborgs have dissociated themselves from physical space: the consciousness of these bodiless actors floats around in cyberspace (Featherstone and Burrows, 1995; Hables, 1995).

7 'Ashton tries hard to keep up his appearance. He had always been a sloppy dresser, but he found that his appearance was important to his job. Now he regularly visits the Bodini Day Spa for full personal makeovers and appearance consulting. He also sees a personality consultant to fine-tune his disposition and demeanour...Ashton's personal life-style consultant tells him he needs to socialise more than he does now. Based on this advice, Ashton decides to have a small dinner party that evening. Jerzy and other guests eat the Angolan feast Ashton cooks, for which he consulted an African chef on the Compuserve Video Forum'(Coates et al., 1997, 439).

8 Cyborg science, game theory and modern economics included, frequently displays the military fascination with 'command, control and information' (Mirowsky, 1996, 4). It is not only future visions which take their starting point from this background. Also the rhetoric of computer advertising follows these paths (Oksanen-Särelä, 1999). As Edwards put it: 'Computers were

developed to support a closed world discourse with centralized computerized military command and control' (Edwards, 1995, 69).

9   American future studies own a lot to the early military problems of modelling a human being. In these theories human intentionality is not different from the self-regulation of machines. Social and human actor act like an autocorrelated servomechanism. Compare these aspects, for instance, with the following: 'The knowbot he has named "CyberJean" is programmed to anticipate Ashton's information needs based on his interests, profession, place of residence, background, and intellectual type'(Coates et al., 1997, 438).

APPENDIX: SAMPLE OF FUTUROLOGICAL TEXTS ANALYSED

Abrahamson, V., Meehan, M. and Samuel, L. (1998). *The future ain't what it used to be. The 40 cultural trends transforming your job, your life, your world*. New York: Riverhead Books.

Brown, D. (1997). *Cybertrends. Chaos power and accountability in the information age*. London: Viking.

Cerf, V. G. (1997). When they're everywhere. In *Beyond Calculation. The next fifty yearts of computing*, edited by P. Denning and R. M. Metcalfe, pp. 33–42. New York: Springer-Verlag.

Cetron, M. and Davies, O. (1997). *Probable Tomorrows. How science and technology will transform our lives in the next twenty years*. New York: St Martin's Press.

Coates, J., Mahaffie, J. and Hines, A. (1997). *2025. Scenarios of US and Global Society reshaped by science and technology*. Greensboro: Oakhill Press.

Denning, P. and Metcalfe R. M. (1997). *Beyond Calculation. The next fifty years of computing*. New York: Springer-Verlag.

Dertouzos, M. (1997). *What will be. How the new world of information will change our lives*. New York: Harper Edge.

Doheny-Farina, Stephen (1996). *The Wired Neighborhood*. New Haven and London: Yale University Press.

Durning, A. T. (1992). *How Much Is Enough? The Consumer Society and the Future of the Earth*. Worldwatch environmental series. London: Earthscan.

Dyson, F. (1997). *Imagined Words*. Cambridge, Mass.: Harvard University Press.

Farrell, W. (1998). *How hits happen, forecasting predictability in a chaotic market*. New York: Harper Business.

Feather, F. (1997). *The Future Consumer. Predictable developments in personal shopping and customer-centered marketing on the information superhighway*. Toronto: Warwick Publishing.

Jensen, R. (1999). *The Dream Society*. New York: McGraw-Hill.

Jones, S. G. (1995). *Cybersociety. Computer-mediated Communication and Community*. Thousand Oaks: Sage.

de Kerchove, D. (1995). *The Skin of Culture. Investigating the New Electronic Reality*. Edited by C. Dewdney. London: Kogan Page.

Knoke, W. (1996). *Bold New World. The essential road map to the twenty-first century*. New York: Kodansha International.

Kreitzman, L. (1999). *The 24 Hour Society*. London: Profile Books.

Latour, B. (1999). *Virtual Society. The social science of electronic technologies*. Http://www.brunel.ac.uk/research/virtsoc/text/events/latour2.htm

Meadows, D. H., Meadows, D. L. and Randers, J. (1992). *Beyond the Limits*. London: Earthscan Publications.

Millett, S. and Kopp, W. (1996). The Top 10 Innovative Products for 2006: A Technology with a Human Touch. *The Futurist*, **July–August 1996,** 16–20.

Mirowski, Philip (1996). *Machine Dreams. Economic Agents as Cyborgs*. Second Draft. University of Notre Dame.

Pine J. and Gilmore, J. (1999). *The Experience Economy*. Boston: Harvard Business School Press.

Popcorn, F. (1991). *The Popcorn Report. Faith Popcorn on the future of your company, your world, your life*. New York: Doubleday, Currency Book.

Roberts, S. (1998). *Harness the Future. The 9 keys to emerging consumer behaviour*. Toronto: John Wiley & Sons Canada Ltd.

Rushkoff, D. (1996). *Playing the Future. How kids culture can teach us to thrive in an age of chaos*. New York: Harper Collins.

Warwick, K. (1997). *March of the machine. Why the new race of robots will rule the world*. London: Century Books.

Visions of the futures (1996). Philips, Eindhoven.

von Weizsäcker, E., Lovins, A. and Lovins, H. (1997). *Factor Four. Doubling wealth, halving resource.* Club of Rome. London: Earthscan Publications Ltd.

Yu, A. (1998). *Creating the digital future. The secrets of consistent innovation at Intel.* New York: Free Press.

Chapter 13

EPILOGUE: CONVENTIONAL CONSUMPTION

Jukka Gronow and Alan Warde

ROUTINES VS. REFLEXIVE CONSUMPTION

In emphasising the amazing variety of the uses and meanings of the rapid increase in consumer goods sociologists have, understandably, paid more attention to the more visible, spectacular and extra-ordinary—and often individual—acts of consumption than to the less discernible, often almost automatic, repetitive and habitual forms of consumer behaviour. In searching for new meanings and uses they have tended to look for consumption involving action and through which a goal is reached. Thus there has been a tendency to overlook forms of consumption which are more habitual and social, which consist of repetitive social patterns of behaviour rather than of people's conscious, more or less imaginative choices. Many everyday shopping routines and eating habits, for instance, are good examples of such social routines, as discussed in Kaj Ilmonen's and Bente Halkier's contributions to this volume.

Such unconscious, non-reflexively applied routines are but one area of consumption in which people engage daily, automatically and often without any further reflection. Many items of consumption are also either parts of a complex pattern of behaviour or elements of com-bined actions. In such cases the different parts and aspects usually cannot clearly be discerned from each other. The consumption of items like electricity or water supplies, discussed in Elizabeth Shove and Heather Chappells' article, is an example. Electricity is used to multiple purposes, warming the house, cooling the fridge, heating food, etc. Only a negligible part of the water consumed is actually drunk; flushing the toilet, watering the lawn or washing dishes or clothes in a machine or, say, circulating it in the system of central heating, might in individual cases take the greatest proportion. At the end of the month the household, however, receives a bill for the total amount consumed.

The same is often true of many other items of consumption from cars to cooking utensils. Driving a car or cooking a dinner are complex acts in the sense that they both activate many utensils and items. They can also serve many different purposes and have different meanings to the individuals in question. Driving a car can be enjoyed as a particularly pleasurable activity and be conducted for its own sake or it can be instrumental in delivering goods or people to different places. As Tim Dant and Pete Martin point out, driving a car simultaneously makes use of the services of many people and the products of many industries, from gas stations and police forces to tyre manufacturers and road constructors. To most of these we only occasionally pay any attention. We become conscious of them usually only when they are causing problems and not functioning properly. They are hardly ever displayed to significant others. Listening to radio, in a rather absent minded manner while engaged simultaneously in other activities demanding more involvement—like driving a car or ironing clothes—is another example of complex actions, often conducted quite routinely and without further reflection (see Brian Longhurst, Gaynor Bagnall and Mike Savage's chapter).

In thinking about consumption one often brings to mind the act of shopping, choosing some objects from among a multitude of more or less clearly discernible alternatives. One is, then, by definition, selecting a particular item. Picking them from the shelves of a shop one clearly is 'consuming' some well defined or discernible objects. Similarly, with activities as watching a movie or eating a dinner in a restaurant or dressing oneself for a particularly festive occasion, it is often possible to discern a 'unit act of consumption'. (However these seemingly individual acts often are socially embedded; social resources and networks are mobilized and activated as shown by Shou-Cheng Lai's study.) But in other types of practices of consumption this is seldom the case.

CLASS DISTINCTIONS AND THE HIERARCHY OF LIFE STYLES

One understandable reason which might explain the tendency to concentrate on more visible and conscious forms of consumption is that in the sociological tradition acts and objects of consumption have mainly been of interest as signs of distinction or as symbols of social status. This is equally true both of those sociologists interested in consumption as expressions of class or other social cleavages in society and of those who emphasise the demand and the ability of the modern individual to construct his or her own identity with the help of commodities. In both cases, objects of consumption are mainly understood to function as signs of inclusion and exclusion: people like me or us prefer objects like ours whereas the 'others' choose, dress, or design and use theirs otherwise, as with the interiors of kitchens in Dale Southerton's study. Often dislikes or feelings of antipathy are more important than shared positive preferences in marking such social boundaries.

Pierre Bourdieu's *Distinction* (1984) has preserved its status as a classic of the sociology of consumption, as evidenced by many contributions to this volume. It was actually not a consumption study as such: it was rather a study of life styles and tastes and the—eternal—struggle between social classes for social power (see Rahkonen, 1996). It has, however, become the critical starting point or target of critique in many consumption studies today. Bourdieu presented a plausible explanation of rapidly changing lifestyles and the ensuing dynamics of consumption. While participating, out of necessity, in the eternal social struggle for distinction and recognition, members of middle and upper social classes keep the wheel of consumption going, with ever more new products being needed to serve as signs of the small distinctions made during this struggle. In this respect, Bourdieu's is the most developed and refined version of the classical sociological conception of the use of consumer goods as status symbols and markers of social wealth which was first presented by Thorstein Veblen (1961) at the end of the last century in his treatise on conspicuous consumption.

Bourdieu's sociology of taste and style has been criticised from two angles. First, the rigidity of tastes and life styles can be questioned. The activity of Bourdieu's new upper and middle classes, engaged in the struggle for the good, legitimate taste and social power, is mainly characterised by small distinctions. As a consequence, their taste becomes more and more refined. There is good reason to doubt whether such continuous refinement gives a plausible picture of the tastes of the growing middle classes in the advanced societies. It could also be asked whether the flexibility, elasticity and sovereignty, which Bourdieu's theoretical scheme reserved only for the higher echelons of society, in fact can be extended to comprise more or less all 'modern' consumers. The degrees of freedom in interpreting and acting out social rules would seem to be much greater than Bourdieu would let us understand, an argument supported by several of the contributions to this volume.

Recent empirical studies in North America have produced a thesis about increasing omnivorousness. According to Peterson and Kern (1996; see also Peterson, 1997), on the basis of a study of musical tastes, the main distinguishing feature of the taste of the upper class was not its exlusiveness but rather its inclusiveness. Members of those social groups who have a great deal of cultural capital liked and preferred to listen to all kinds of music, even to those genres that have traditionally been associated with less educated or less cultured social classes, like Country and Western or Gospel. Cultivated people distinguished themselves from others basically not by the exclusiveness of their taste but by its all-encompassing range. (See also Warde et al., 1999).

As Holt (1997b and 1998) observes, these empirical results do not necessarily reveal the whole truth, for there might be other kinds of taste dispositions which cannot be identified from lists of preferences for musical styles or performers. While liking the songs of, say, Dolly Parton, people with high cultural capital might have different, even opposing, motivations for doing so. Higher social classes might, for instance, appreciate her as a genuine representative of American folk music whereas the lower ones admire her because she sings about their own lives and loves. The latter might identify with her sentimentality, or like those songs that remind them about some 'fateful' moments of their own lives, whereas the former, if challenged, might engage in lengthy discussions of the relative merits of different recordings or 'vintages'. As Holt concluded, in a highly developed consumer culture it is hardly possible to study the hierarchy of tastes solely by analysing individual choices and preferences concerning musical genres or individual artists. The issue is not solely which item is preferred but also the manner in which music is appreciated and the different practices in relation to the object in question.

By emphasising the individual dispositions behind taste preferences, Holt proves a more orthodox Bourdieusian than Peterson. Mere classification of different objects of art forms or artists was not for Bourdieu the main methodological device of analysis. On the contrary, he stressed the role of habitual dipositions, often corporeally distinctive ones, which are expressed in such choices or preferences. Dale Southerton's study of the differences in kitchen design in an English town consequently emphasised, following Lamont's (1992, 9) earlier comparison of the tastes of the middle classes in the United States and France, the importance of 'symbolic boundaries' and categorical frameworks used as 'mental maps' to categorise objects, people, practices and even time and place. This approach also underlines the importance of analysing the various contexts and practices of different forms of consumption.

It is all but impossible to analyse such social dispositions and tastes by survey methods alone, which means that it is difficult to get information concerning tastes of social classes and populations as a whole. To study the dispositions and motivations a more reflexive method is required, indepth analyses of localities and smaller social groups being useful—as evidenced by several of the present studies. These might then be complemented by interviewing experts in relevant fields of consumption, reading journals and technical magazines of groups of enthusiasts, for instance, in order to get to know the 'objective aesthetics' applied in this area.

The social presentation of status in a developed and highly differentiated but relatively homogeneous society, has become a very delicate and multidimensional matter. Both making distinctions and interpreting them presumes much cultural capital or competence. If we are to believe Holt, Lamont and others working in the same tradition, the lack of simple and conspicuous social distinctions makes us all, or at least all members of the educated middle classes, connoisseurs with a blasé attitude, who can at the same time be sensitive and indifferent to everything, and for whom everything and nothing is good enough.

Bourdieu's second disputable premise is the presumption of a strong hierachy of tastes. Though readily admitting the existence of varied tastes and that members of different social groups have different dispositions to consumption, it is much more problematic to prove that these tastes are hierarchically ordered. Even if the taste of a professor might radically differ from the taste of a farmer there is no saying which is better taste. To be better—or legitimate—taste it must be recognised as such both by those who presume to have it and by others who aspire to get it. Explanation of the dynamics of consumption in terms of a status struggle falls in the absence of a hierarchy of tastes.

SOCIAL REGULARITIES BETWEEN THE INDIVIDUAL AND THE MASS

If the conception of social classes and their socially determined hierarchically ordered tastes were to be abandoned, it would become tempting to interpret behaviour in one of two opposite ways: either the consumers have become totally individualised, each having his or her individual and more or less private taste, or they are all homogeneous parts of one single 'grey' mass. In the first case, the consumer is presumed to be left alone to make his or her own choices—within the limits of available economic resources, of course. As Terhi-Anna

Wilska's study shows, people living on social benefits in Britain suffer exclusion from ordinary consumption. (There are other kinds of social limitations and restrictions, too, such as anti-drug legislation, but these do not generally and directly discriminate against any particular social groups.) In the second case, people make no choices but rather follow 'opinion leaders' or copy everyone else. The former would result in a totally individualised society, the latter would suggest the classical impression of a mass society.

In the classical theories of a mass society (Le Bon, 1899, Tarde, 1903, etc.), modern commercial society and life under monetary relations of exchange was often seen as consisting of one single homogenous mass of human beings without individuality and subjectivity. In buying and selling things no real distinctions are made any more, and everyone just repeats the example of everyone else. Thus people act as if they were imitating themselves (Tarde)—by imitating others who are, in all essentials, just like they are. This was the 'society of ants' feared by Max Weber. Money paints everything grey and makes everything commensurable thus destroying all genuine distinctions, and with it, everything elevating and sublime, as Georg Simmel (1950), like many of his contemporaries following Nietzsche, also thought.

In sociology, it is difficult to conceptualise socially shared practices or habits which cannot be explained as characteristic or distinctive of the behaviour of social groups, whether determined by class, gender, age, ethnicity or geographic location. Such distinctions have by no means disappeared from modern societies. There are, however, social regularities and behavioural patterns which are socially shared—where people act as if following rules—but which are not group or class specific. Regularities can be identified among many people in daily consumption which lack other common features explicable by some common 'background variables'. (See, for instance, Gronow et al.'s study (1998) of daily eating habits in the Nordic countries).

Recent sociological discussions, and in the sociology of consumption in particular, have considered the role of social habits and even individual routines. (See Ilmonen's contribution to this volume.) What is the role of routines and habits, often followed unconsciously and almost automatically, in everyday life? In the absence of strong religious or other traditional norms governing, for instance, the proper times and contexts of eating, regulation is weak in modern societies. The decision what and when and with whom to eat is mostly left to the individual to decide, at least in the case of adults. Why, then, do people behave in a habitual manner when there are no clear social norms or sources of authority that could force or effectively persuade them to do so?

HABITS, ROUTINES AND INDIVIDUAL ACCOUNTABILITY

Habit was, according to Camic (1986), a central concept in classical social theory at the turn of the century but it disappeared almost totally from later sociological discourse. For instance, Max Weber, who is best known for his sociological typology of intentional social actions, claimed in his *Economy and Society* that, empirically, habitual behaviour or routines are in every society the most prevalent form of social behaviour. Even Emile Durkheim, the analyst of social norms, emphasised the great role of unconscious, automatic, permanent and habitual social routines in everyday social interaction and social order.

Camic explained the neglect of such forms of social behaviour in later sociology by the historical conditions of the emerging new social science. Sociology had to distinguish itself clearly from psychological behaviorism. The opaqueness of the concept of habit might have played an equally important role in this respect: habits or routines were hard to grasp theoretically. Consequently, they were often treated as a kind of a residual category the nature of which it was difficult to determine in any greater detail. Habit was simply based on repetition or caused by blind imitation. The reputation of the concept was certainly not improved by its association with the theories of mass society (cf. Gustave Le Bon's mass soul or 'Völkerpsychologie' of Moritz Lazarus (*s.a.*),[2] one of Simmel's teachers at Berlin).

There might, however, be an even more important explanation for the neglect of habits or socially shared routines in sociology. Max Weber was programmatically interested mainly in individually meaningful and purposeful social action because he believed that only those historical transformations which could be accounted for in the terms of purposefully acting individuals were satisfactorily explained. Modern capitalism, for instance, had to thank for its emergence a multitude of empirical historical factors but the crucial one was the new disposition of methodical conduct introduced by Protestantism. Durkheim distinguished social norms, and not individual actions or dipositions, as the prime explanandum in social science. This social sphere *sui generis* was the sphere of ethical norms. There might thus be an analogy between classical sociology and the present day sociology of consumption: both paid attention to the accountability of the ethical dispositions of the individual actor or the (lack of) ethical norms prevailing in a society.

The classical duality—either conscious action or blind, routine, non-action—can be identified in the recent theories of the modern world and the individual condition. In both Giddens' and Beck's diagnoses of modern times, or the conditions of life in a 'risk society', the emphasis is on rational, calculative action: 'Living in the "risk society" means living with a calculative attitude to the open possibilities of action, positive and negative, with which, as individuals and globally, we are confronted in a continuous way in our contemporary social existence.' (Giddens, 1990, 28). In modernity we are dealing with the increasing 'reflexivity of the self'; individuals are increasingly faced with the task of making choices in their life, 'making themselves into what they are and what they want to be'. Biographies are 'do-it-yourself biographies'. We are faced with a process of individualization or, expressed in other words, detraditionalization (Beck and Beck-Gernsheim, 1996).

As Colin Campbell (1996, 149) has argued, many accounts of individualisation or, what often amounts to the same thing, detraditionalization are misleading in making us believe that 'a decline in the power and influence of tradition automatically leads to a world in which individuals engage in more reflexive forms of conduct.' In his opinion these diagnoses grossly exaggerate the free and reflexive nature of our daily behaviour; they are to be blamed for, what might be called, a voluntaristic fallacy. Campbell rightly pointed out that contrasting traditions and traditional conduct with voluntary action is too gross. Campbell's main argument is the same as Weber's: our daily conduct is everywhere dominated by habits and routines. It would simply be impossible to turn every form of conduct into action. Individuals simply could not possibly monitor every aspect of their daily conduct. Life without routines would be impossible to live (*ibid.*, 165).[3]

The core of Campbell's argument is that life in modern societies could at the same time become detraditionalized *and* more habitual. We could, if we only wanted to, act in another way, but mostly our daily life is dominated by 'taken-for-granted' routines and habits. The first meaning is the Schutzean, phenomenological one: some things are simply taken for granted in the sense that they constitute the background for individual actions. They usually go unnoticed rather than possess any authority as such. They could be changed if the author wanted, if they were challenged by other alternatives or obstacles, or even if they were merely drawn into the author's attention. Such routines are usually followed not because of any 'power of tradition' but because of social inertia: they remain intact unless there is some reason to change them. Traditions, on the other hand, represent another kind of 'taken-for-grantedness' where it is not easy even to think or imagine that things might be done otherwise.

One of the problems of the above discussion was that the conceptual alternatives were limited to traditions or reflexive action. Campbell drew attention, in addition, to the role of individual routines and their natural inertia, and the possibility of the reflexive application of traditions. The 'consequences of modernity', described in these terms, may certainly catch something of the life experience, or existential situation, of a modern individual who often is free to make use of opportunities without the 'heavy burden' of traditions yet, at the same time, is forced to face the risks offered by an 'abstract and anonymous social system'.

What is often forgotten in contrasting traditional institutions with modern individuality and freedom of action is the origin of socially shared habits and customs or, to put it simply, the role of social institutions. They are too often explained functionally, by the necessity for coordinating action and diminishing complexity in decision making and to make our behaviour predictable and trustworthy to others.

HABITUALNESS AND CONVENTIONALITY

Bourdieu, through his emphasis on the habitualness of action and consumption, overcame, or at least tried to overcome, the duality between goal-oriented action premised upon conscious choices by the individual and socially shared, more automatic practices or habits. According to Bourdieu, every individual is capable and forced to make his or her own choices out of a multitude of alternatives solely relying on his or her own individual taste. People subjectively like or dislike, say, some kind of music or food and genuinely express such preferences in their choices. Yet, at the same time, in so doing they only act according to their innate dispositions, following their own habitus, dictated by their relative social position determined by their relative quantities of economic, cultural and social capital. To Bourdieu, like to many pragmatists before him (see Kilpinen, 1999), individual action and its rationality on the one hand, and social habits on the other, are not necessarily opposites but, rather, mutually presume and support each other.

In *Economy and Society*, Weber (1968, 29–31) recognised three possible types of social regularities: customs, conventions and laws. Customs are social routines, social regularities that are repeated unconsciously and without reason. Their 'power' is based on repetition alone, on social inertia, if you like. Law, on the contrary is an explicit norm the following of which is externally sanctioned. The most interesting category, however, lies between the two pure types, that of a convention.

For Weber many forms of eating and dress, usually regulated by an etiquette, are good examples of convention. Less explicit than laws but more explicit than customs, conventions are more closely observed and sanctioned by others than customs but less so than laws. In general, conventions are sanctioned by social approval or disapproval alone. We may be aware of the conventions we follow, but do not necessarily have to be. A law and a custom are always socially shared, whereas routines and habits can be private. Conventions are socially shared. But often they are more loosely observed and shared by a smaller social group or circle than are laws. In other words, in Weber's typology of social action conventions lie between normatively regulated behaviour and pure social habits and individual routines.

MODERN CONSUMER AS A CONVENTIONAL SELF-MANAGER

Many objects of consumption are instruments of self management but in a broader sense than is commonly understood in many present-day technological utopias. As shown by Katja Oksanen-Särelä's and Mika Pantzar's analyses, the typical pattern of consumption of new technical gadgets in the techno-futurological literature is that they are deployed as instruments of control or substitutes or extensions for one's self-control. As shown by Pasi Mäenpää's analyses of the multiple and creative uses of mobile phones, gadgets are, in fact, used in a much more varied manner to arrange one's social relations and interactions. Thus, they create and support an ideal combination of control and freedom. All personal encounters and commitments, can be left open and flexible up to the last moment yet life is still experienced as within personal control. One gets the impression that mobile telephone owners seek social relations without any permanent routines and social conventions. They live a life only in the present, without any undue commitments.

One recurrent theme in this volume is that in utilising various kinds of consumer goods, from cars to mobile phones to the use of gyms, people are managing their personal lives. It is a question of self-management in a world where commitment is avoided—and, with commitment, rule-governed behaviour—until the last minute, and where as many options as possible are left open. This is most clear in the case of mobile phones, but equally characteristic among Roberta Sassatelli's 'body builders' and Tim Dant's and Pete Martin's car drivers. The central issue is how to be in charge of one's self, one's social relations and interpersonal social practices.

The modern consumer is, as shown by Roberta Sassatelli, not just any hedonist but a calculating one. He or she sets her or his own spatial or chronological limits to enjoyment and pleasure in order to be able to continue consuming in the future. These limits can be over-stepped, but only under strictly regulated circumstances. She or he enjoys life and its pleasures but does not take unnecessary risks or, for instance, endanger health. Consumption is part of an overall project of self-management.

This condition contrasts interestingly with the more traditional, but in many ways similar, case of British second home owners on holiday in France, described in Davina Chaplin's study, who create their own 'artificial' world where they labour following their own self-imposed routines and rules, which can become rituals. Such consumption practices do not emphasise the peculiarity or individuality of their author. Often the opposite is true: these self-managers are self-made conformists rather than individualistic heroes of consumption. As Brian Longhurst, Gaynor Bagnall and Mike Savage showed, the radio listeners living in middle class areas in Manchester emphasised their conventionality. In interviews, they exhibited the social competence of ordinariness. The middle classes increasingly seem to want to appear ordinary, to be ordinary and consume in an ordinary way. Such ordinariness or conformity does not, by any means, exclude all signs of individuality. On the contrary: 'However, once ordinariness has been established, or while it is being constructed, the individual may feel the need to differentiate themselves from the rest of the ordinary community.' (p. 140)

THE PROCESS OF INFORMALIZATION

Such a general picture of modern consumers as expressing their individuality while conforming to some standard of normalcy is reminiscent of analyses of the informalization of etiquette and conventions in modern Europe. In another theoretical tradition, inspired by Norbert Elias' analysis of the civilizing process, there has been discussion about the formalization and informalization of the rules of conduct or etiquette. Cas Wouters (1987, see also 1995a and b) has, in studying changes in the European books of good behaviour after the Second World War, suggested that, even if an overall trend of informalization is noticeable, there have been cycles of formalization too. Following Elias, Wouters explained these changes in terms of transformations in power constellations and in the hierarchical social differentiation in the society.

According to Wouters (1987, 406), formalization is characterized by a process of the 'dominant modes of social conduct tending towards greater strictness, hierarchy and consensus', whereas informalization is equal to 'greater leniency, variety and differentiation' (*ibid.*, 405). There are thus two dimensions of informalization, a leniency-strictness dimension and a variety-uniformity dimension. Both are further connected to the hierarchy of rules. The more hierarchical the society is, and the more hierarchical the rules of the etiquette are, the more probable it is that such rules are strict and do not allow for much variation and individual interpretation.

In Elias' analysis of the process of civilization, greater leniency and variety allowed by the rules of an etiquette—say in regulating the relations between the sexes—presumes, as a matter of fact, that human instincts and impulses have become increasingly self-constrained. External control, as represented by explicit, strict social rules and sanctions, becomes internalized, demanding greater flexibility and reflexivity in the adaptation of those rules. Thus informalization precludes general, universal social norms of conduct.

Whatever one thinks of Elias' basically Freudian conception of the gradual substitution of a strong super ego for the equally strong social other, his discussion is relevant for the present purposes in another respect. Namely, if the internalization of norms succeeds, the overt behaviour and appearance of individuals can be left to a more lenient and variable etiquette. For instance, a more informal etiquette typically allows for more escape clauses, individual application and interpretation, as well as greater variety in conduct. As Wouters' comparative studies of European etiquettes also showed, informalization and individualization can go hand in hand with increasingly complex rules of etiquette, which become more nuanced at the same time as more democratic and liberal. In this sense, increasing conventionality and individuality need not be social opposites.

CONCLUSION

Longhurst and co-authors observed that their interviewees expressed their unique personal identity within a general framework of ordinariness, as personal narratives rather than in terms of wider social groupings. One could probably extend this to other areas of consumption and social interaction too. The new informal etiquette of the expanded middle classes in modern societies helps to establish general normalcy and ordinariness while, at the same time allowing for individual variation, flexibility and interpretation. Individual variation, or the individuality of consumption practices, may more often be expressed in terms of personal routines—or even family traditions, as in the case of radio listeners—than individual experimentation emphasising creativity, even though these are by no means the only alternatives. To be personal, a lifestyle—or a pattern of consumption—does not need to be extraordinary or spectacular. It may well be thoroughly ordinary. It is personal because it can combine ordinary routines and conventions in a way that is peculiar only to the person in question (see Gronow, 1997). These routines and conventions may also be appplied in a flexible way, making them differ slightly from each other. Thus, they preserve their conventionality while allowing for individual variation.

Under such conditions, the world of material culture in general is characterized by the simultaneous tendencies of the increasing variety of commodities on offer and their increasing homogeneity, as shown, for instance, by the development of modern food culture. Ever new commodities are simultaneously available all over the world both enriching local cultures and making them apparently more similar. Yet this does not necessarily mean, as feared by some, a general levelling out of all real cultural differences. While older differences are preserved and new ones become possible, all can be recognized as being part of one and the same common or ordinary style of life. After all, as pointed out by Max Weber (1968, 30) among others, despite its emphasis on novelty, fashion, as a social phenomenon, does not differ from a convention: people who follow it and look for something totally new are just repeating others. In fashion, as in their daily life and habits of consumption, people simultaneously both imitate others and express their individuality.

REFERENCES

Aatola, L. and Viinisalo, M. (1995). *Kohtuullinen kulutus—määrittelyn ja mittaamisen mahdollisuuksia ja ongelmia* [Defining and measuring reasonable consumption—prospects and problems]. National Consumer Research Centre. Publications 1:1995.

Abercrombie, N. and Longhurst, B. (1998). *Audiences: A Sociological Theory of Performance and Imagination.* London: Sage.

Akrich, M. (1992). The de-scription of technical objects. In *Shaping Technology/Building Society—Studies in Sociotechnical Change,* edited by W. Bijker and J. Law. Cambridge, Mass.: MIT Press.

Akrich, M. (1995). User representations practices, methods and sociology. In *Managing Technology in Society. The Approach of Constructive Technology Assesment,* edited by A. Rip, T. Misa and J. Schot. London: Pinter Publisher.

Akrich, M. and Latour, B. (1992). A summary of convenient vocabulary for the semiotics of human and nonhuman assemblies. In *Shaping Technology/Building Society-Studies in Sociotechnical Change,* edited by W. Bijker, and J. Law. Cambridge, Mass.: MIT Press.

Alasuutari, P. (1992). *Desire and Craving. A Cultural Theory of Alcoholism.* Albany: State University of New York Press.

Aldridge, A. (1994). The construction of rational consumption in *Which?* magazine: The more blobs the better? *Sociology,* **28**, 899–912.

Alexander, J. (1995). *Fin de Siècle Social Theory. Relativism, Reduction and the Problem of Reason.* London: Verso.

Altshuler, A.; Anderson, M.; Jones, D.; Roos, D.; Womack, J. (1984). Can Automobility Endure? In *The Future of the Automobile: The Report of MIT's International Automobile Program,* pp. 47–76. London: George, Allen and Unwin.

Anderson, B. (1983). *Imagined Communities.* London: Verso.

Antaki, C. (1994). *Explaining and Arguing. The Social Organization of Accounts.* London: Sage.

Appleby, J. O. (1978). *Economic Thought in Seventeenth-Century England.* Princeton: Princeton University Press.

Atkinson, A. B. (1995). *Incomes and the Welfare State. Essays on Britain and Europe.* Cambridge: Cambridge University Press.

Bachelard, G. (1969 [1958]). *The Poetics of Space.* Boston: Beacon Press.

Bagnall, G. (1996). Consuming the Past. In *Consumption Matters: The Production and Experience of Consumption,* edited by S. Edgell, K. Hetherington and A. Warde, pp. 227–247. Oxford: Blackwells/Sociological Review.

Bagnall, G. (1998). Mapping the Museum: The Cultural Consumption and Production of Two North West Heritage Sites. Unpublished PhD Thesis. Institute for Social Research and Department of Sociology, University of Salford.

Bagnall, G., Longhurst, B. and Savage, M. (1997). Social Class, Lifestyles and Urban Networks. Paper to the Annual Conference of the British Sociological Association, University of York.

Ballard, J. G. (1995 [1973]). *Crash.* London: Vintage.

Bardini, T. and Horvath, A. T. (1995). The social construction of the personal computer user. *Journal of Communication,* **45**(3), 40–65.

Baudrillard, J. (1990). *Fatal Strategies.* London: Pluto Press.

Baudrillard, J. (1996 [1968]). *The System of Objects.* London: Verso.

Bauman, Z. (1988). *Freedom.* Milton Keynes: Open University Press.

Bauman, Z. (1989). Hermeneutics and modern social theory. In *Social Theory of Modern Societies,* edited by D. Held and J. B. Thompson. Cambridge: Cambridge University Press.

Bauman, Z. (1990). *Thinking Sociologically.* Cambridge: Blackwell.

Bauman, Z. (1992). *Intimations of Postmodernity.* London: Routledge.

Bauman, Z. (1993). *Postmodern Ethics.* Oxford: Blackwell.

Bauman, Z. (1995). *Life in Fragments*. Oxford: Blackwell.

Bauman, Z. (1997). *Postmodernity and its Discontents*. Cambridge: Polity Press.

Bauman, Z. (1998). *Work, Consumerism and the New Poor*. Buckingham: Open University Press.

Beck, U. (1992). *Risk Society: Towards a New Modernity*. London: Sage.

Beck, U. and Beck-Gernsheim, E. (1996). Individualization and 'precarious freedoms': perspectives and controversies of subject-oriented sociology. In *Detraditionalization. Critical Reflections on Authority and Identity*, edited by P. Heelas, S. Lash and P. Morris. Cambridge and Oxford: Blackwell.

Becker, H. S. (1963). *Outsiders. Studies in the Sociology of Deviance*. New York: The Free Press.

Becker, H. S. and McCall, M. M. (editors) (1990). *Symbolic Interaction and Cultural Studies*. Chicago: University of Chicago Press.

Bell, C. (1992). *Ritual Theory, Ritual Practice*. Oxford: Oxford University Press.

Berg, A.-J. (1996). *Digital Feminism. (A Gendered Socio-Technical Construction: The Smart House)*. Senter for teknologi og samfunn. Norges teknisk-naturvitenskaplige universitet. Rapport nr. 28, 1996.

Berger, P. and Luckmann, T. (1987). *The Social Construction of Reality*. Harmondsworth: Penguin Books.

Beynon, H. (1973). *Working for Ford*. Harmondsworth: Allen Lane.

Bijker, W. E. and Pinch, T. (1987). The social construction of facts and artefacts. In *The Social Construction of Technological Systems: New Directions in the Sociology and History of Technology*, edited by W. E. Bijker, T. Hughes and T. Pinch, pp. 17–50. Cambridge, Mass.: MIT Press.

Blanks, T. (ed.) (1998). *The Body Shop Book of Well-being: Mind, Body, Soul*. London: Ebury Press.

Bocock, R. (1993). *Consumption*. London: Routledge.

Boltanski, L. and Thévenot, L. (1991). *De la Justification. Les Economies de la Grandeur*. Paris: Gallimard.

Bordo, S. (1993). *Unbearable Weight. Feminism, Western Culture and the Body*. Berkeley: University of California Press.

Bourdieu, P. (1984). *Distinction: a Social Critique of the Judgement of Taste*. London: Routledge; Cambridge, Mass: Harvard University Press.

Bourdieu, P. (1986). The forms of capital. In *Handbook and Theory for the Sociology of Education*, edited by J. G. Richardson, pp. 241–258. New York: Greenwood Press.

Bourdieu, P. (1989). Social space and symbolic power. *Sociological Theory*, 7, 18–29.

Bourdieu, P. (1990). *In Other Words*. Cambridge: Polity Press.

Bourdieu, P. (1990). *The Logic of Practice*. Cambridge: Polity Press.

Bryson, B. (1996). 'Anything but Heavy Metal': Symbolic exclusion and musical dislikes. *American Sociological Review*, 61, 884–899.

Bryson, B. (1997). What about the univores? Musical dislikes and group-based identity construction among Americans with low levels of education. *Poetics*, 25, 141–156.

Butenschon, P. (1998). Design, youth, consumption. *ICSID Information, 3/98*.

Böök, S.-A[o]. and Ilmonen, K. (1989). Problems of contemporary cooperatives: Consumer cooperatives in Sweden and Finland 1960–1980. *Economic and Industrial Democracy*, 19, 499–515.

Camic, C. (1986). The matter of habit. *American Journal of Sociology*, 91, 1039–1087.

Campbell, C. (1986; 1987). *The Romantic Ethic and the Spirit of Modern Consumerism*. Oxford and New York: Blackwell.

Campbell, C. (1996). Detraditionalization, character and the limits of agency. In *Detraditionalization. Critical Reflections on Authority and Identity*, edited by P. Heelas, S. Lash and P. Morris, pp. 149–169. Cambridge, Mass.: Blackwell.

Campbell, C. (1996a). *The Myth of Social Action*. Cambridge: Cambridge University Press.

Campbell, C. (1996b). Half-belief and the paradox of ritual instrumental activism: A theory of modern superstition. *British Journal of Sociology*, 47, 151–165.

Campbell, C. (1996c). The meaning of objects and the meaning of action. *The Journal of Material Culture*, 1, 93–105.

Carrabine, E. and Longhurst, B. (1999). Mosaics of omnivorousness: Suburban youth and popular music. *New Formations*, 38, 125–140.

Castells, M. (1998). *End of Millennium*. Oxford: Blackwell.

Centre for Alternative Technology (CAT) (1998). Interview for the Domus Project. June.

de Certeau, M. (1984). *The Practice of Everyday Life*. Berkeley, Los Angeles and London: University of California Press.

Chesner, C. (1997). *Colonizing Virtual Reality. Construction of the Discourse of Virtual Reality, 1984–1992*. CULTRONIX (htpp://eng.hss.cmu.edu/Cultronix/chesher/default.html.)

Chinoy, E. (1955). *Automobile Workers and the American Dream*. Boston: Beacon.

Coffey, A. and Atkinson, P. (1996). *Making Sense of Qualitative Data. Complementary Research Strategies*. London: Sage.

Connerton, P. (1989). *How Societies Remember*. Cambridge: Cambridge University Press.

Corrigan, P. (1997). *The Sociology of Consumption*. London: Sage.

Corsten, M. (1999). Ecstasy as 'this-worldly path to salvation': The techno youth scene as a proto-religious collective. In *Alternative Religions among European Youth*, edited by L. Tomasi, pp. 91–124. Aldershot: Ashgate.

Cowan, R. S. (1983). *More Work for Mother: The Ironies of Household Technology from the Open Hearth to the Microwave*. New York: Basic Books.

Crisell, A. (1994). *Understanding Radio*. Second edition. London: Routledge.

Crompton, R. (1993). *Class and Stratification. An Introduction to Current Debates*. Cambridge: Polity Press.

Crook, S., Pakulski, J. and Waters, M. (1992). *Postmodernisation: Change in Advanced Society*. London: Sage.

Cross, G. (1993). *Time and Money. The Making of Consumer Culture*. London: Routledge.

Cross, G. (1997). The suburban weekend: perspectives on a vanishing twentieth century dream. In *Visions of Suburbia*, edited by R. Silverstone, pp. 108–131. London and New York: Routledge.

CSO (Central Statistical Office) (1992). *Social Trends*, **22**. London: HMSO.

CSO (Central Statistical Office) (1994). *Social Trends*, **24**. London: HMSO.

Danmarks Naturfrednings Forening (1989). *Den Miljøvenlige Husholdning*. København.

Dant, T. (1999). *Material Culture in the Social World: Values, Activities, Lifestyles*. Buckingham: Open University Press.

Davis, E. (1998) How can we all cash in on efficiency. *New Statesman Special Supplement*, 24 July, XXI.

DeVault, M. (1991). *Feeding the Family: the Social Organization of Caring as Gendered Work*. Chicago: University of Chicago Press.

Dewey, J. (1958). *How We Think*. Boston: D. C. Heath Co. Publishers.

Douglas, M. (1982). *Natural Symbols. Exploration in Cosmology*. New York: Pantheon Books.

Douglas, M. (1984) *Purity and Danger*. London: Routledge & Kegan.

Douglas, M. and Gross, J. (1981). Food and culture: measuring the intricacy of rule systems. *Social Science Information*, **20/1**, 1–35.

Durkheim, E. (1915). *The Elementary Forms of the Religious Life: A Study in Religious Sociology*. New York: Macmillan.

Durkheim, E. (1956). *Education and Sociology*. New York: Free Press.

Durkheim, E. (1964). *The Rules of Sociological Method*. New York: Free Press.

Durkheim, E. (1983). *Pragmatism and Sociology*. Cambridge University Press: Cambridge.

The Economist, February 24th, 1996, pp. 30–32.

Eden, S. E. (1993). Individual environmental responsibility and its role in public environmentalism. *Environment and Planning*, **25**, 1743–1758.

Edwards, P. N. (1995). From impact to social process. Computers in society and culture. In *Handbook of Science and Technology Studies*, edited by S. Jasanoff, G. E. Markle, J. C. Petersen and T. Pinch, pp. 257–285. Thousand Oaks: Sage.

Eisenhardt, K. and Brown, S. (1998). Time pacing: Competing in markets that won't stand still. *Harvard Business Review*, **March-April**, 59–69.

Elgin, D. (1981). *Voluntary Simplicity*. New York: William Morrow and Co.

Elias, N. (1995). Technization and civilization. *Theory, Culture and Society*, **12**, 7–42.

Elias, N. and Dunning, E. (1986). *Quest for Excitement: Sport and Leisure in the Civilizing Process*. London: Basil Blackwell.

Elliott, P. (1974). Uses and gratifications research: A critique and a sociological alternative. In *The Uses of Mass Communications*, edited by J. G. Blumler and E. Katz. London: Sage.

Enger, A. (1995). *Forholdet mellem Forbrukerens Holdning og Handling*. Lysaker: SIFO.

Environment Agency (1998). *Resource Demand Management Techniques for Sustainable Development*. March.

Erickson, B. (1996). Culture, class and connections, *American Journal of Sociology*, 102, 217–251.

Eriksson, P., Oksanen-Särelä, K. and Pantzar, M. (1998). *Just a Tool. Metaphors of Personal Computers in Advertising Texts*. Helsinki: Kuluttajatutkimuskeskus julkaisuja 13.

Esping-Andersen, G. (1990). *The Three Worlds of Welfare Capitalism*. London: Polity Press.

Falk, P. (1994). *The Consuming Body*. London: Sage.

Featherstone, M. (1990). Perspectives on consumer culture. *Sociology*, 24(1), 5–22.

Featherstone, M. (1991). *Consumer Culture and Postmodernism*. London: Sage.

Featherstone, M. and Burrows, R. (1995). *Cyberspace/Cyberbodies/Cyberpunk—Cultures of Technological Embodiment*. London: Sage.

Finger, M. (1994). From knowledge to action? Exploring the relationships between environmental experiences, learning and behaviour. *Journal of Social Issues*, 50, 141–60.

Firat, A. F. and Dholakia, N. (1998). *Consuming People*. London and New York: Routledge.

Flink, J. (1975). *Car Culture*. Cambridge, Mass.: MIT Press.

Flink, J. (1988). *The Automobile Age*. Cambridge, Mass.: MIT Press.

Forty, A. (1986). *Objects of Desire: Design and Society Since 1750*. London: Thames and Hudson Ltd.

Forty, A. (1990). Design and mechanization: The standardised product. In *History of Industrial Design: 1815–1918. The Great Emporium of the World*, edited by C. Pirovano, pp. 52–67. Milan: Electa.

Foucault, M. (1976). *La Volonté de Savoir*. Paris: Gallimard.

Foucault, M. (1979). *Discipline and Punish: The Birth of the Prison*. New York: Vintage.

Foucault, M. (1988). The subject and power. In *Michel Foucault: Beyond Structuralism and Hermeneutics*, edited by H. Dreyfus and P. Rabinow. Chicago: The University of Chicago Press.

Frisby, D. (1985). *Fragments of Modernity: Theories of Modernity in the Work of Simmel, Kracauer and Benjamin*. Cambridge: Polity Press.

Fuller, L. and Smith, V. (1991). Consumers reports: Management by customers in a changing economy. *Work, Employment and Society*, 15, 1–16.

Gabriel, Y. and Lang, T. (1995). *The Unmanageable Consumer. Contemporary Consumption and its Fragmentations*. London: Sage.

Gadamer, H.-G. (1993). *Truth and Method*. London: Sheed and Ward.

Gallup for *Berlingske Tidende*. (1999). Økologi er en Folkesag. 7.4.

Garfinkel, H. (1967). *Studies in Ethnomethodology*. New Jersey: Prentice Hall Inc.

Garrett, P. (1997). Who do we think we are? *Utility Week*, 4 April, 12–13.

Gartman, D. (1994). *Auto Opium: A Social History of American Automobile Design*. London: Routledge.

du Gay, P. (1997). *Consumption and Identity at Work*. London: Sage.

du Gay, P. et al. (1997). *Doing Cultural Studies. The Story of the Sony Walkman*. London: Sage.

Gellings, C. W. (1996). Then and now: The perspective of the man who coined the term 'DSM'. *Energy Policy*, 24, 285–288.

Giddens, A. (1976). *New Rules of Sociological Method: a Positive Critique of Interpretative Sociology*. London: Hutchinson.

Giddens, A. (1979). *Central Problems in Social Theory: Action, Structure and Contradiction in Social Analysis*. London: MacMillan.

Giddens, A. (1984; 1986). *The Constitution of Society*. Cambridge: Polity Press.

Giddens, A. (1990). *The Consequences of Modernity*. Cambridge: Polity Press.

Giddens, A. (1991). *Modernity and Self-Identity*. Cambridge: Polity Press.

Ginsburg, N. (1993). *Divisions of Welfare*. London: Sage.

Goffman, E. (1959). *The Presentation of Self in Everyday Life*. New York: Anchor Books.

Goffman, E. (1963). *Behaviour in Public Places: Notes on the Social Organisation of Gatherings*. New York: Free Press.

Goffman, E. (1963a). *Stigma. Notes on the Management of Spoiled Identities.* Englewood Cliffs: Prentice-Hall.

Goffman, E. (1971a [1959]) *Presentation of Self in Everyday Life.* Harmondsworth, Middlesex: Pelican Books.

Goffman, E. (1971b). *Relations in Public: Microstudies of the Public Order.* New York: Basic Books.

Goffman, E. (1972). *Interaction Ritual: Essays on Face-to-Face Behaviour.* Garden City, NY: Anchor Books.

Goffman, E. (1974). *Frame Analysis: An Essay on the Organization of Experience.* New York: Harper and Row.

Goldthorpe, J. H., Lockwood, D., Bechhofer, F. and Platt, J. (1968). *The Affluent Worker: (1) Industrial Attitudes and Behaviour; (2) Political Attitudes and Behaviour.* Cambridge: Cambridge University Press.

Gorz, A. (1985). *Paths to Paradise: On the Liberation from Work.* London: Pluto Press.

Gosling, P. (1996). The race for grid positions: Councils may move into the energy business by selling surplus supplies. *The Independent*, 14 August, 17.

Gow, D. (1998). Scots become world power. *The Guardian*, 8 December, 19.

Graham, S. and Marvin, S. (1996). *Telecommunications and the City. Electronic Spaces, Urban Places.* London: Routledge.

Graves Brown, P. (1997). From highway to superhighway: The sustainability, symbolism and situated practices of car culture. *Social Analysis*, 41, 63–75.

Gray, C. (1995). *The Cyborg Handbook.* New York: Routledge.

Gronow, J. (1993). Taste and fashion: The social function of fashion and style. *Acta Sociologica,* 36, 89–100.

Gronow, J. (1997). *The Sociology of Taste.* London and New York: Routledge.

Gronow J., Mäkelä, J., Kjærnes, U., Ekström, M., Holm, L. and Björkum, E. (1998). A comparative study of Nordic meal patterns. In *Culinary Arts and Sciences II. Global and National Perspectives,* edited by J. S. A. Edwards and D. Lee-Ross. Worshipful Company of Cooks Centre for Culinary Research at Bournemouth University.

Grossberg, L. (1996). Identity and cultural studies—Is that all there is? In *Questions of Cultural Identity,* edited by S. Hall and P. du Gay, pp. 87–107. London: Sage.

Gullestad, M. (1989). *Kultur og Hverdagsliv.* Oslo: Universitetsforlaget.

Gundelach, P. and Riis, O. (1992). *Danskernes Værdier.* København: Forlaget Sociologi.

Guo, C. (1996). Whom do consumers trust most? *Brain*, 248, 87–9. [In Chinese].

Guy, S. and Marvin, S. J. (1995). Reconfiguring urban networks: The emergence of demand side management in the UK. *Journal of Urban Technology*, 2, 45–58.

Guy, S. and Marvin, S. J. (1996). Transforming urban infrastructure provision: The emerging logic of demand side management. *Policy Studies*, 17, 137–147.

Haddon, L. and Skinner, D. (1991). The enigma of the micro: Lessons from the British home computer boom. *Social Sciences Computer Review,* 9:3, 435–449.

Halkier, B. (1997). Miljøhensyn i forbruget. Kropslig fornøjelse eller forsagelse? *Grus,* 52, 37–59.

Halkier, B. (1999). *Miljø til Daglig Brug? Forbrugeres Erfaringer med Miljøhensyn i Hverdagen.* København: Samfundslitteratur.

Hall, D. (1992). The capital(s) of cultures: A nonholistic approach to status situations, class, gender, and ethnicity. In *Cultivating Differences: Symbolic Boundaries and the Making of Inequality,* edited by M. Lamont and M. Fournier, pp. 257–285. Chicago: University of Chicago Press.

Halle, D. (1993). *Inside Culture: Art and Class in the American Home.* Chicago: University of Chicago Press.

Harvey, D. (1989). *The Condition of Postmodernity: An Enquiry into the Origins of Cultural Change.* Oxford: Blackwell.

Haskey, J. (1998). One-parent families and their dependent children in Britain. *Population Trends,* 91. Office for National Statistics.

Hastrup, K. (1992). *Det Antropologiske Projekt. Om Forbløffelse.* København: Gyldendal.

Hastrup, K. (1995). The inarticulate mind: The place of awareness in social action. In *Questions of Consciousness,* edited by A. P. Cohen and N. Rapport. London: Routledge.

Hawkins, N. (1998). Towards the one-stop utility shop. *New Statesman Special Supplement*, 24 July.

Hawkins, R. (1986). A road not taken: Sociology and the neglect of the automobile. *California Sociologist*, 9, 61–79.

Heelas, P., Lash, S. and Morris, P. (editors) (1996). *Detraditionalization and its Rivals. Critical Reflections on Authority and Identity*. Cambridge, Mass.: Blackwell.

Heritage, K. (1984). *Garfinkel and Ethnomethodology*. Cambridge: Polity Press.

Hermes, J. (1995). *Reading Women's Magazines*. Cambridge: Polity.

Hetherington, K. (1997). In place of geometry: the materiality of space. In *Ideas of Difference*, edited by K. Hetherington and R. Munro, pp. 183–199. Oxford: Blackwell.

Hirschman, A. O. (1977). *The Passions and the Interests: Political Arguments for Capitalism before its Triumph*. Princeton: Princeton University Press.

Hirschman, A. O. (1979). *Exit, Voice and Loyalty*. Harvard: Harvard University Press.

Hockerton Housing Project (1998). Interview for Domus Project. August.

Holt, D. (1997a). *Distinction* in America? Recovering Bourdieu's theory of tastes from its critics. *Poetics*, 25, 93–120.

Holt, D. (1997b). Poststructuralist lifestyle analysis: Conceptualizing the social patterning of consumption in postmodernity. *Journal of Consumer Research*, 23, 326–350.

Holt, D. (1998). Does cultural capital structure American consumption? *Journal of Consumer Research*, 25, 1–25.

Honkanen, P. (1995). *Julkinen sektori* [Public Sector]. Helsinki: Hanki ja Jää.

Horrigan, B. (1986). The home of tomorrow, 1927–1945. In *Imagining Tomorrow*, edited by Joseph Corn, pp. 137–164. Cambridge, Mass.: MIT Press.

Hoyer, W. and Brown, S. (1990). Effects of brand awareness on choice for repeat-purchase product. *Journal of Consumer Research*, 17, 141–148.

HS (Helsingin Sanomat), 12 August, 1998.

Hsien, D. (1998). Let the seller beware!—Changing times for consumer protection. *Sinorama*, 3, 108–117.

Hughes, T. P. (1983). *Networks of Power: Electrification in Western Society 1880–1930*. Baltimore: John Hopkins University Press.

Hugman, R. (1994). Consuming health and welfare. In *The Authority of the Consumer*, by R. Keat et al. London: Routledge.

Hundert, E. G. (1994). *The Enlightenment's Fable*. Cambridge: Cambridge University Press.

Hutton, W. (1998). Darkness at the heart of privatisation. *The Observer*, 8 March, 24.

Ihde, D. (1974). The experience of technology: Human-machine relations. *Cultural Hermeneutics*, 2, 267–279.

Ilmonen, K. (1987). From consumer problems to consumer anomie. *Journal of Consumer Policy*, 10, 25–38

Ilmonen, K. (1991) Change and stability in Finnish eating habits. In *Palatable Worlds. Sociocultural Food Studies*, edited by E. Furst et al., pp. 169–184. Larvik: Solum.

Ilmonen, K. (1997). Consumption and routine. Article for *ESA conference*. Essex. August.

Ilmonen, K. and Stø, E. (1997). The consumer in political discourse: Consumer policy in the Nordic welfare states. In *Constructing the New Consumer Society*, edited by P. Sulkunen, J. Holmwood, H. Radner and G. Schulze, pp. 197–217. London: Macmillan.

Iversen, T. (1996). *Miljøproblematikken i Hverdaglivet*. Institut for Antropologi. Københavns Universitet.

Jaakson, R. (1986). Second-home domestic tourism. *Annals of Tourism Research*, 13, 367–391.

Jenkins, R. (1992). *Pierre Bourdieu*. London: Routledge.

Joerges, B. (1989). Romancing the machine-reflections on the social scientific construction of computer reality. In *International Studies of Management & Organization*, 19:4, 24–50.

Johnson, N. (1991). *Reconstructing the Welfare State. A Decade of Change. 1980–1990*. London: Harvester Wheatsheaf.

Jordan, T. (1995). Collective bodies: raving and the politics of Gilles Deleuze and Felix Guattari. *Body and Society*, 1, 125–144.

Joy, A. and Auchinacie, L. (1994). Paradigms of the self and the environment in consumer behaviour and marketing. *Advances in Consumer Research*, 21, 153–57.

JRF (Joseph Rowntree Foundation) (1992). Household budgets and living standards. Social Policy Research Findings, 31. York.

Jäntti, M. (1994). Tulonjako ja tulojen muutos laman aikana. *Talous & Yhteiskunta,* **4:1994,** 64–72.

Kangas, O. and Ritakallio, V.-M. (1996). Eri menetelmät, eri tulokset. Köyhyyden monimuotoisuus [Different Methods, Different Results. Approaches to Multidimensional Poverty]. In *Kuka on köyhä? Köyhyys 1990-luvun puolivälin Suomessa* [Who is Poor? Finnish Poverty in the mid-1990s.], edited by O. Kangas and V.-M. Ritakallio, pp. 177–199. Stakes. Tutkimuksia 65.

Katz, E., Blumler, J. G. and Gurevitch, M. (1974). Utilization of mass communication by the individual. In *The Uses of Mass Communications,* edited by J. G. Blumler and E. Katz, London: Sage.

Kaufman, C. F. and Lane, P. M. (1996). Time and technology. The growing nexus. In *New Infortainment Technologies in the Home,* edited by R. R. Dholakia, R. Mundorf and N. Dholakia, pp. 135–154. Mahwah, New Jersey: Lawrence Erlbaum Associates.

Keynes, J. M. (1964). *The General Theory of Employment, Interest and Money.* New York: Harcourt Brace.

Kilpinen, E. (1999). What is rationality? A new reading of Veblen's critique of utilitarian hedonism. *International Journal of Politics, Culture and Society,* 13, 187–206.

King, J. (editor) (1997). *Family Spending—A Report on the 1996–1997 Family Expenditure Survey.* Office of National Statistics. London: ONS.

Klint, J. (1996). *Er der Salg i Etik?* København: CASA.

Knorr Cetina, K. (1997). Sociality with objects: Social relations in postsocial knowledge societies. *Theory, Culture and Society,* 14, 1–30.

Kortteinen, M. and Tuomikoski, H. (1998). *Työtön. Tutkimus pitkäaikaistyöttömien selviytymisestä.* Helsinki: Tammi.

Kosunen, V. (1997). The recession and changes in social security in the 1990s. In *The Cost of Cuts,* edited by M. Heikkilä and H. Uusitalo. National Research and Development Centre for Welfare and Health, Helsinki.

Kovalainen, A. and Simonen, L. (1995). *Sosiaali- ja terveysalan yrittäjyys.* Helsinki: WSOY.

Kvale, S. (1996). *Inter Views. An Introduction to Qualitative Research Interviewing.* London: Sage.

Læssøe, J. (1990). The making of the new environmentalism in Denmark. In The *Making of the New Environmental Consciousness,* edited by R. Eyerman and A. Jamison, pp. 66–120. Edinburgh: Edinburgh University Press.

Læssøe, J., Hansen, F. and Jørgensen, M. S. (1995). *Grønne Familier.* Institut for Teknologi og Samfund. Danmarks Tekniske Universitet.

Lamont, M. (1992). *Money, Morals & Manners: The Culture of the French and American Upper-Middle Class.* London: Chicago Press; Chicago: University of Chicago Press.

Lave, J. (1988). *Cognition in Practice.* Cambridge: Cambridge University Press.

Lavik, R. and Enger, A. (1995). Environmental conscious consumers. Who they are and what explains the variation in environmental consciousness. Article for *International Conference on Sustainable Consumption.* Lillehammer. January.

Lazarus, M. (*s.a.*). Über Gespräche. *s.l.:* Hensel.

Le Bon, G. (1903 [1899]). *The Crowd.* T. F. Unwin: London.

Lehtonen, T.-K. and Mäenpää, P. (1997). Shopping in the East Centre Mall. In *The Shopping Experience,* edited by P. Falk and C. Campbell, pp. 136–165. London: Sage.

Leidner, R. (1993). *Fast Food, Fast Talk. Service Work and the Routinization of Everyday Life.* Berkeley–Los Angeles–London: University of California Press.

Lenson, D. (1995). *On Drugs.* Minneapolis: University of Minnesota Press.

Leonard, P. (1997). *Postmodern Welfare. Reconstructing an Emancipatory Project.* London: Sage.

Levins, H. (1998). A growing US audience reads the net. *Editor & Publisher,* February 21.

Lieblich, A., Tuval-Mashiach, R. and Zilber, T. (1998). *Narrative Research: Reading, Analysis and Interpretation.* Thousand Oaks, California: Sage.

Liikkanen, M. and Pääkkönen, H. (editors) (1993). *Arjen kulttuuria.* Helsinki: Statistics Finland, Culture and Mass Media 3.

Liniado, M. (1996). *Car Culture and Countryside Change.* Cirencester, Glos.: The National Trust.

Longhurst, B. and Savage, M. (1996). Social class, consumption and the influence of Bourdieu: some critical issues. In *Consumption Matters: The Production and Experience of Consumption*, edited by S. Edgell, K. Hetherington and A. Warde, pp. 274–301. Oxford: Blackwell/The Sociological Review.

Lorente, S. (1996). The Global House. New user telecommunication opportunity in automation and information. Paper submitted to the COST248 Home Group, electronic house inline, 1996, http://www.hometeam.com/article/s _report.htm.

Lovins, A. B. (1996). Negawatts—Twelve Transitions, Eight Improvements and One Distraction. *Energy Policy*, **24**, 331–343.

Luckmann, T. (1989). On meaning in everyday life and sociology. *Current Sociology*, **37**, 17–30.

Lunt, P. and Livingstone, S. (1992). *Mass Consumption and Personal Identity*. Milton Keynes: Open University Press.

Lupton, D. (1996). *Food, the Body and the Self*. London: Sage.

Lury, C. (1994). Planning a culture for the people? In *The Authority of the Consumer*, by R. Keat, N. Whitley and N. Abercrombie. London: Routledge.

Lury, C. (1996). *Consumer Culture*. Cambridge: Polity Press.

Macnaghten, P. and Urry, J. (1998). *Contested Natures*. London: Sage.

Maffesoli, M. (1989). The sociology of everyday life. Epistemological elements. *Current Sociology*, **37**, 1–16.

Maffesoli, M. (1996). *The Contemplation of the World: Figures of Community Style*. Minneapolis: Minnesota University Press.

Malbon, B. (1997). Clubbing: consumption, identity and the spatial practices of every-night life. In *Cool Places. Geographies of Youth Culture,* edited by T. Skelton and G. Valentine. London: Routledge.

Malinowski, B. (1948). *Magic, Science and Religion*. New Jersey: Doubleday and Co.

Markussen, R. (1995). Constructing easiness—historical perpectives on work, computerization and women. In *The Cultures of Computing,* edited by S. Leigh Star, pp. 158–181. Oxford: Blackwell Publishers.

Marris, R. (1996). *How to Save the Underclass*. London: MacMillan Press.

Matza, D. (1967). *Becoming Deviant*. New York: Prentice-Hall.

McCracken, G. (1988). *The Long Interview*. London: Sage.

McCracken, G. (1990). *Culture & Consumption. New Approaches to the Symbolic Character of Consumer Goods and Activities*. Bloomington and Indianapolis: Indiana University Press.

McEvoy, D., Gibbs, D. C. and Longhurst, J. W. S. (1999). The prospect for improved energy efficiency in the UK residential sector. *Journal of Environmental Planning and Management*, **42**, 409–424.

McLuhan, M. (1994 [1964]). *Understanding Media: The Extensions of Man*. Cambridge, Mass.: MIT Press.

McLuhan, M. and Powers, B. R. (1989*). The Global Village: Transformations in the World Life and Media in the 21st Century*. New York: Oxford University Press.

McShane, C. (1999). The origins and globalization of traffic control signals. *Journal of Urban History*, **25**, 379–404.

Mick, D. and Fournieur, S. (1998). Paradoxes of technology: Consumer cognizance, emotions, and coping strategies. *Journal of Consumer Research*, **25**, 123–143.

Miles, S. (1998). *Consumerism—as a Way of Life*. London: Sage.

Miljøstyrelsen (1996). *En Styrket Produktorienteret Miljøindsats*. København.

Miller, D. (1987). *Material Culture and Mass Consumption*. Oxford: Blackwell.

Miller, D. (1988). Appropriating the State on the Council Estate. *Man*, **23**, 353–372.

Miller, D. (editor) (1995). *Acknowledging Consumption: a Review of New Studies*. London: Routledge.

Miller, D. (1997). Consumption and its consequences. In *Consumption and Everyday Life*, edited by H. Mackay, pp. 13–50. London, Thousand Oaks and New Delhi: Sage.

Miller, D., Jackson P., Thrift, N., Holbrook, B. and Rowlands, M. (1998). *Shopping, Place and Identity*. London: Routledge.

Miller, P. and Rose, N. (1997). Mobilizing the consumer. Assembling the subject of consumption. *Theory, Culture & Society*, **14:1**, 1–36.

Misztal, B. (1996). *Trust in Modern Societies*. Cambridge: Polity Press.

Moorhouse, H. F. (1983). American automobiles and workers' dreams. *Sociological Review,* 31, 403–426.

Moorhouse, H. F. (1991). *Driving Ambitions: An Analysis of the American Hot Rod Enthusiasm.* Manchester: Manchester University Press.

Morgan, D. (1991). Ideologies of marriage and family life. In *Marriage, Domestic Life and Social Change,* edited by D. Clark. London: Routledge.

Morgan, D. L. (1997). *Focus Groups as Qualitative Research.* London: Sage.

Morris, L. (1994). *Dangerous Classes. The Underclass and Social Citizenship.* London: Routledge.

Mortensen, N. (1986). Knowledge problems in the sociology of the 80's. *Acta Sociologica,* 29, 325–36.

Mortensen, N. (1991). Modsætninger og forsoninger mellem strukturer og aktører. *Politica,* 23, 42–59.

Mortensen, N. (1992). Future norms. In *From Voters to Participants,* edited by P. Gundelach and K. Siune, pp. 194–207. A[o]rhus: Politica.

Muller, J. Z. (1993). *Adam Smith in His Time and Ours: Designing the Decent Society.* New York: Free Press.

Mumford, L. (1963). *Technics and Civilization.* San Diego: Harcourt Brace Jovanovich.

Murcott, A. (1982). On the social significance of the 'cooked dinner' in South Wales. *Social Science Information,* 21, 677–696.

Murroni, C., Irvine, N. and King, R. (1998). Tuning into the public interest in radio. *Cultural Trends,* 30, 35–67.

Mäenpää, P. (1993). *Niin moni tulee vastaan* [You Come Across So Many People]. Proceedings of the City Planning Office, no. 14 Helsinki.

Nadel, S. and Geller, H. (1996). Utility DSM—What have we learned? Where are we going? *Energy Policy,* 24, 289–302.

Nahapiet, J. and Ghoshal, S. (1998). Social capital, intellectual capital and the organizational advantage. *Academy of Management Review,* 23, 242–266.

Negroponte, N. (1996). *Being Digital.* London: Hodder & Stoughton.

Niemi, I. and Pääkkönen, H. (1989). *Ajankäytön muutokset 1980-luvulla.* [Changes in the Use of Time in the 1980s.] Helsinki: Central Statistical Office of Finland. Studies 153.

Nowotny, H. (1994). *Time. The Modern and Postmodern Perspective.* Cambridge: Polity Press.

Nye, D. E. (1992). *Electrifying America: Social Meanings of a New Technology, 1880–1940.* London: MIT Press.

O'Connell, S. (1998). *The Car and British Society: Class, Gender and Motoring, 1896–1939.* Manchester: Manchester University Press.

Oksanen-Särelä, K. (1999). *Tehokas, rationaalinen käyttäjä. Tietokonemainonnan kuluttajakuva.* [The efficient, rational user. The consumer image of computer advertising.] Helsinki: Helsingin yliopisto.

Olin Wright, E. (1979). *Class, Crisis and the State.* London: Verso.

Orwell, G. (1955). *Nineteen Eighty-Four.* London: Secker & Warburg.

Osborn, D., Arnell, N., Barber, J. and Lascelles, D. (1998). *Independent Advisory Panel on Long-Term Environmental Issues Facing the Water Industry.* A Report to Severn Trent plc.

Palast, G. (1998). Power Games. *The Guardian,* 3 September, 13.

Palojoki, P. (1997). *The Complexity of Food-related Activities in a Household Context.* Helsinki: Department of Teacher Education, University of Helsinki. Research Report 172.

Pantzar, M. (1996). Rational choice of food: on the domain of the premises of consumer choice theory. *Journal of Consumer Studies and Home Economics,* 20, 1–20.

Pantzar, M. (1996a). *Kuinka teknologia kesytetään. Kulutuksen tieteestä kulutuksen taiteeseen* [Domestication of technology. From science of consumption to art of consumption]. Helsinki: Tammi.

Pantzar, M. (1999). Consumption as work, play and art—Representation of consumer in future scenarios. Forthcoming in *Design Issues.*

Pantzar, M. (2000). *Invention of Needs.* Forthcoming. Helsinki: Otava.

Parkkinen, P. (1996). Hyvinvoivat keski-ikäiset. *Talous & Yhteiskunta,* **1996:3,** 55–60.

Partanen, J. (1992*). Sociability and Intoxication. Alcohol and Drinking in Kenya, Africa and the Modern World.* Helsinki: The Finnish Foundation for Alcohol Studies.

Peterson, R. A. (1992). Understanding audience segmentation: From elite and mass to omnivore and univore. *Poetics,* **21,** 243–258.

Peterson, R. A. (1997). The rise and fall of highbrow snobbery as a status marker. *Poetics,* **25,** 75–92.

Peterson, R. A. and Kern, R. M. (1996). Changing highbrow taste: from snob to omnivore. *American Sociological Review,* **61,** 900–907.

Pinto, L. (1990). Le consommateur: agent économique et acteur politique. *Revue Franc[,]aise de Sociologie,* **31,** 179–198.

Pocock, J. G. A. (1985). *Virtue, Commerce, History.* Cambridge: Cambridge University Press.

Potter, J. (1996). *Representing Reality. Discourse, Rhetoric and Social Construction.* London: Sage.

Preston, L. (1996) Women and alcohol: defining the problem and seeking help. *International Journal of Sociology and Social Policy,* **16,** 5–6, 52–72.

Prättälä, R. et al. (1993). Continuity and change in meal pattern: The case of urban Finland. *Ecology of Food and Nutrition,* **31,** 87–100.

Rahkonen, K. (1996). Le goût vu comme une lutte: Bourdieu et Nietzsche. *Sociétés,* **53,** 283–297.

RAJAR (1999a). Quarterly Summary of Radio Listening, 1999/3. www.rajar.co.uk/summary/993/summarytable.cfm.

RAJAR (1999b) Rajar Insight 3, Radio Listening in Car. www.rab.co.uk/publications/insights/insight3.htm.

Ritakallio, V.-M. (1994). *Köyhyys Suomessa 1981–1990. Tutkimus tulonsiirtojen vaikutuksista* [Poverty in Finland 1981–1990. A Study of Effects of Income Transfers]. Stakes. Tutkimuksia 39.

Roche, M. (1992). *Rethinking Citizenship. Welfare, Ideology and Change in Modern Society.* Polity Press: Cambridge.

Roos, J. P. (1993). 300 000 Yuppies? Mobile phones in Finland. *Telecommunications Policy,* **17,** 446–458.

Roos, J. P. (1999). *Miksi Suomi on johtava matkapuhelinmaa* [Why Finland is the leading country in mobile phones]. Internet site: http://www.valt.helsinki.fi/staff/jproos/matkap.htm

Rose, N. (1996). Authority and the genealogy of subjectivity. In *Detraditionalization. Critical Reflections on Authority and Identity,* edited by P. Heelas, S. Lash and P. Morris, pp. 294–327. Cambridge, Mass.: Blackwell.

Rybczynski, W. (1988). *Home: a Short History of an Idea.* London: Heinemann.

Rybczynski, W. (1992). *Waiting for the Weekend.* London: Penguin.

Sachs, W. (1992). *For Love of the Automobile: Looking Back into the History of Our Desires.* Berkeley: University of California Press.

Sassatelli, R. (1995). Power Balance in the Consumption Sphere. Reconsidering Consumer Protection Organizations, SPS Working Papers, 5. Florence: European University Institute.

Sassatelli, R. (1997). Consuming ambivalence: eighteenth century public discourse on consumption and Mandeville's legacy. *Journal of Material Culture,* **2,** 339–360.

Sassatelli, R. (1999). Interaction order and beyond. A field analysis of body culture within fitness gyms. *Body and Society,* **5,** 2–3, 227–248.

Savage, M., Bagnall, G. and Longhurst, B. (1999). The Ambiguity of Class Identities in Contemporary Britain. Paper presented to the Annual Conference of the British Sociological Association, University of Glasgow.

Schnaars, S. (1989). *Megamistakes. Forecasting and the Myth of Rapid Technological Change.* New York: Free Press.

Schulze, G. (1995). *The Experience Society.* London: Sage.

Schutz, A. (1962). *Collected Papers. Vol.1.* The Hague: Martinuss Nijhoff.

Schutz, A. (1975). *Hverdagslivets Sociologi.* København: Hans Reitzel.

Sedgewick, E. K. (1992). Epidemics of the will. In *Incorporations,* edited by J. Crary and S. Kwinter. New York: Zone.

Seies, E.-L. (1987). Finns eat like Europeans. *Talouselämä,* 22.

Selden, D. B. (1962). Alcohol and complex society, In *Society, Culture and Drinking Patterns,* edited by D. J. Pittman and C. R. Snyder. New York: John Wiley.

Sennett, R. (1977). *The Fall of Public Man.* Cambridge: Cambridge University Press.

Shields, R. (1991). *Places on the Margin. Alternative Geographies of Modernity.* London: Routledge.

Shove, E. (1997). The science of comfort and the comfort of science. Proceedings of Workshop on Nytenkning omkring effektiv energibruk og baerekraftig forbruk I husholdninger, 23–24 May, pp. 18–21. Oslo: Norges forskningsrad.

Shove, E. (1998). Consuming automobility. Discussion paper presented to SCENESUSTECH. May 1998, Bologna.

Shove, E. and Warde, A. (1998). Inconspicuous consumption: the sociology of consumption and the environment. Paper presented at seminar on Consumption, Environment and the Social Sciences, Oxford University, 6–7 July.

Shove, E. and Wilhite, H. (1999). Energy policy: what it forgot and what it might yet recognise. Energy Efficiency and CO2 reduction: the dimensions of the social challenge. Proceedings of the European Council for an Energy-Efficient Economy (ECEEE) Summer Study, May 31–June 4, Mandelieu, France.

Simmel, G. (1950). The metropolis and mental life. In *The Sociology of Georg Simmel,* edited by K. H. Wolff, pp. 409–424. Glencoe, Ill.: Free Press.

Simmel, G. (1957). Fashion. *The American Journal of Sociology,* LXII, 541–558.

Simmel, G. (1991). The problem of style. *Theory, Culture and Society,* 8, 63–72.

Simmel, G. (1998). *Hvordan er Samfundet Muligt? Udvalgte Sociologiske Skrifter.* København: Gyldendal.

Siohansi, F. P. (1996). DSM in transition: from mandates to markets. *Energy Policy,* 24, 283–284.

Siohansi, F. P. and Davis, E. H. (1989). Information technology and efficient pricing—Providing a competitive edge for electric utilities. *Energy Policy,* 17, 599–607.

Slater, D. (1997). *Consumer Culture and Modernity.* Cambridge: Polity.

Slaughter, R. A. (1993). Looking for the real 'megatrends'. *Futures,* Oct., 827–849.

Smith, A. (1981 [1776]). *An Enquiry into the Nature and Causes of the Wealth of Nations.* Indianapolis: Liberty Classics.

Somers, M. (1994). The narrative constitution of identity: A relational and network approach. *Theory and Society,* 23, 605–650.

South, N. (editor) (1998). *Drugs. Cultures, Controls and Everyday Life.* Sage: London.

Southerton, D. (1999). Capital Resources and Geographical Mobility: Consumption and Identification in a New Town. PhD Thesis, Lancaster University.

Spradley, J. P. (1979). *The Ethnographic Interview.* Fort Worth: Holt, Rinehart and Winston.

Stanley, L. R. and Lasonde, K. M. (1996). The relationship between environmental issue involvement and environmentally-conscious behaviour. *Advances in Consumer Research,* 23, 183–88.

Statistics Finland (1996). Income and Consumption, 1996:4.

Stern, P. C. and Aronson, E. (1984) *Energy Use: The Human Dimension.* New York: Freeman.

Stone, M. (1997). Keeping the partly faithful. *Utility Week,* 18 April, 18–19.

Stones, R. (1991). Strategic context analysis: A new research strategy for structuration theory. *Sociology,* 25.

Stuart, L. (1998). Now consumers can plug that choice gap. *The Guardian,* 5 September, 8.

Sulkunen, P., Alasuutari, P., Nätkin, R. and Kinnunen, M. (1997). *The Urban Pub.* Helsinki: Stakes.

SYF (Statistical Yearbook of Finland) (1996). Statistics Finland, Helsinki.

Säylä, M. (1996). Suomalaisten omaisuuksia tutkimassa. *Hyvinvointikatsaus,* 1996:1, 4–8.

Tannen, D. (editor) (1993). *Framing in Discourse.* Oxford: Oxford University Press.

de Tarde, G. (1962 [1903]). *The Laws of Imitation.* Gloucester, Mass.: Peter Smith.

Thoreau, H. D. (1985 [1854]). Walden. In *Henry David Thoreau,* edited by R. F. Sayre, pp. 321–588. New York: The Library of America.

Thøgersen, J. (1994). *Forbrugeradfærdsundersøgelser med Miljømæssigt Sigte.* København: Miljøstyrelsen.

Townsend, P. (1979). *Poverty in the United Kingdom. A Survey of Household Resources and Standard of Living.* London: Harmondswordth.

Tseng, S.-F. (1997). Hard times for software pirates. *Sinorama*, 5, 92–117.

Tuan, Y.-F. (1998). *Escapism*. Baltimore and London: Johns Hopkins University Press.

Tucker, W. T. (1968). The development of brand loyalty. In *Perspectives in Consumer Behaviour* by H. Kassarijan and T. Robertson. Glenview: Scott, Foresman and Company.

Turkle, S. (1996). *Life on the Screen. Identity in the Age of the Internet*. London: Weidenfeld & Nicolson.

Turner, S. (1994). *The Social Theory of Practices. Tradition, Tacit Knowledge and Presuppositions*, pp. 114–120. Cambridge: Polity.

Turner, V. (1967). *The Forest of Symbols: Aspects of Ndembu Ritual*. Ithaca: Cornell University Press.

Twine, F. (1994). *Citizenship and Social Rights. The Interdependence of Self and Society*. London: Sage.

Urry, J. (1995). *Consuming Places*. London: Routledge.

Urry, J. (1999). Automobility, car culture and weightless travel: A discussion paper, Department of Sociology, Lancaster University: http://www.comp.lancs.ac.uk/sociology/soc008ju.html

Valverde, M. (1998). *Diseases of the Will: Alcohol and the Dilemmas of Freedom*. New York: Cambridge University Press.

Veblen, T. (1961 [1899]). *The Theory of the Leisure Class*. New York: Random House.

Vesterga[o]rd, M. (1999). Øko-salg halter. *Information*, 5.1.

Virilio, Paul (1994): *Katoamisen estetiikka* [The Aesthetics of Disappearance]. Tampere: Gaudeamus.

Vogel, D. (1995). *Trading Up. Consumer and Environmental Regulation in a Global Economy*. Cambridge, Mass.: Harvard University Press.

Waddams, C. (1998). Taking the utilities to market. *New Statesman Special Supplement*, 24 July, IV–V.

Walsh, K. (1994). Citizens, charters and contracts. In *The Authority of the Consumer*, by R. Keat et al. London: Routledge.

Wandel, M. et al. (1995). *Change and Stability in Food Habits*. Lysaker: SIFO Rapport no. 4.

Warde, A. (1994). Consumers, identity and belonging: Reflections on some theses of Zygmunt Bauman. In *The Authority of the Consumer*, edited by R. Keat and N. Abercrombie, pp. 58–74. London: Routledge.

Warde, A. (1994a). Consumption, identity-formation and uncertainty. *Sociology*, 28, 877–898.

Warde, A. (1997). *Consumption, Food and Taste*. London: Sage.

Warde, A., Martens, L. and Olsen, W. (1999). Consumption and the problem of variety: cultural omnivorousness, social distinction and eating out. *Sociology*, 33, 105–127.

Warde, A., Shove, E. and Southerton, D. (1998). Convenience, schedules and sustainability. Draft paper for ESF Workshop on sustainable consumption, Lancaster, March 27–29, 1998.

Weber, M. (1949 [1917]). *The Methodology of the Social Sciences*. New York: Free Press.

Weber, M. (1964). *The Theory of Social and Economic Organization*. New York: Free Press.

Weber, M. (1968). *Economy and Society*. New York: Bedminster Press.

Weber, M. (1978). *Economy and Society 2*. Berkeley: University of California Press.

Weil, P. (1993). *A Quoi Revent les Années 90*. Paris: Seuil.

Wieman, C. (1996). Infrastructure. *Technology Review*, **May/June**, 49–55.

Wilhite, H. (1994). Market signals fall short as policy instruments to encourage energy savings in the home. Human dimensions of energy consumption. Proceedings of the American Council for an Energy Efficient Economy (ACEEE) Summer Study.

Williams, R. H. (1982). *Dream Worlds. Mass Consumption in Late Nineteenth Century France*. Berkeley: University of California Press.

Willis, P. (1990). *Common Culture*. Milton Keynes: Open University Press.

Winpenny, J. (1994). *Managing Water as an Economic Resource*. London: Routledge.

Wise, J. M. (1997). *Exploring Technology and Social Space*. London: Sage.

Wolfe, A. (1989). *Whose Keeper? Social Science and Moral Obligation*. Berkeley: University of California Press.

Wong, C. and Coombes, M. (1996). Growing up in poverty. In *The Population of Britain in the 1990s. A Social and Economic Atlas*, by T. Champion, C. Wong et al. Oxford: Clarendon Press.

Wouters, G. (1987). Developments in the behavioural codes between the sexes: The formalization of informalization in the Netherlands, 1930–85.' *Theory, Culture & Society,* **4**, 405–427.

Wouters, G. (1995a). Etiquette books and emotion management in the 20th Century: Part one—The integration of social classes. *Journal of Social History,* **29**, 107–123.

Wouters, G. (1995b). Etiquette books and emotion management in the 20th Century: Part two—The integration of sexes. *Journal of Social History,* **29**, 325–339.

Yang, M. (1994). *Gift, Favors and Banquets: The Art of Social Relationship in China*. Ithaca: Cornell University Press.

NOTES ON CONTRIBUTORS

Gaynor Bagnall is a lecturer specialising in the Sociology of Consumption in the School of Education, Community & Social Science at Liverpool John Moores University in England. She has recently completed her doctorate which examined the cultural production and consumption of heritage sites in the north west of England. Current research focusses on issues of lifestyle, consumption, identity and social integration in middle class communities around Manchester.

Davina Chaplin was Senior Lecturer in Tourism at the University of Central Lancashire, Preston, UK, where she taught international tourism and strategic hospitality management. Just before her death she completed a PhD project about the consumption of second homes in France; recent publications include papers in *Leisure Studies* and the *Journal of Consumer Studies and Home Economics*. Other research interests included the interface between tourism and leisure provision and consumption, and themed environments, especially Las Vegas: an article on the latter is forthcoming in *The Hospitality Review*.

Heather Chappells is a researcher in the Centre for Science Studies at Lancaster University. She has interests in the consumption of domestic utility services and everyday technologies. Her on-going PhD research investigates the dynamics of utility sectors and questions what it means to consume energy, water and waste in the context of recent environmental and institutional change and how this might influence the relationships between providers and consumers. She has also worked on a European Union project—DOMUS—which explored consumer involvement in utility provision.

Tim Dant lectures in Sociology at the University of East Anglia. His doctoral work on the sociology of knowledge was published as *Knowledge, Ideology and Discourse* (Routledge, 1991). In the past he has researched and published on homelessness, community care and elderly people. More recently he has published articles on material culture, planning, the sociology of knowledge and is the author of *Material Culture in the Social World* (Open University Press, 1999).

Jukka Gronow is a senior researcher at the Academy of Finland, Helsinki whose research interests are in social theory and the sociology of consumption. His recent publications include *The Sociology of Taste* (Routledge, 1997) and, with Arto Noro and Pertti Töttö, *The Classics of Sociology* (in Finnish; Gaudeamus, 1997). He has just finished two research projects, one on the eating habits in the Nordic countries and another on the birth of the Soviet consumer in Stalin's time, publications of which are forthcoming.

Bente Halkier is educated in sociology in England and political science in Denmark. Her PhD thesis is about how consumers handle environmental consideration in consumption in an everyday life sociological perspective. She is associate professor in sociology of knowledge at Communication Studies, Roskilde University, Denmark.

Kaj Ilmonen is a professor of sociology at the University of Jyväskylä, Finland. In addition to the sociology of consumption, his research interests are in social movements, the cooperative movement in particular, and labour unions. His publications include *The End of Cooperative Movement* (TTT, 1994), *New and Old Movements* (in Finnish; Gaudeamus, 1998) and *Modernity and Morality* (in Finnish; Vastapaino 1998).

Shou-Cheng Lai is a doctoral student in the Department of Sociology at Lancaster University. His current research interest is in the cultural intermediary, modern advertising, consumer culture and consumption processes with special emphasis on East Asian countries. He is currently completing his thesis on the transformative relation between consumption processes and modern advertising in Taiwan.

Brian Longhurst is a Senior Lecturer in Sociology and Director of the Institute for Social Research at the University of Salford, UK. His books include *Popular Music and Society* (Polity, 1995), *Audiences: A Sociological Theory of Performance and Imagination* (with N. Abercrombie; Sage, 1998) and *Introducing Cultural Studies* (with E. Baldwin, S. McCracken, M. Ogborn and G. Smith; Addison Wesley Longman, 1999).

Pasi Mäenpää is a PhD candidate in the Department of Sociology at the University of Helsinki. He has written on urban experience, shopping, digital culture and urban planning. His forthcoming PhD thesis combines theories and practices of urban culture and consumerism. He is also the co-author of *Hitting the Jackpot. Lives of Lottery Millionaires* (Berg, 1999). He is currently working at City of Helsinki Urban Facts research institute as a project researcher.

Peter J. Martin is Dean of Undergraduate Studies in the Faculty of Economic and Social Studies at the University of Manchester. He studied at the universities of Edinburgh and Manchester, and is a former Head of Sociology at Manchester. His main research interests have been in the sociology of culture, social theory, social stratification, and interactional analysis. Publications include *Sounds and Society—Themes in the Sociology of Music* (Manchester University Press, 1995) and *Understanding Classical Sociology* (Sage, 1995) with J. Hughes and W. W. Sharrock.

Katja Oksanen-Särelä is a sociologist (MA). Her master's thesis was about the construction of the computer/pc user in pc advertisements. Currently she is working as a researcher in the Helsinki University of Art and Design, Media Lab. She is interested in the social construction of technology and effects of technological change on everyday life, and sociology of consumption. She has published an article (with Inkeri Korhonen) in a book *Semioottisen sosiologian näkökulmia* (*Semiotic Sociology*; Gaudeamus, 1997) and (with Päivi Eriksson and Mika Pantzar) an article 'Just a tool. Metaphors of personal computers in advertising texts' which was presented in *Samples of the Future, A Conference on Organizations Research*, Stanford University, Cal., September 1998.

Mika Pantzar is an economist (PhD), senior researcher in Academy of Finland and Helsinki School of Economics. He has published articles within consumer research, design and technology studies, rhetoric of economic policy, food studies, systems research, future studies etc. His latest book *Domestication of technology. From science of consumption to art of consumption* (in Finnish; Tammi, 1996) will be followed by *The Invention of Needs* (in Finnish; Otava, 2000). (In the 1990s he has been working as research manager both in National Consumer Research Centre and University of Art and Design Helsinki.)

Roberta Sassatelli teaches cultural sociology at the University of East Anglia (Norwich, UK) and history of sociological thought at the University of Bologna (Italy). Her current research interests are in the Theories and History of Consumer Culture and the Sociology of the Body and Leisure. She is author of *Anatomy of the Gym. Commercial Culture and Body Discipline*, il Mulino, Bologna, 2000.

Mike Savage is Professor and Head of the Department of Sociology at Manchester University. His recent publications include *Gender, Careers and Organisations* with Susan Halford and Anne Witz (Macmillan, 1997) and *Class Analysis and Social Transformation* (Open University Press, 2000). His research interests are in social stratification, social mobility, social networks and cultural analysis.

Elizabeth Shove is Director of the Centre for Science Studies at Lancaster University. She has written about energy policies and practices and has been responsible for a number of research projects at the interface of sociology, technology studies, and the built environment. Elizabeth is interested in the sociology of comfort, cleanliness and convenience, and has recently co-ordinated a series of events on the subject of consumption, sustainability and everyday life, funded by the European Science Foundation.

Dale Southerton is a Research Fellow at the ESRC Centre for Research on Innovation and Competition, The University of Manchester, U.K. He has recently completed his PhD thesis, entitled *Capital Resources and Geographical Mobility: consumption and identification in a New Town*, at Lancaster University, U.K.

Alan Warde is Professor of Sociology and Director of the Centre for Research on Innovation and Competition at the University of Manchester. His research interests are in the field of the sociology of consumption and recent work has concentrated on food. Recent books include *Consumption, Food and Taste: culinary antinomies and commodity culture*, (Sage, 1997) and, with Lydia Martens, *Eating Out: social differentiation, consumption and pleasure*, (Cambridge University Press, 2000). He also was joint editor, with S. Edgell and K. Hetherington, of *Consumption Matters*, Sociological Review Monograph Series A (1996).

Terhi-Anna Wilska is a Ph.D. (Soc.) with special interests in consumption, age and generations, and the welfare state and welfare policy. Her PhD thesis 'Survival with Dignity? The Consumption of Young Adults during Economic Depression.' (Turku School of Economics, Serie A-3: 1999) was completed at Lancaster University, U.K. in 1999. She works as a lecturer in Economic Sociology at the Turku School of Economics and Business Administration, and as a researcher in the project 'Welfare State—Resource or Constraint' funded by the Academy of Finland.

Index